FUNDAMENTAL THEORY OF SINGULARITY

(FTS)

Prabhakaran Natesan

Scan for web-link

SHANATCO PUBLISHING

Self-published by **Shanatco Publishing**

Home Address: 63B, Kattabomman Street, Sri Karumariamman Nagar Extn, Perumattunallur, Chengalpattu District, Tamil Nadu, India. Pin code – 603202. Email: [shanatcop@gmail.com]

Purpose: Contribute for worldwide education

Pages: 192

Year of Publication - 2024

Copyright © Prabhakaran Natesan 2024

FUNDAMENTAL THEORY OF SINGULARITY

<h1 align="center">THE PROPOSAL – Page 1</h1>

EXISTING STUDY	NEW STUDY
THEORY OF RELATIVITY **by Albert Einstein**	**THEORY OF SINGULARITY** **by Prabhakaran Natesan**
1) Length contraction & Time dilation – Observations are true but interpreted at surface level only (reason for its failure).	Length contraction & Time dilation - True interpretation with in-depth visualization (leading to quantum physics).
2) The idea drives the study away from reality resulting in science fictions such as time travel.	The idea leads towards the ultimate reality and helps in formulating the fundamental study of space-time.
3) Time dilation is a measure of variation in time in terms of slow / fast ticking of the clock.	Time dilation is a measure of variation in length in terms of bending space line.
4) Length in meters and time in minutes are the units conveniently assumed for human perspective.	Space and time are same in linear scale in reality or singular perspective.
5) Concept based on thought experiments only. The theory basically needs two objects or references to relate each other.	Study based on real dimensions along with real-time illustrations. Dependency factor that holds back is solved to move deeper and deeper.

EXISTING STUDY	NEW STUDY
THEORY OF RELATIVITY **by Albert Einstein**	**THEORY OF SINGULARITY** **by Prabhakaran Natesan**
6) Evidently failed to explain quantum mechanics and does not serve a fundamental study.	Serves one fundamental for general relativity and quantum mechanics, the two major branches of physics.
7) Human perspective suffers and it is struck between all dual nature and dualities.	One-eye perspective is free from dualities to see through the reality and takes the singular path clearly.
8) Gravitation is at intermediate level (macro-scale).	Gravitation explained at point level (Quantum scale).
9) Theory is known for its impracticality such as travelling of an object or a person at the speed of light to check relative effect.	Theory explains the limitations of relativity and solves the mysteries of existing studies through real dimensions of space-time.
10) General theory of relativity is incomplete for education due to its incompatibility with the behavior of quantum objects or nature.	Ready for education as it would acknowledge general relativity by extending it to show the connection with quantum physics without any contradictions to actually exist.

1.0 LIGHT

Travelling of light has the ultimate speed limit of the Universe that nothing can travel faster than light. The speed of light in vacuum is measured to be 3 x 10^8 m/s. The experimentation with speed of light resulted in two observations such as **Length contraction** and **Time dilation.** The new and correct visualization of the same is the basis for all the topics discussed under theory of singularity.

We know the formula,

$$\text{Speed} = \frac{\textbf{Distance travelled (Km)}}{\textbf{Time taken (Hr)}}$$

Here, the distance is a fixed one. For example, a vehicle travelling at the speed of 60 Km/hr means the distance of 60 Km to be reached in one hour time, if uniform speed is maintained. Change in speed to be slow or fast, results in change in estimated time. So, the speed and the time are varying factors depending upon conditions. However, for a constant speed again, time is a fixed value to calculate.

Now, what is happening with speed of light?

The same formula is applicable even for light travelling in space. However, the experimentation that verified distance and time for a constant speed of 3 x 10^8 m/s resulted in some strange variations.

There was a delay in time over the calculated time. As per the formula, time cannot change for a constant speed. Thus, the variation is accounted as dilation in time instead of **time-delay** which means same calculated time is assumed to have slowed down with slow ticking of clock.

This obviously made the scientist to think of distance also to have variation in terms of shortening of length with respect to time dilation. Means, the object travelling at the speed of light undergoes contraction in its length.

Speed of light = Length contraction / Time dilation

The above two variations happening together led to the conclusion that space and time are two different manifestation of the same thing and to be called as **spacetime,** a single entity.

The term time dilation has become popular as slowing down of time is a fascination that travelling at high speed in space would slow down the aging of the person. The above said observations are not visualized clearly and declared with following misconceptions rather.

a) Length contraction and time dilation are said to be continuous and tending to zero.

b) Speed of light is approaching time zero, means the present time slows down, and ultimately stops ticking to remain at time zero. The object travelling at this speed experiences no time. Thus, the photons are said to be timeless.

c) It is also obvious that if length contraction tends to zero then the travelling distance taken or the destination to be reached is almost instantaneous, as the distance is zero.

How the above declarations are misconceptions?

i) Evidently, to travel from one galaxy to the other even at the speed of light, it takes light years of time. Means, even for the light photons which are said to be timeless, takes time in years to reach the destination. Which also means the travelling distance (length) is also not shortening for the light. So, both the observations did not work, the way it is imagined.

ii) Further, people might ask, length contraction is about the length of the travelling object and nothing to do with the distance. Truth is, the observations are not diagrammatically visualized is the major problem in space-time studies that general relativity could not extend itself to reach or explain quantum mechanics.

Now, how to visualize Length contraction and time dilation in reality. We are entering into an equipment-less methodology of studying space-time, only by being a simple and natural human.

Let us consider space and time to be a line. Even though these two aspects are inseparable, to observe the variations we equally divide the line into two halves as shown in Fig 1.

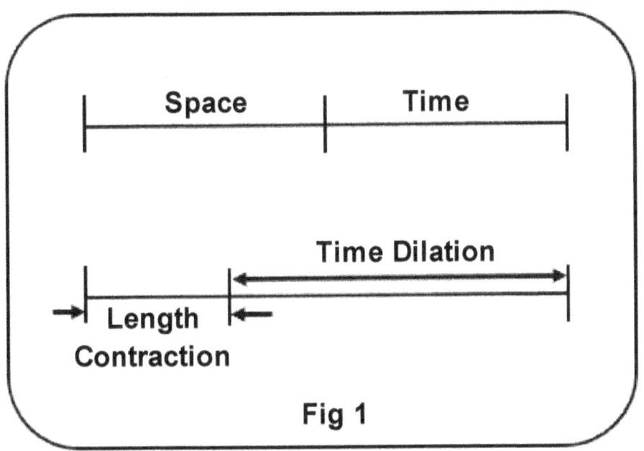

Fig 1

Here, the change in one observation has obvious change in the other, constituting a dual observation. Hence space and time are not two different things but a single entity to be called as **spacetime**.

Length contraction means a direct contraction in space whereas time dilation implies a slow ticking of clock which could be considered as reduction in time. Then the above two aspects are together undergoing a reduced scale imagined as follows,

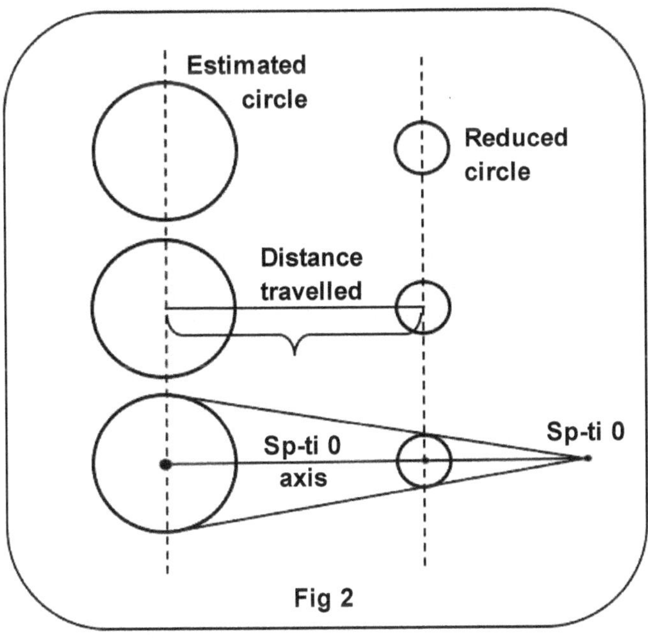

Fig 2

[11]

Fig 2 shows,

a) Estimated circle of space and time by us and there is a reduced circle representing the actuals in terms of length contraction and time reduction.

b) The reduced circle is shown at a distance from estimated one which means that, the variations are observed only with the speed of light photon that has travelled a distance.

c) The tangents drawn to touch the two circles are extended to meet at a point called **Sp-ti 0**. Thus, the axis connecting the three center points is called as **Sp-ti 0 axis**.

d) These two tangents also represent the value of length contraction and time dilation which were assumed to be continuous to reach space zero and time zero respectively for speed of light.

e) Further, the object travelling at the speed of light would achieve time zero which implies travelling faster than light would enter time negative, enabling us for time travel back in time.

f) With this, even twin theory was imagined that, twin siblings one living on earth and the other allowed to travel in space at the speed of light, on his return sees his brother on earth have grown older while he finds himself remain younger.

g) It implies, that the person travelled at light speed have now entered into the future on earth, where several years would have been passed relative to his travel in space only for a while.

h) Entering into the past is not believed based on the paradox that a grandson travelling to the past, if kills his grandfather then there is no possibility for him to take birth and live now at the present. Moreover, there is nobody showed up from the future to the present world, so travelling back in time is said to be impossible.

All the above assumptions could be simply rectified with the following visualization,

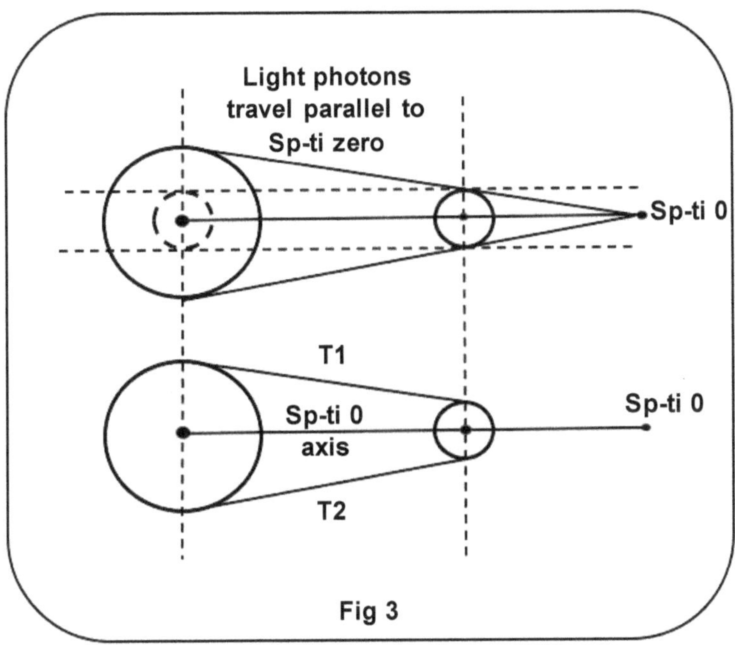

Fig 3 denotes the following points,

i) The light photons even without having to travel a distance with its speed, it is near to Sp-ti 0 with its volume.

ii) Therefore, the speed of light is never approaching zero and it is running parallel to Sp-ti 0 axis. The very photon is almost near to space zero with its volume.

iii) Here, space zero is same as time zero in a single point, as space-time was discovered to be a single entity, to be noted.

iv) The diagram also shows the tangents T1 and T2 to have solved and not reaching Sp-ti 0, which means length contraction and time dilation observed with the speed of light are finite values and never tending to zero.

v) For a constant speed value of light, the variations observed obviously must have fixed values. Further, the indication of length contraction and time dilation in reality shows light photon to exist at a reduced scale, at some depth of the Sp-ti medium.

2.0 REDUCED SP-TI SCALE

How to locate or mark the above said estimated circle and reduced circle in space-time medium. And where does this point of Sp-ti 0 exist? Here, the estimated circle is pertaining to human perspective, numbers and calculations whereas the reduced circle is a hidden factor unknown in existing studies and projected in our new theory of singularity. What does the reduced space-time scale indicate? Shall be understood with the following real-time illustration.

Consider a water well with symmetry that looks like a cylinder as shown in Fig 4. There are two identical circles on top and bottom of the well. When we look into the well from top, the bottom circle appears smaller and situated well within the top circle.

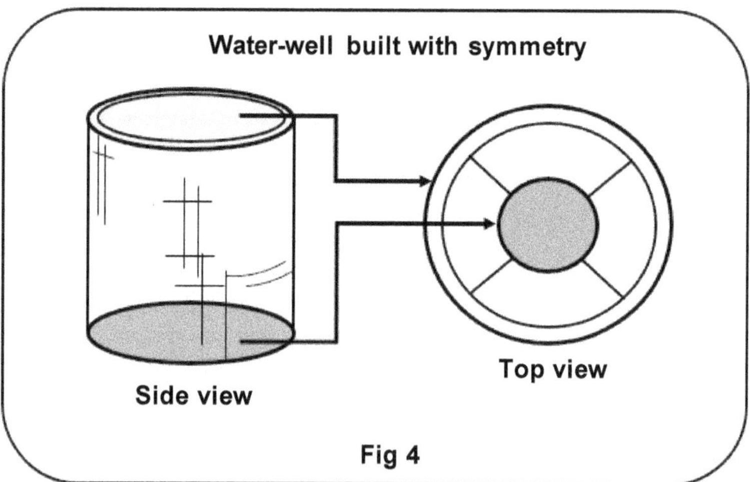

We know, this difference indicates the depth of the well. However, what do we mean by depth in our day-to-day life? It is a measurement made from top to bottom and vice versa is called as height. This way of understanding did not affect our calculations and technology in anyway. But depth is an important factor when it comes to space-time study. In reality we are not measuring the depth anywhere. It is only the height measured in two opposite ways.

Now, we are going to project the depth of the well, the way it appears. Let the two circles have the height difference but the depth is distinguished with different sizes of the circles as shown in Fig 5.

[14]

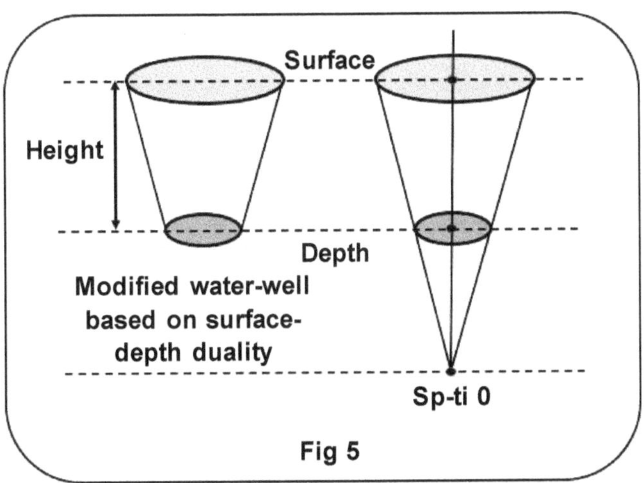

In Fig 5, height of the well is shown with double headed arrow such that measurement from top to bottom is not the depth. Moreover, depth has a duality of its own surface. If the depth of the well is further projected, it ends up with the point of Sp-ti 0.

From the discussions so far, we obtain a cone of depth leading to Sp-ti 0. If this Sp-ti 0 is the depth of space-time, then does it exist at the center of the Universe? The answer is no, first of all, the cone is not a fixed one. It is an appearance pertaining to the human vision. That means, the Sp-ti 0 is distributed throughout the Universe. Entire Sp-ti medium is made up of Sp-ti 0 points. The cone begins with a wide opening and ends with the apex point called Sp-ti 0 in any direction.

The reduced space-time scale means that space-time medium has surface and depth, where depth is not physically seen in any direction in the space we live. So, it requires diagrammatic representation to make a projection of the same for our understanding.

In case of water well, the depth is only a shadow such that, it is possible to reach the point of depth as it is constituting a deep appearance only. However, in case of light, it is really deep and travelling of photons happens in deeper space.

Thus, by applying cone of depth for light in space-time medium, the observations such as length contraction and time dilation are projected to the surface as shown in Fig 6.

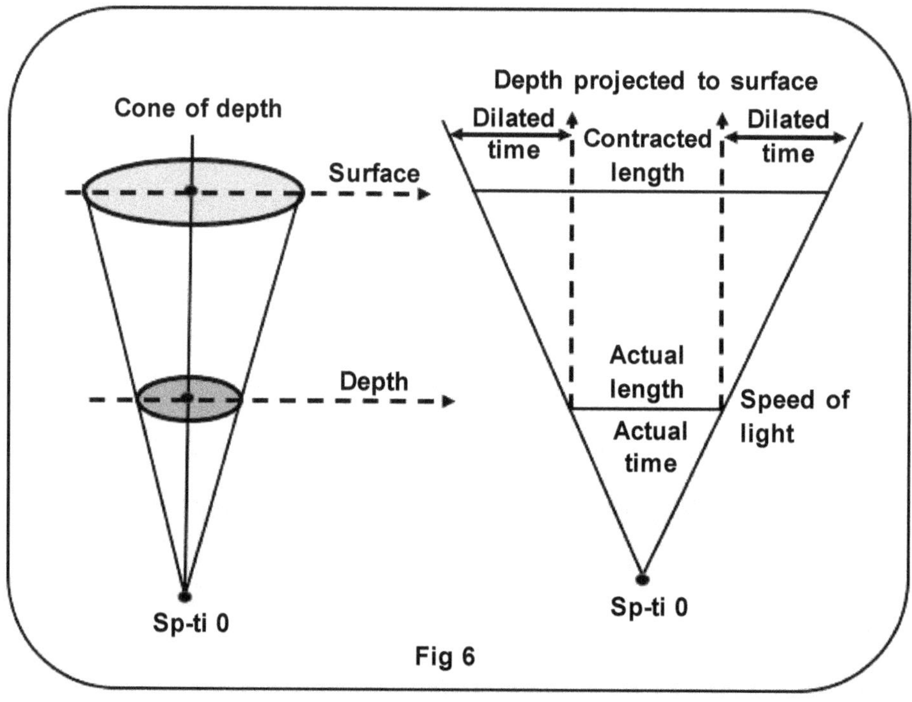

Fig 6

Moreover, the gap between estimated and reduced circles shown in Fig 2 is no more a distance but a depth. The representation of reduced circle actually contains length contraction and time dilation in terms of space contraction and time reduction in it, could be better understood in the fore coming topics.

Fig 6 shows the actual length by actual time of light at certain depth which is appearing as shortened or contracted length and measured as dilation in time respectively on the surface we live.

The above diagram is the basic one and more supporting ideas and illustrations are discussed in the fore coming topics.

3.0 SHADOW CONE

(Impression of real dimensions)

The term shadow cone implies that there is some real cone to exist and we are seeing only its impression constituting a cone like appearance. In that case what the real cone is about? If travelling of light is concerned with real cone, what makes it inaccessible that it can only be projected to the surface for our study? Shall be seen in the course of the theory. We will see another illustration to understand the shadow cone clearly,

a) The cone appearance unrealized, when person standing in midst of trees.

b) A straight line or a road that is clear from any objects in its track.

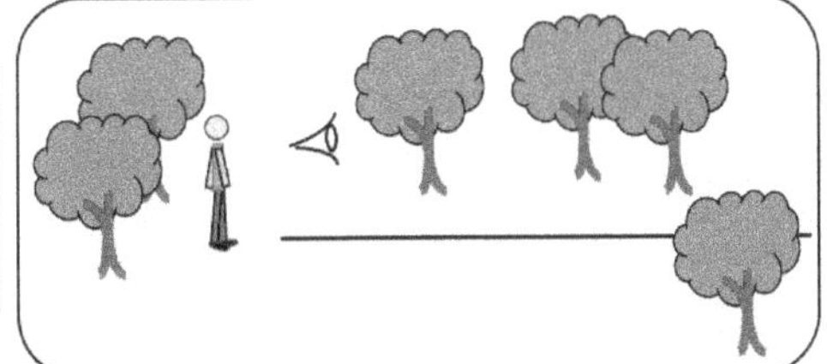

c) The shadow line raises.

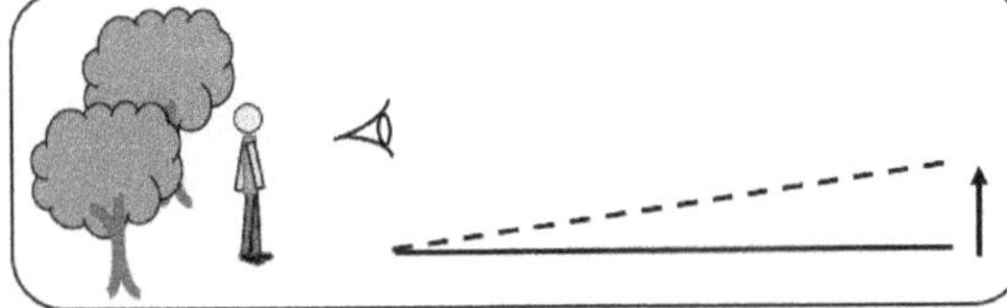

d) The shadow slant line generates a shadow cone with the end point of Sp-ti 0 (apex).

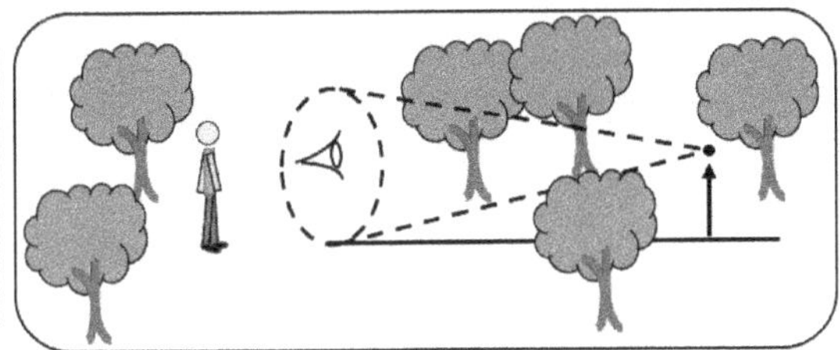

Fig 7 [(a) (b) (c) & (d)]

[17]

From Fig 7, we clearly see the shadow cone formation. The observer standing in a high way tunnel sees this cone clearly. This appearance makes the observer to see the trees near to the end point are reducing in size Fig 8(b).

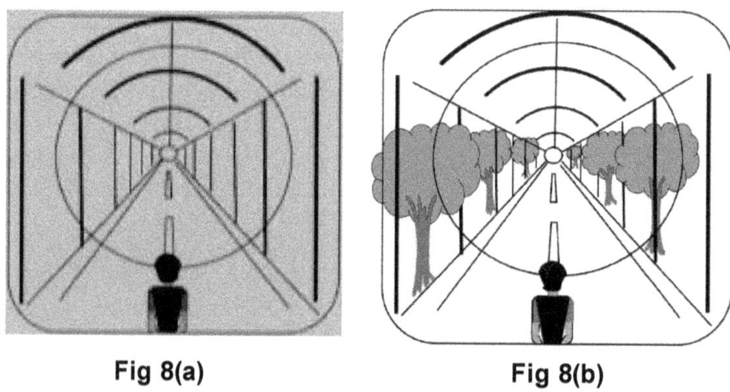

Fig 8(a)   **Fig 8(b)**

Whereas, the observer-2 from the side view does not see any variation with the size of the trees and thus, solves the perspective of observer-1 telling him that changes in appearance does not imply any physical changes happening out there in space-time.

Based on this, there is a misconception in the thought experiment of relativity visualized as follows,

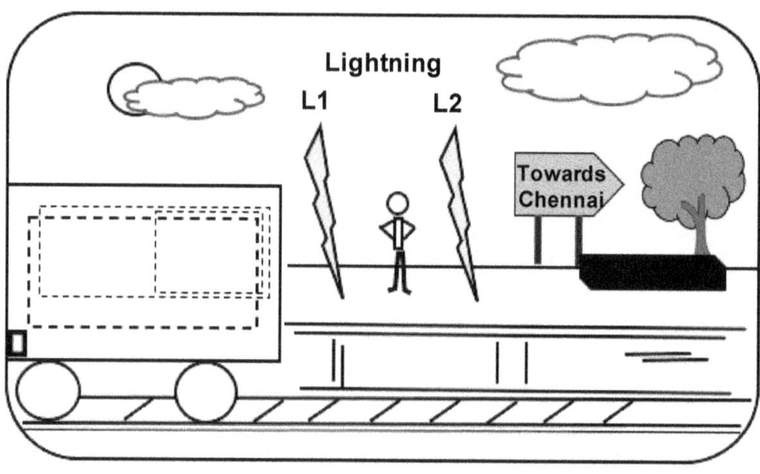

Fig 9(a)

[18]

Fig 9(a) shows an observer standing in a platform and sees two equal lightning strikes on either side of him. He finds both to be striking the ground at the same time. However, another observer in the train approaching the platform sees the same situation differently.

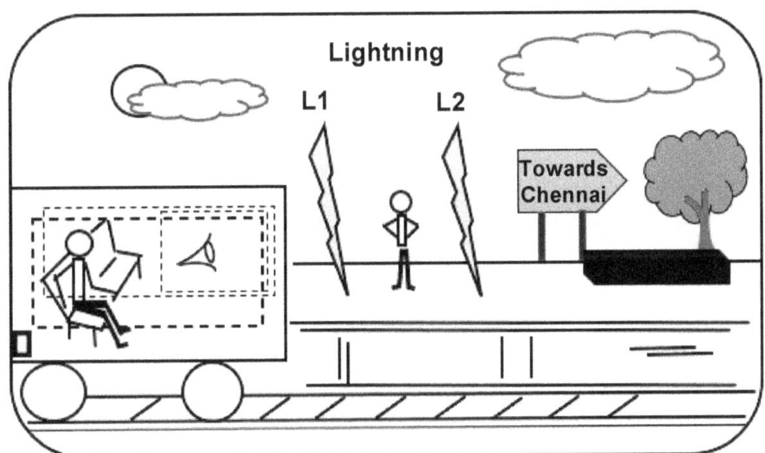

Fig 9(b)

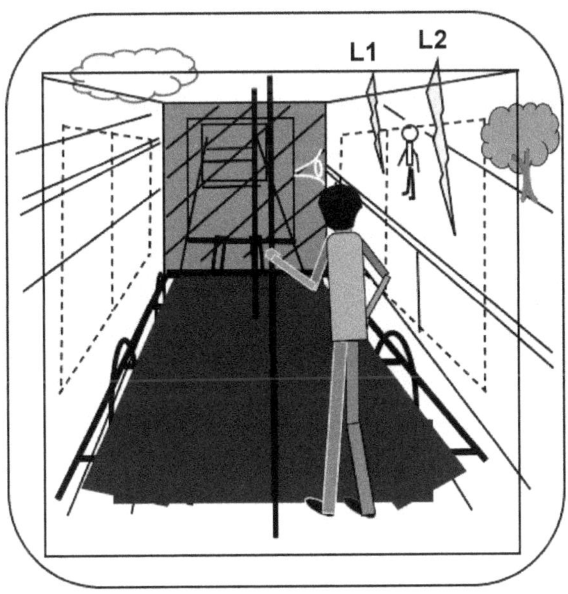

Fig 9(c)

[19]

Fig 9(c) shows that the lightning strike differs in such a way that L2 towards the observer in train, appears to strike the ground first and L1 later. Also, the length of L2 appears bigger than L1 which is farther. Here, it is obvious that the two considered frames are referring to each other like, if one view is straight, the other one is cross. This perspective of comparison is assumed for space and time to be relative for observers of different reference frames, in existing studies.

Whereas, with the shadow cone in Fig 7, the observation from the side view is clearly showing that, there is no physical change happening out there and it is just about the appearance of cone shape for observer-1. Theory of relativity has taken it in opposite manner not knowing the geometry of appearance in space-time and had no objective.

It was assumed only on the basis of angle of observation made. Further, the reference frames of observers vary from one another and captures different angle of views without having one main correct frame for reference. So, same like speed, space and time are also said to be relative for observers of different reference frames.

Fig 9 (say) more or less contains the square picture frame in which, the angle of view is taken as it is by relativity for real whereas in singularity study, we have shown it only as a shadow cone of appearances, to be noted. Also, even if this cone is considered as a reference frame, it required only two frames for correction between observer 1&2. Thus, the phrase "Observers of all reference frames must be reduced to only two Sp-ti frames namely straight frame and angled frame.

The observer who says that the two lightnings strike the ground at equal distance on either side of him at the same time holds the main reference frame. While all the other frames come under angled frame irrespective of whatever angle it differs, would have to refer to the main frame. Theory of relativity basically has a requirement of two objects for comparison.

Even in this thought experiment, the theory meets its limitation. Consider Fig 9(c), the observer in train holds the angled frame. What if the observer gets down from the train and stands in-line (zero degree) with the other person standing in the platform? Now he says he could see only one lightning (L2) and does not see L1 right behind L2, at all. Then this reference frame does not support the theory at all, to be noted. How, for speeds other than light speed are said to be relative is also a misconception, shall be discussed in fore coming topics, as it requires more details for explaining the same.

4.0 DIMENSIONS IN EXISTING STUDIES

Even after the discovery of space-time to be a single entity, the existing studies still follows three spatial dimensions and time as fourth dimension in one direction separately.

The three spatial dimensions are based on the conventional graph comprised of x, y and z axes with an origin as shown in Fig 10(a). As it is known that space is a curvature instead of straight lines, the x, y and z axes are understood for latitude, longitude and altitude perpendicular to each other.

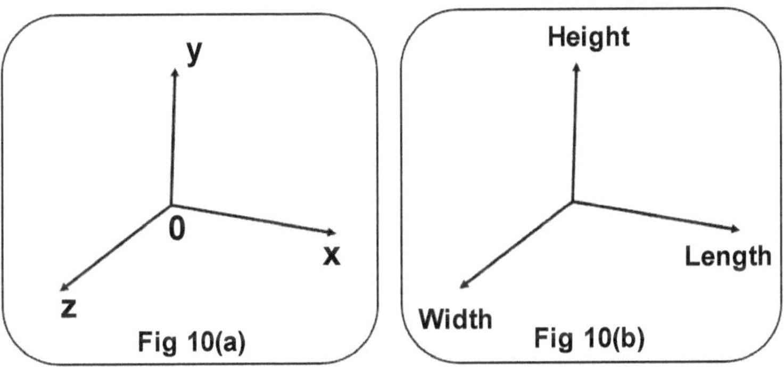

The arrow of time is managed to draw in the same graph indicating 3-dimensional space is moving forward in fourth dimension called time. Thus, space-time together is said to be four dimensional in nature.

We see all the three axes representing length, width and height are distinct from each other that, width cannot be more than a length and height is a measure different from the other two. However, these dimensions in terms of measurements, are only pertaining to the object and not describing anything about space.

Further, we claim that latitude, longitude and altitude are unlike the straight-line measurements and curvilinear in nature which is describing the curve nature of space and so, they could serve as three spatial dimensions. A word is generic, a term is specific which more than a word is and a dimension is something special and stuffed more than a term. So, dimensions must contain the knowledge of space-time like a seed that contains the tree in it.

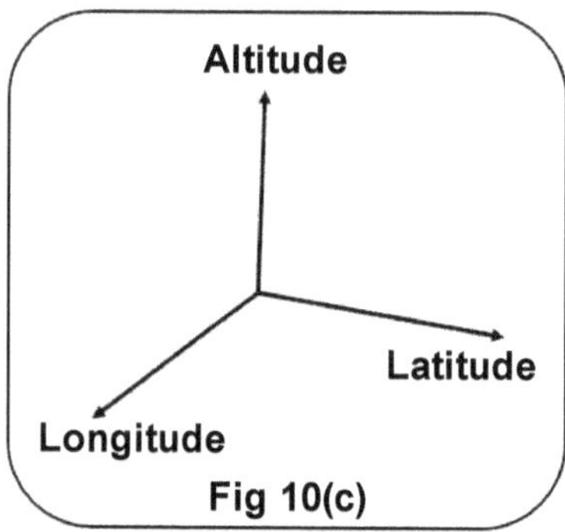

We will now analyze and check what could be done with the above shown conventional 3-D graph.

All the three axes are just a measure of distance 'D' between two points. The graph could be modified as shown in Fig 11(a). However, in case of latitude or longitude, as it is curved, it can be traced to end up at the same point where it is started, Fig 11(b).

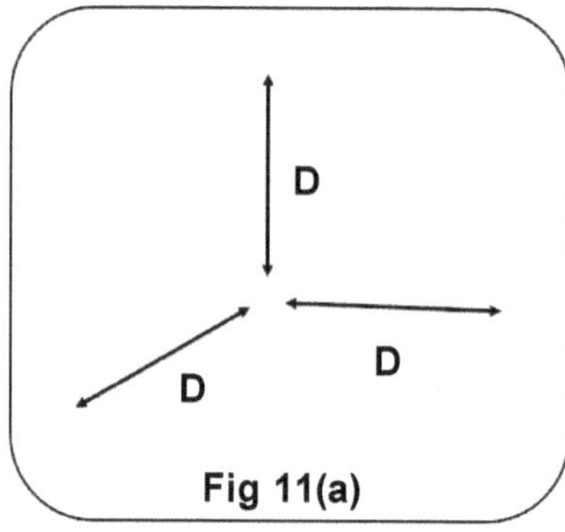

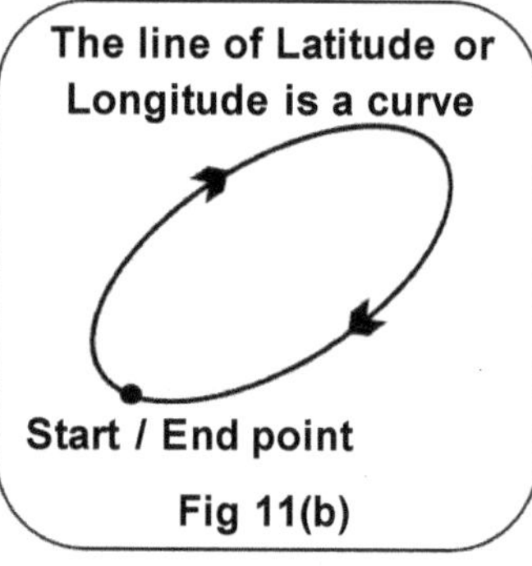

Latitude and longitude together being perpendicular to each other, constitute a sphere and describes the Universe to be spherical in shape. No other details could be extracted out of this. Further the above spatial dimensions are also, more or less object oriented such that without a big object such as the Earth, these lines are imaginary and could not be found to exist in empty space-time. If Universe is a sphere, obviously there is an in & out duality (Fig 11(c)) with a boundary line, which raises the question of what is beyond the Universe? So, we move on to discovering the real dimensions that would contain the knowledge of the Universe such as structure, evolution, behavior of objects and nature of space-time medium. Thus, the problems of existing studies mainly on the limitations of theory of relativity due to its contradiction with quantum physics, shall be applied with dimensions and solved in singular perspective.

5.0 REAL DIMENSIONS OF SPACE-TIME

(Geometrical aspects)

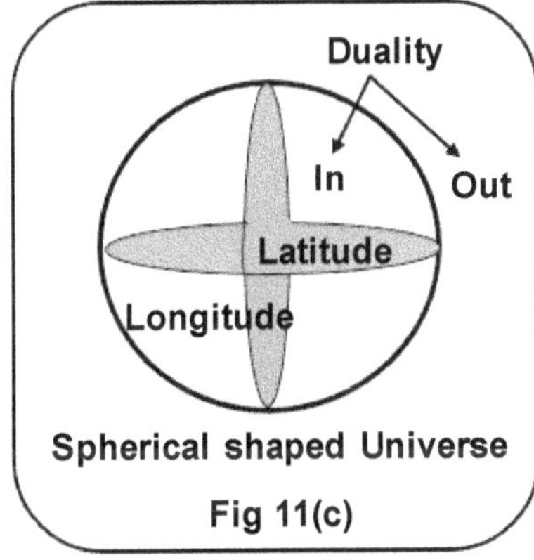

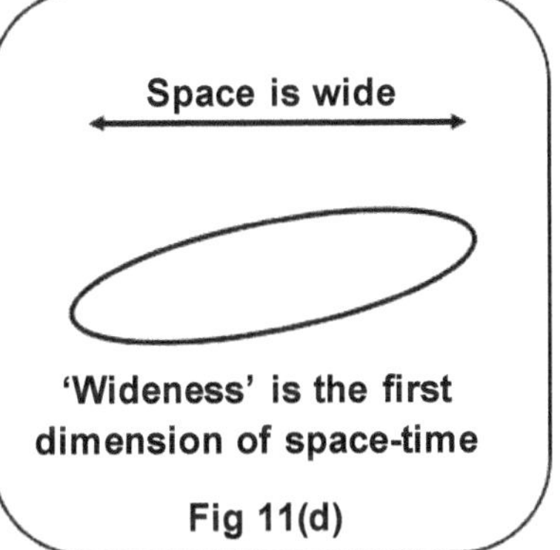

The dimensions are supposed to be like first dimension of space-time, second, third and so on without separating space and time. We shall see how to derive those dimensions from empty space-time as follows,

i) The first dimension of Space-time is simply, as we see in Fig 11(a) that space-time is 'wide' in any direction. Wideness shall not be confused with width because wide is describing the nature of space-time medium whereas width is specific about a side (measurement) of an object.

ii) Moving on to second dimension, let us consider two objects A and B separated by a distance D between each other. We see both the objects are different in sizes. How to denote the size difference of the objects is unknown. One may say, it could be represented with radius R but again radius is same like length or width understood on the object side. So,

[23]

what is the solution to get a dimension describing the nature of space-time medium? We make use of the shadow cone here.

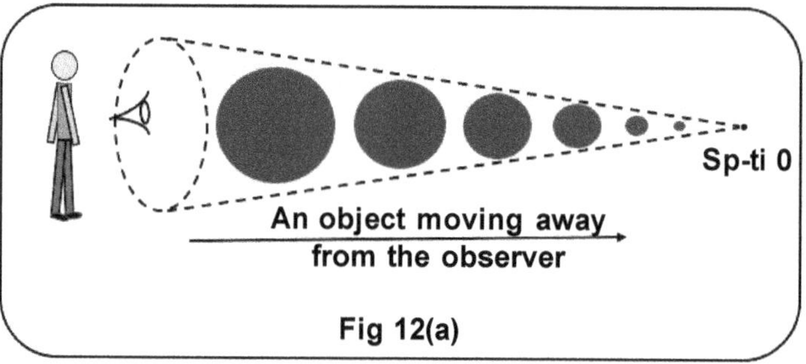

Fig 12(a)

1) The object appears to diminish in size as it moves away from the observer and at certain point (i.e.,) Sp-ti 0, it completely vanishes from the sight.
2) It is not the limitation of human sight, but the object is actually moving through a different dimension.
3) We shall go for a thought experiment to understand this variation.

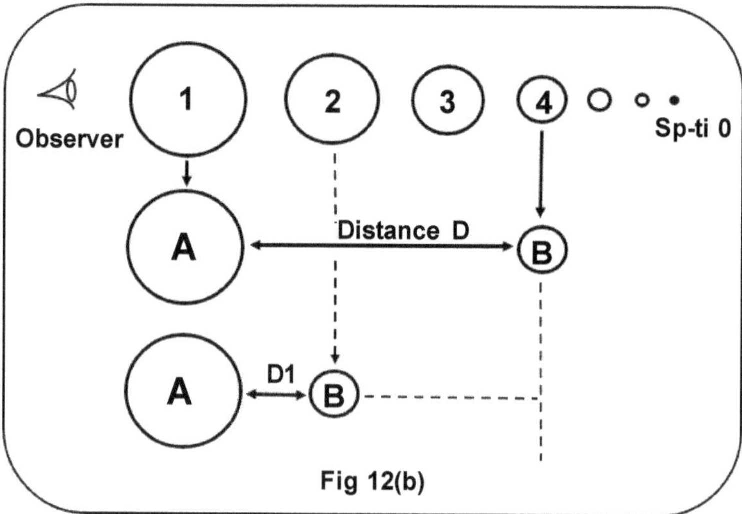

Fig 12(b)

- Mark the different positions of the object moving in a direction.
- Consider two objects A and B matching with positions 1 and 4 respectively separated by a distance 'D'.

[24]

- Now, assume object B shifted to position 2 with the new distance 'D1'. Here, changing the distance between the two objects did not help to understand the hidden dimension.
- Means, distance D and D1 are measured only in wide dimension. So, we move on for a different representation.

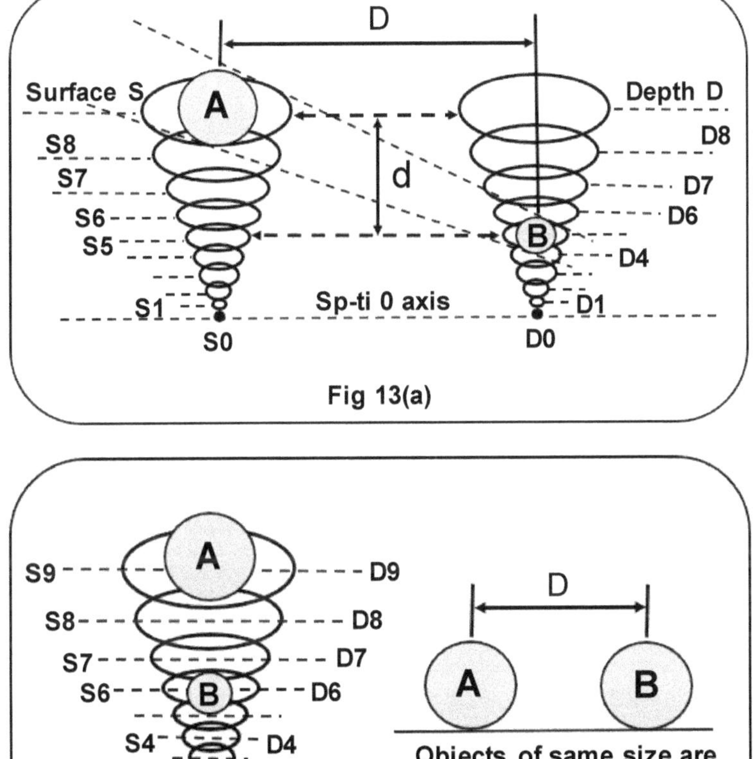

Fig 13(a) shows the two considered objects A and B separated by a distance 'D' in wide dimension. It also has a difference in a scale denoted as 'd' indicating object B at a depth D5 from object A at D9. Here, surface and depth are an inseparable duality and hence it could also be understood as object A at a surface S9 from object B at S5. This scale reduces to reach Sp-ti 0 axis with level S0-D0.

Fig 13(b) shows both the objects could be represented in the same scale. In case of objects of same size, are said to be on the same surface or depth level and separated by a distance D, only in wide dimension.

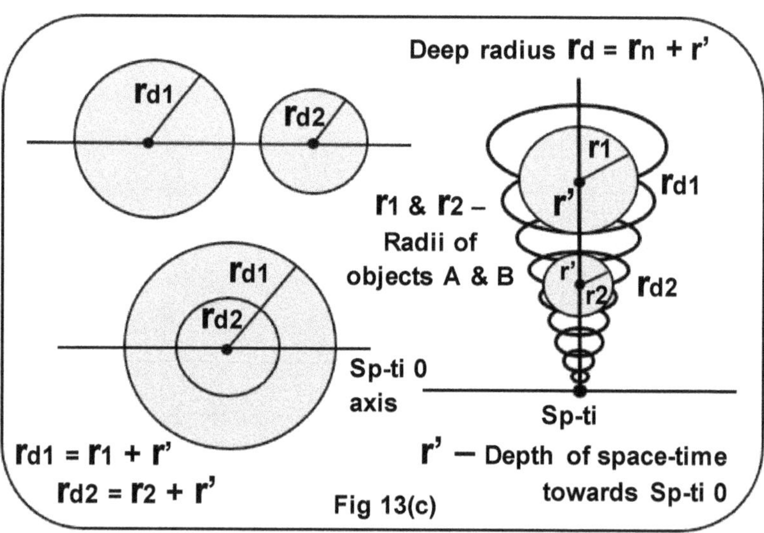

The two objects of different sizes with its positions in sp-ti scale could be shown to be dimensionally one within the other, Fig 13(c). Here, r_{d1} & r_{d2} are deep radii of objects 1 & 2 respectively.

In general, $r_{dn} = r_n + r'$

Where r_n is the surface radius of the object and r' is the hidden depth of space-time towards Sp-ti 0.

Important notes:

- It is now clear that objects of same size are on the same surface or depth levels and said to be separated only by the Distance D in wide dimension, on the other hand considering the estimated and reduced circles (Fig 2) in case of speed of light, it is not a distance but only the depth levels between the two circles.
- It means there is no distance travelled and time taken between estimated and reduced circles however, they both still contain

[26]

the values of space and time whose difference is shown with sizes of the circles. Estimated circle indicates calculation of distance and time at macro-scale (Human perspective) and reduced circle means the variations such as space contraction and time reduction together indicating reduced Sp-ti scale in nature.

- Moreover, the length contraction and time dilation for speeds other than light speed could be represented with a special aspect called **Sp-ti bubble** of the object (will be discussed in detail with drawings). This object range has a limit between large to small sizes called as macro-scale objects.

- In case of light, the variations need to be projected to the surface of the medium for understanding. Suppose, if light photons also had Sp-ti bubble same as other macro-objects, we would have not observed any variations such as length contraction and time dilation, as it would be contained and varying within the bubble itself.
- The Sp-ti bubble includes volume as well as mobility of the individual object in space-time medium as shown in Fig 14. However, only the mobile space-time available for the object undergoes changes with speed factor and not the volume. Hence length contraction is neither associated with change in distance taken nor with length of the object itself, to be noted.

- In addition, it is not only the speed but also the size factor of the bubble that shows the variations in mobile space-time of the macro-objects.
- Understanding Sp-ti bubble is more important as it solves the incompatibility between general relativity and quantum mechanics.

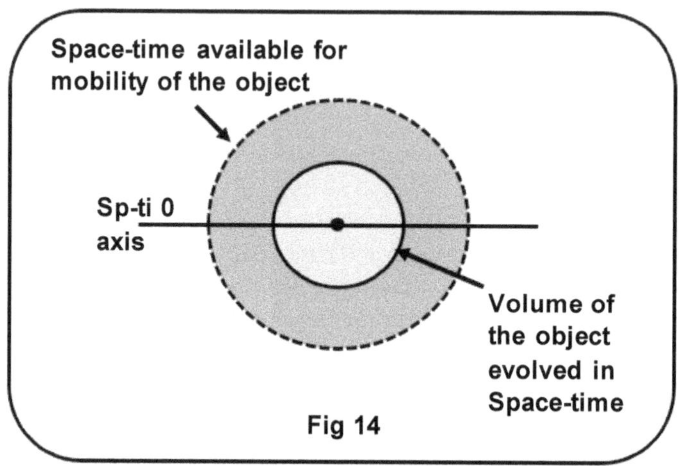

Fig 14

With the discussions so far, we have derived two dimensions in terms of aspects describing the nature of the space-time medium,

- ❖ **Wide** (curvilinear) is the first dimension of space-time.
- ❖ **Deep** (Radial) is the second dimension of space-time.

The above aspects could be represented as a dimensional cone, Fig 15(a).

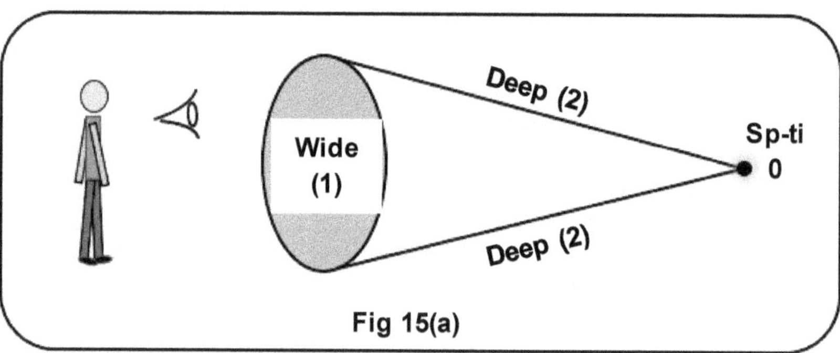

Fig 15(a)

iii) To derive third dimension of space-time, we need to analyze the objects along with the Sp-ti grid at its background. Starting from macro-objects towards Nano or quantum objects, we could observe and find exactly, where is the point of contradiction? That is believed to exist between general theory of relativity (classical physics) and quantum mechanics (modern physics) in space-time medium.

[28]

6.0 GRID CONFIGURATION OF SP-TI MEDIUM

Sir Albert Einstein discovered Space-time to behave like a fabric in which heavy objects are said to cause curvature in it. It could be imagined in the same way it is described, Fig 16.

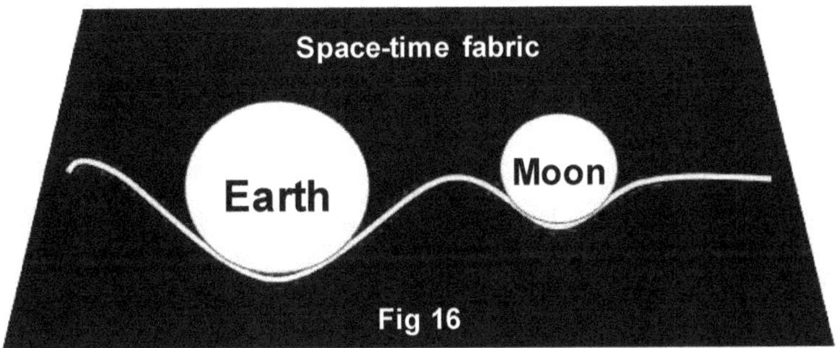

A fabric in general is weaved by threads. Same way we assume the above darkness of sp-ti fabric made up of two kinds of threads called space and time. So, multi-dimensionally the Sp-ti medium could be shown as square grid of space and time lines to be perpendicular to each other for our understanding and ease of observing the variations.

Consider an object in this grid configuration. There are two types of bending of space-time lines by the objects.

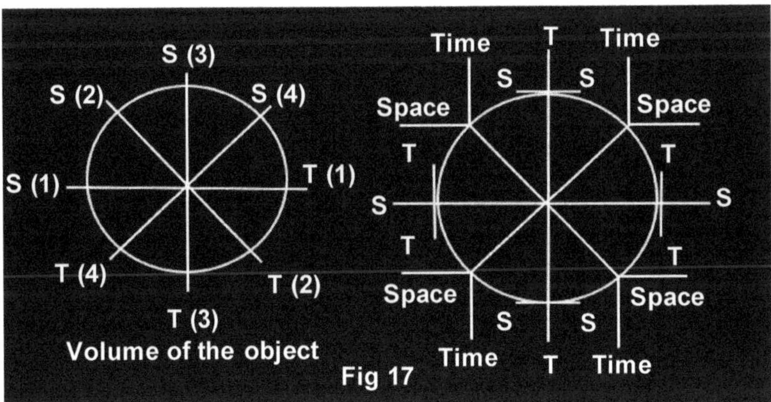

However, only one type of bending shown in Fig 16 is known in the existing studies which is due to the density of the object. The more basic one is bending of sp-ti lines due to volume of the object (Fig 17), new to studies (introduced in this book).

[29]

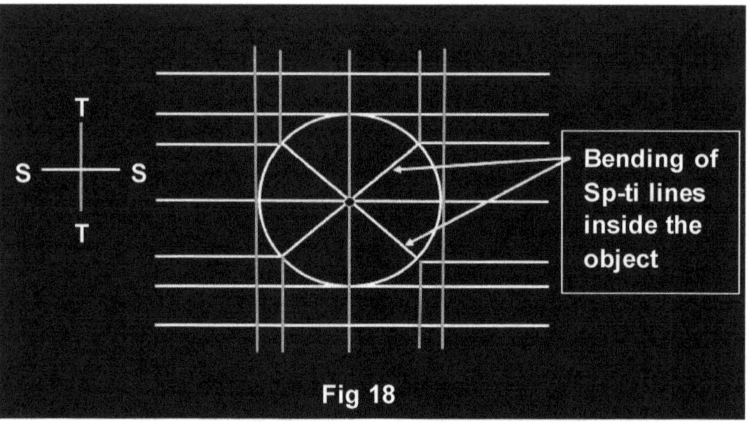

Applying the Sp-ti bubble to contain space and time variations pertaining to mobility (Speed factor) and position of the object in Sp-ti scale (size factor) the above diagram is further modified, Fig 19.

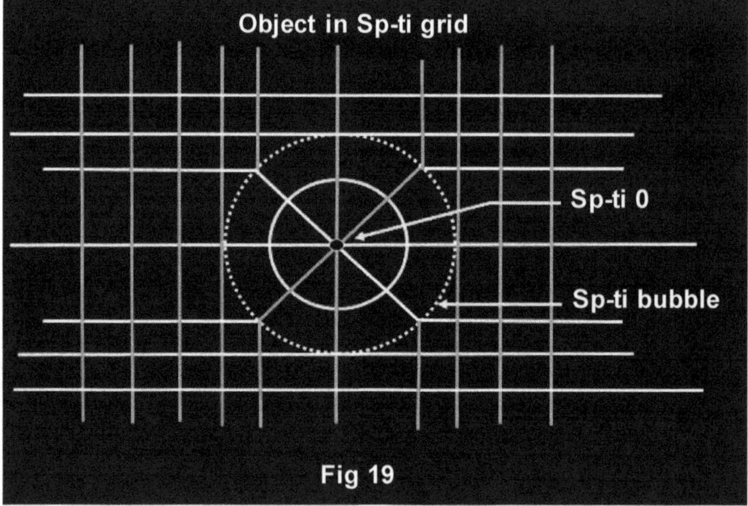

Here, the sp-ti bubble contains space-time for volume as well as mobility of the object. However, the direction of space-lines of volume is away from Sp-ti 0, indicating its evolution, whereas the direction of mobile space-time is towards the Sp-ti 0 indicating certain pressure acting upon the volume of the object by the sp-ti medium externally.

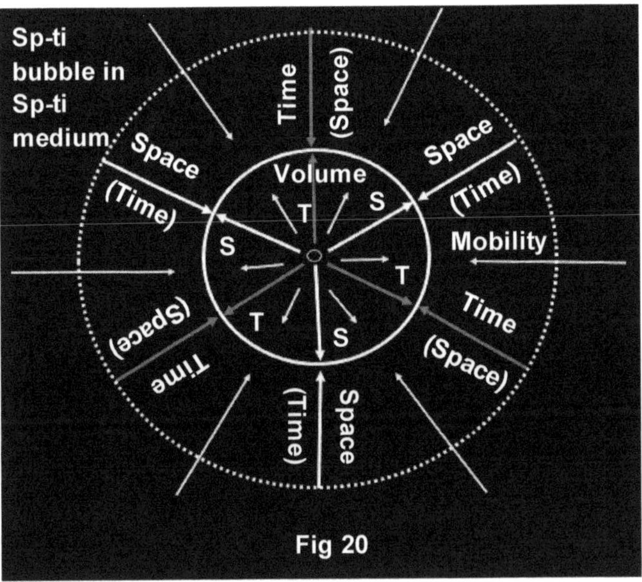

Fig 20

This could be indicated with arrow heads in opposite directions as shown in Fig 20. The space and time lines are shown separately for our simple understanding otherwise they are dual aspects in reality, to be noted.

The yellow arrow lines indicate direction of pressure of space-time aspects within the Sp-ti bubble. The pressure due to the creation and evolution from inside the object pushes the medium away from Sp-ti 0, whereas the medium has the pressure over the object towards Sp-ti 0 and causes variation in mobile space-time available for the object's motion according to speed (changing) and size (fixed) factors.

Now, let us see how length contraction and time dilation in terms of space contraction and time reduction together varies within a Sp-ti bubble with two cases, one is for a constant speed and the other is uniformly increasing speed of the object in Sp-ti medium.

We shall make markings for these variations in the available mobile space-time within Sp-ti bubble. For changes in space, it is denoted as virtual resistance Vr and for change in time, denoted as virtual delay Vd. Virtual resistance decreases from Vn to reach V0 beyond which the medium touches the volume of the object and offers Real resistance Rr and Real delay Rd.

[31]

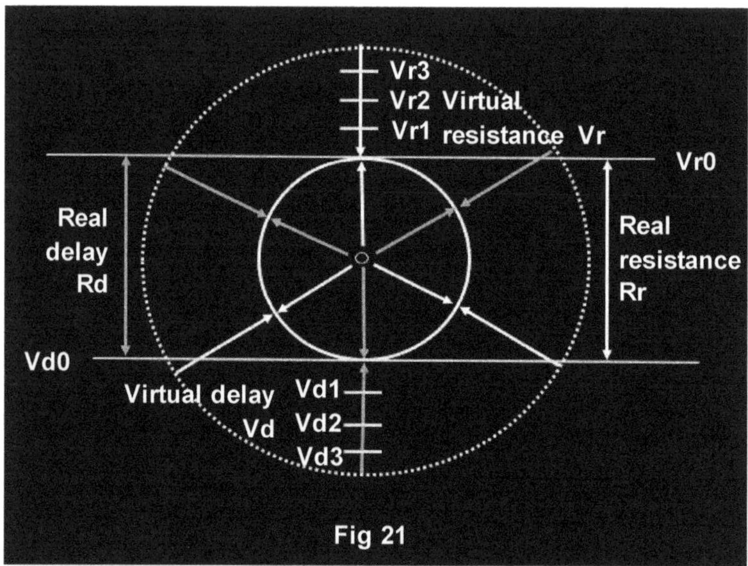

Fig 21

So, for a constant speed of the object, the Sp-ti bubble shrinks to the measure of (say) Vr2 and Vd2 and for uniformly increasing speed the bubble keep reducing in size to reach Vr0 and the point beyond which the real resistance of the medium act on the object.

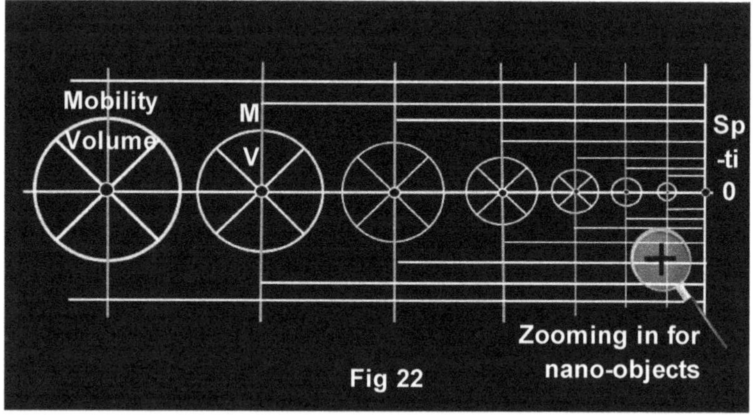

Fig 22

For variation of Sp-ti bubble in case of size factor, it is a fixed one for a single object as the size does not change and we need to compare the objects of various sizes. Means, size of the Sp-ti bubble is proportional to the size of the object itself. Here we assume uniformly increasing or decreasing sizes of the objects in a space-time grid, Fig 22. So, for

[32]

variation of Sp-ti bubble differing between the two cases such as speed and size factors could be represented as follows,

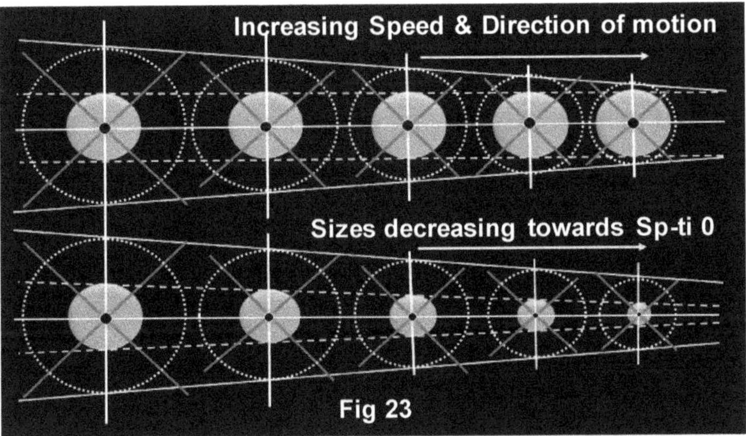

Fig 22 shows a range of objects from large to small sizes in a row along with the Sp-ti grid at its background. This range has limit on either side. We have to zoom in to see the objects at nano scale near to Sp-ti 0 to know what happens to Sp-ti bubble beyond the smallest macro-object.

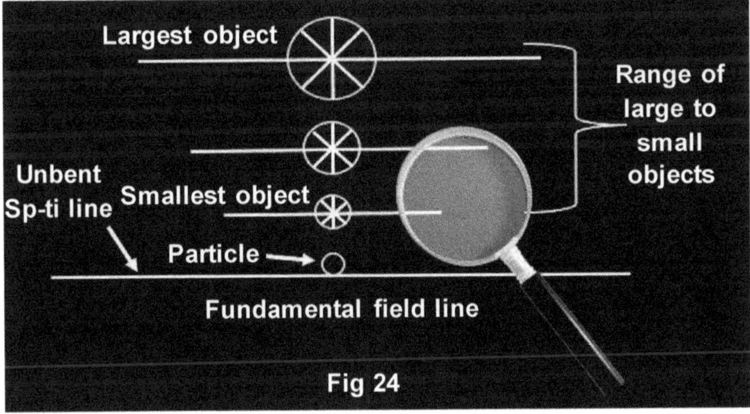

Fig 24 zoomed in to show the objects beyond smallest macro-object where the object is not bending the sp-ti lines anymore and said to be floating in Sp-ti medium. The unbent sp-ti line is free and restored in its own wave nature, to be noted. Thus, the objects that are not capable of bending the space-time with its volume are said to be minute objects and

[33]

their region of existence is called quantum range along with quantum sp-ti grid.

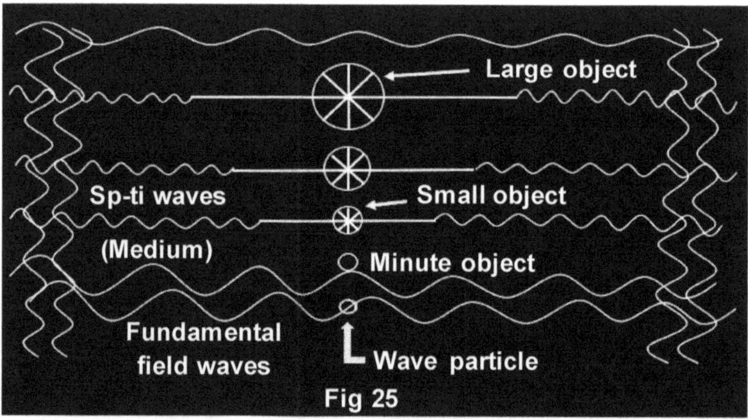

Fig 25

The third dimension of space-time is **'minute'** in nature. Now, applying first and second dimensions of space-time and comparing objects of two different sizes in sp-ti grid, Fig 26.

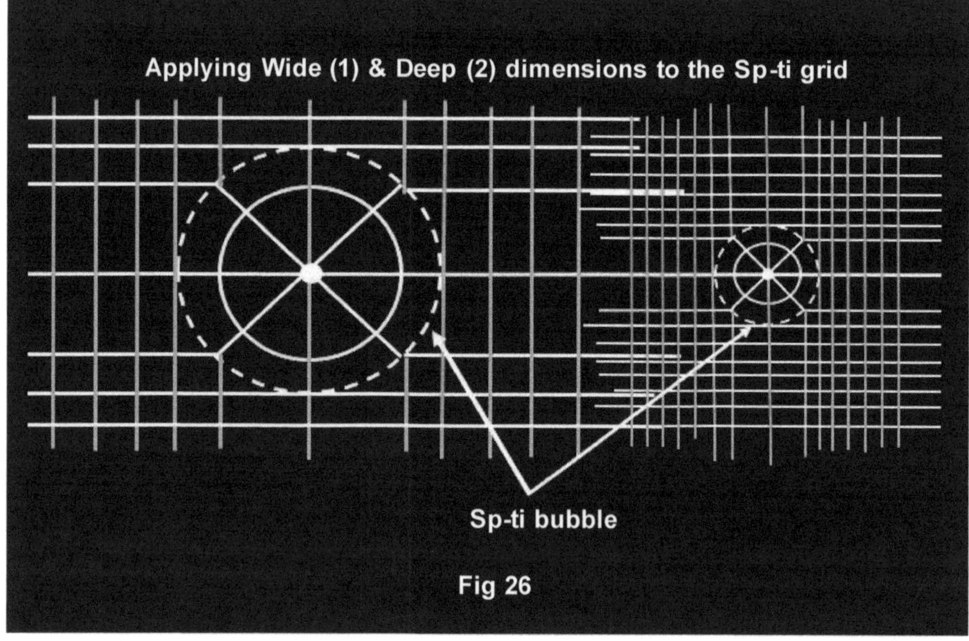

Fig 26

[34]

The thickness of the Sp-ti threads also differs along with the size of the objects. From the discussion so far, the Sp-ti bubble is also limited to macro-objects range between largest to smallest. Before going to check the other extreme beyond largest object, let us complete the dimensional cone with three new dimensions in terms of aspects and tabulate the same.

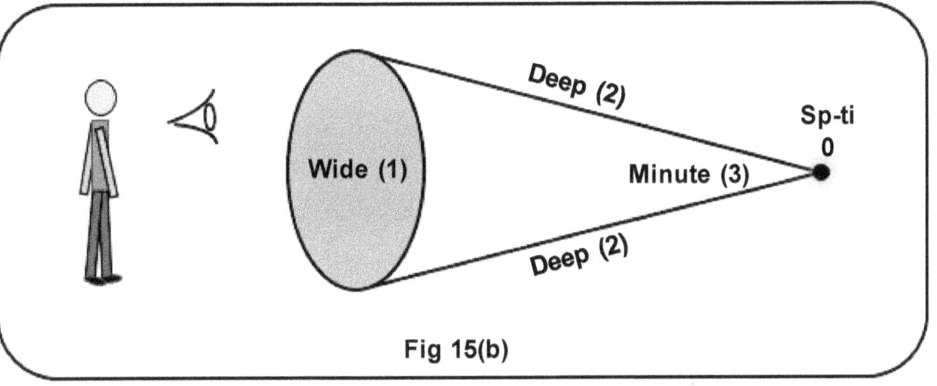

Fig 15(b)

Table of Real dimensions

S. No.	Real dimensions of space-time	Path / Nature
1(a)	**Wide (1D)** - Length	Curvilinear
1(b)	**Wide (1D)** - Width	Curvilinear
1(c)	**Wide (1D)** - Height	Curvilinear
1(d)	**Wide (1D)** – Surface Radius	Curvilinear
2	**Deep (2D)** - Deep radius	Radial
3	**Minute (3D)** - Waveform	Oscillation

We discovered minute dimension by zooming into the sp-ti grid near to Sp-ti 0 where the objects are floating on the space-time waves. Now moving on to the point next to the largest object, the variation in Sp-ti bubble is further consumed by the object itself, not in terms of volume but with its mass density.

The bending of sp-ti lines by volume and mass of the object sounds to be same, as mass is constituting the volume or volume is occupied by the mass in either way but still there is a minute difference between the two. Bending of Sp-ti lines by different mass densities, Fig 28.

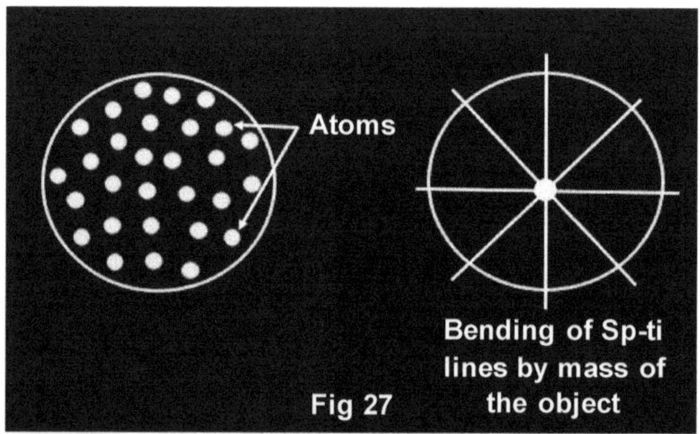

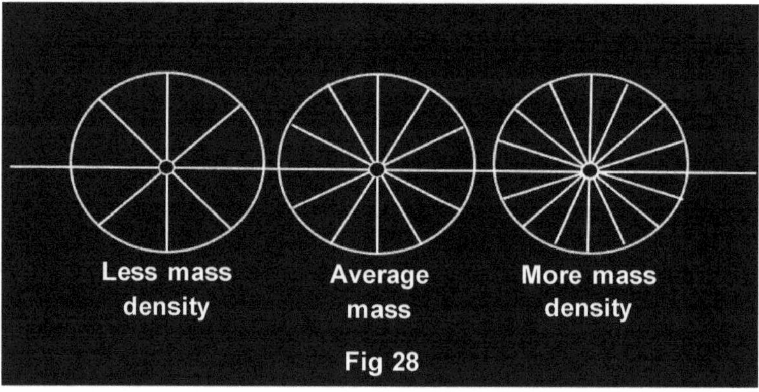

Comparison between mass and volume of the objects in space-time medium, Fig 29. Mass-volume is an inseparable duality.

a) Volume:

- Changes pertaining to length of the bending sp-ti lines.
- Length of the bending sp-ti lines extends between surface and depth.

[36]

b) Mass:

- Changes pertaining to No. of bending sp-ti lines.
- No. of bending sp-ti lines depends upon density or packing of atoms in an object.

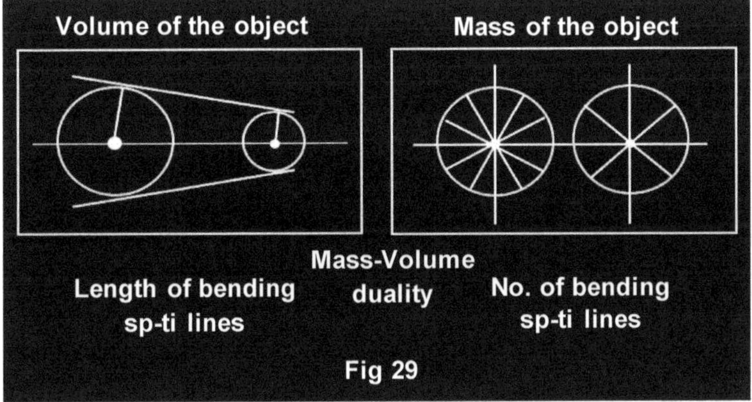

Fig 29

Beyond certain limit, the density of the object exceeds the maximum number of sp-ti lines and starts bending the lines of sp-ti grid itself. This type of bending caused in sp-ti fabric is described by Einstein. So, such objects are more than the largest objects and shall be called as heavy objects in space-time medium, Fig 30.

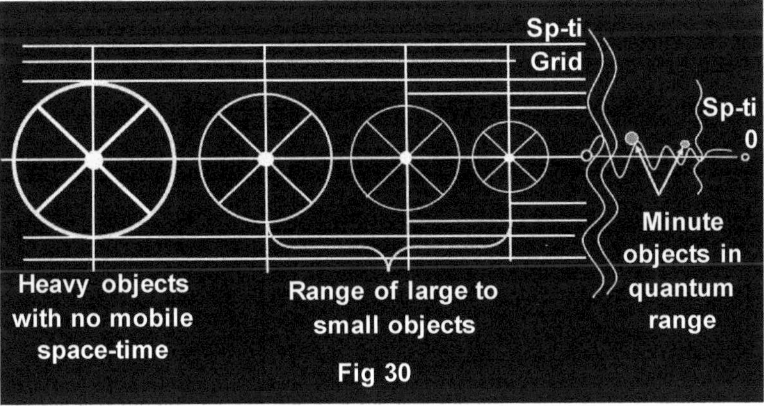

Fig 30

The objects becoming heavy would completely use up the mobile space-time available for its free motion in sp-ti medium. The Fig 30 shows the

[37]

object to have reached min sp-ti tolerance point beyond which the Sp-ti grid lines would bend, as the object starts to bite it with its mass density.

This could be discussed in detail under the topic of gravitation. Now, we move on to particle physics based on real dimensions of space-time. The point where we found the unbent sp-ti lines set free to be waves, on which the minute objects are floating, the general physics is shown to connect with the modern quantum physics without any contradictions, to be noted.

We shall see the representation of all the three real dimensions of space-time, Fig 31.

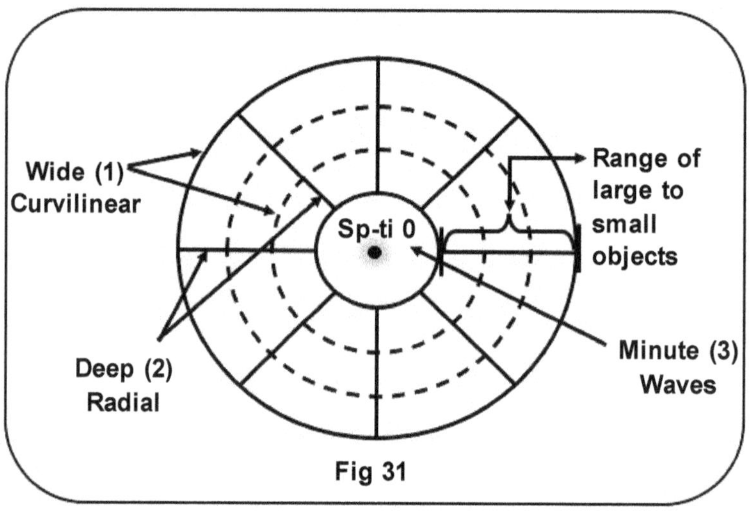

Fig 31

7.0 SP-TI OCEAN

We have seen that the minute objects such as particles float on the waves. These waves are unlike sea waves as there is no shore in space-time medium. However, the Universe we live is evolved from this wave of shoreless Dark Ocean. The specialty of this wave is oscillating in the same position and called multi-dimensional standing waves. Somehow, we imagine the same as shown in Fig 32.

Sea waves
Standing waves of Sp-ti
Particle
Fig 32(a)

Multi-dimensional Sp-ti waves
Fig 32(b)

Fig 32(c)
Male Energy
Sp-ti 0
axis
Sp-ti 0
Female Energy
Mating of
waves
Sp-ti 0
Male wave
Sp-ti
Nucleus
Female wave

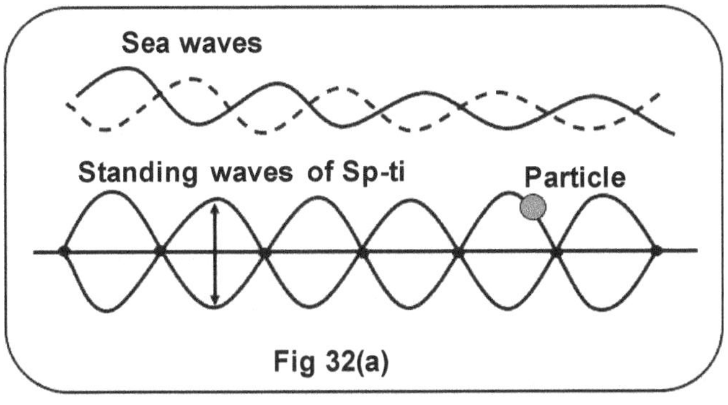

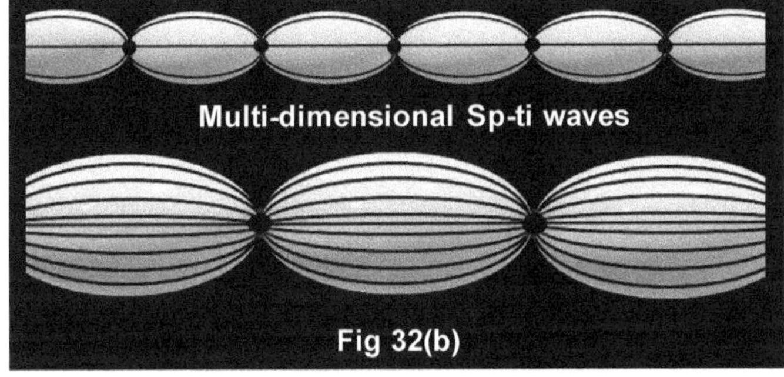

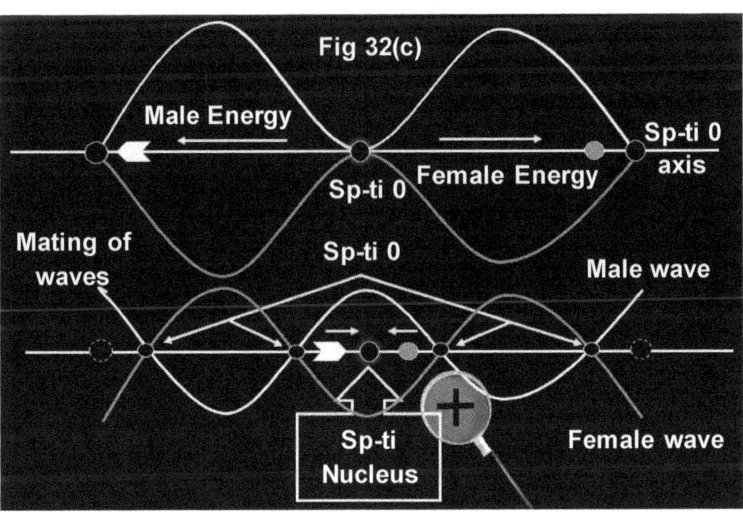

[39]

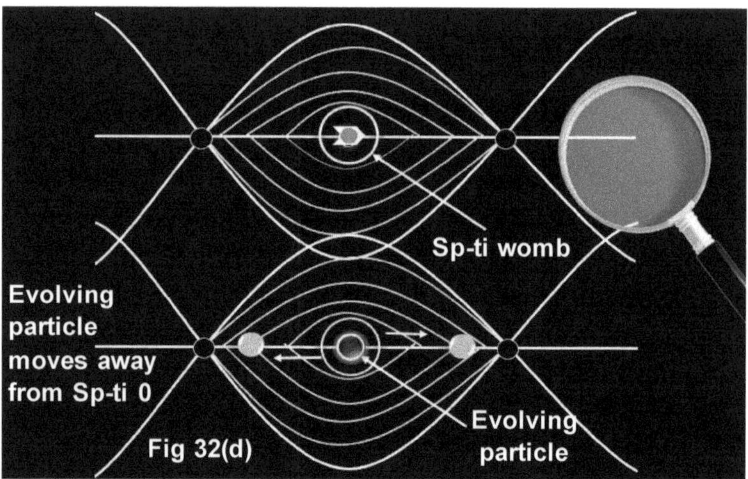

Multi-dimensional Sp-ti wave contain numerous wave pairs with a minimum of at least one pair of waves and not a single line wave. Depending upon the path of the evolving particle, there are lot of characteristics associated with it like charges, spin, up, down types etc.

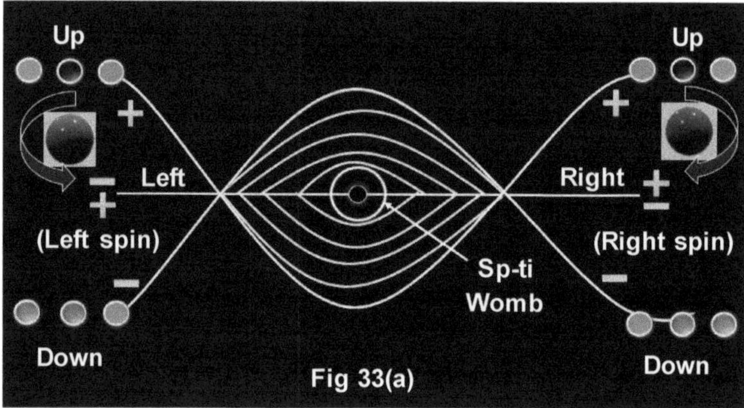

Sp-ti womb is created as a result of male-female sp-ti waves mating, from which the fundamental particles evolve.

We see the minute dimension of a single bead of wave at quantum range again contains wide, deep and minute dimensions in it, Fig 33(b). Minute womb for creation of the particle, Radial path for its growth and Wide dimension with curvilinear path is available for moving particles. So, the three real dimensions exists together at any point of space-time.

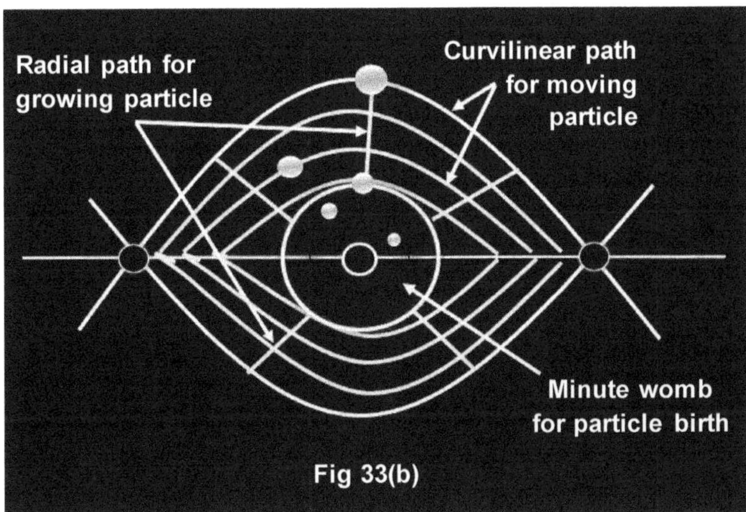

Fig 33(c) shows the representation of sp-ti pond, in which particle detached from fundamental field has particle nature, particle along with the field is a duality of wave-particle nature and considering the field alone has wave nature same as sp-ti medium.

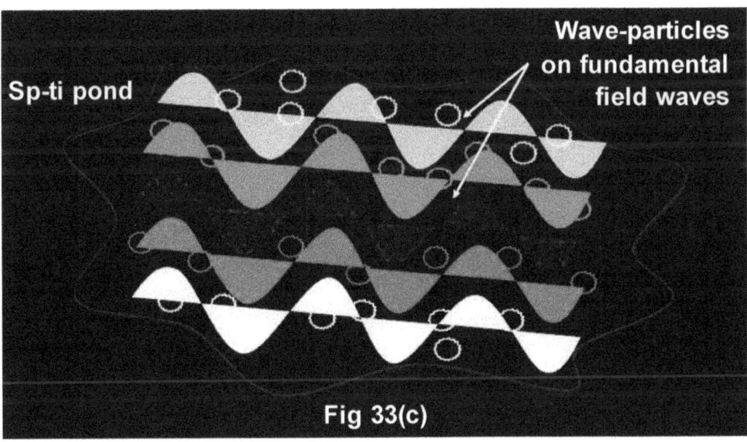

Fundamental field waves are originally Sp-ti waves and it could be distinguished only with colors. The letters written in the sp-ti pond denotes fundamental sound notes associated with dimensions. For our understanding the colors of different fundamental fields are shown in Fig 33(c).

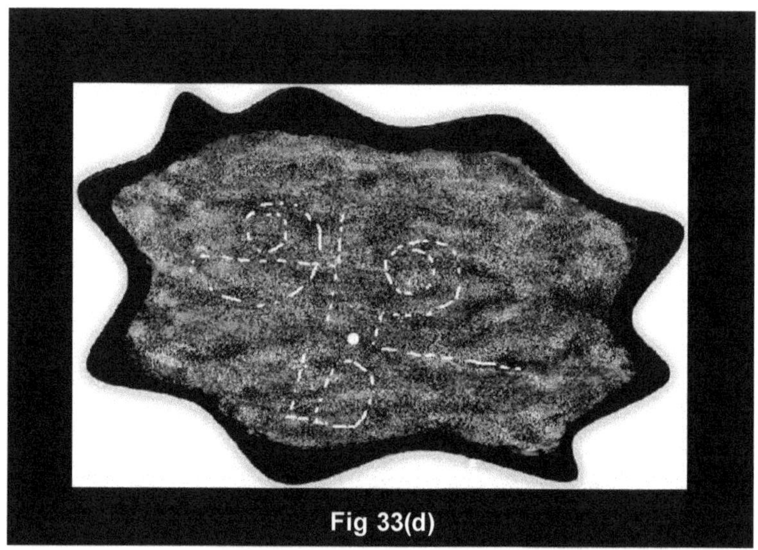

Fig 33(d)

Thus, Fig 34 shows the representation of dimensions along with the Sp-ti waves that is present over the entire existence. The fundamental field waves are shown within the minute dimension range. However, in reality they are like pool of mixed colors, Fig 33(d).

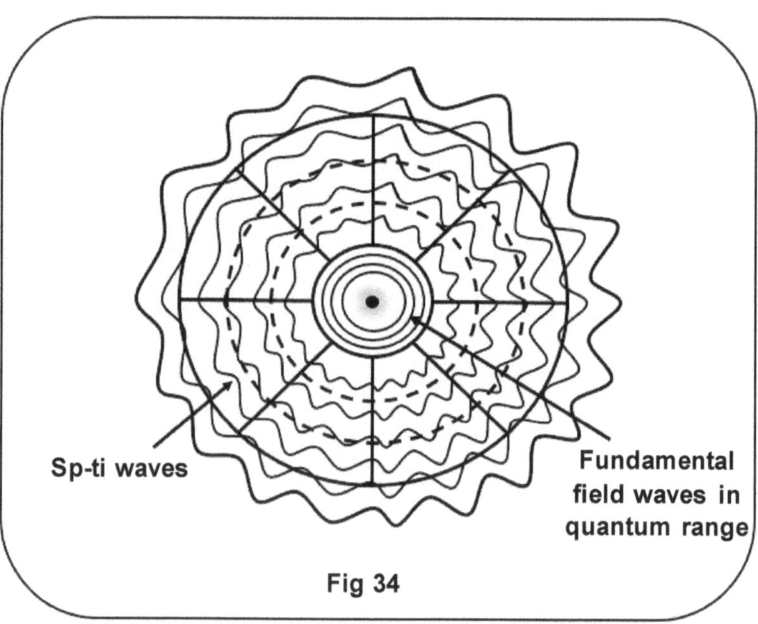

Fig 34

In Fig 34, since, the field waves are shown to have accumulated in the center of the representation, we call it as Sp-ti pond. In reality, there is no pond of fields in one particular location in the medium, to be noted.

8.0 PARTICLE PHYSICS; PART-1

The particle physics have only five main points to be discussed as follows,

i)   Dual nature of the particle to behave as particle as well as wave.

ii)   Collapsing of wave function into a particle when an observation is made.

iii)   Super position of a particle, to exist at multiple positions at the same time.

iv)   Quantum entanglement – communication between two particles at instantaneous speed irrespective of distance.

v)   Disappearing of particle at one point and re-appearing at another point by even crossing the barriers.

The particle has only one nature of being a particle. Means, the wave behavior of particle is actually indicating the nature of space-time medium itself, at its background. The observation we make on particle is on the tail end of fourth dimension. The diagrams discussed so far clearly shows that the particles are minute objects that are free floating on fundamental field waves which in turn is along with sp-ti waves.

There is an obvious point where the particle detaches itself from the wave. Fig 25 shows a wave-particle in its fundamental field wave at a point below the actual particle about to exist.

The problem of mysteries in physics is due to lack of dimensions, visualization and continuity, starting from the point of evolution of a fundamental particle to macro-object.

Before the particle attains a purpose of evolving to surface of life, it is obviously in a non-directional region of space-time medium. Only when it is called, even (say) for an observation, it becomes directional and serves the purpose.

Even without a need for fourth dimension and mathematical expressions, it is possible to visualize the same with simple drawings. All the major problems of physics could be solved with the only idea or understanding that, space-time medium has surface and depth.

a) Super position of a particle in terms of space:

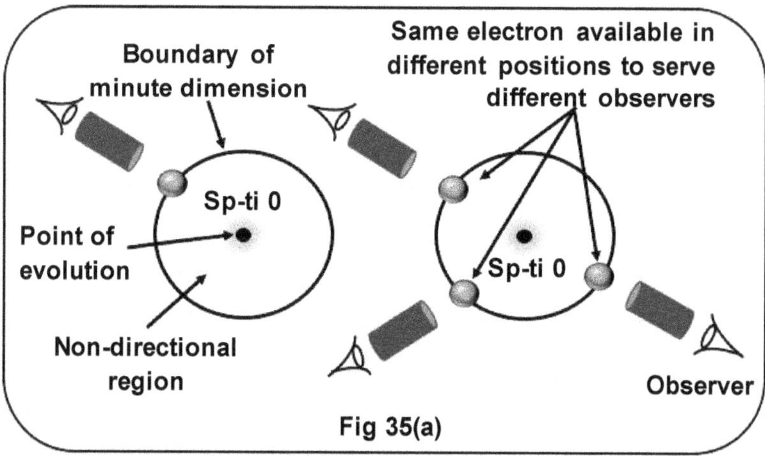

Fig 35(a)

Here, for simplicity consider an observer is observing an electron evolved from Sp-ti 0. This electron must be away from zero so that if the same electron is observed by another observer from a different direction, it must be available for his observation as well.

Nature has made a special dimension for a particle to be spherically available in all the directions. Hence the minute dimension is said to be a non-directional region with a boundary and beyond this line the particle has purpose (say) even for an observation and so a direction in space-time medium.

b) Super position of a particle in terms of time:

The representation of three real dimensions discussed so far, we divide the same into 8 sections as shown in Fig 32(b) and consider one of the sections with a macro-object on wide dimension and a particle such as an electron along the boundary of minute dimension, for comparison.

This diagram could be further taken for a straight-line path of both macro and quantum object to observe its motion in time. One moment for an object in macro-scale is equal to several moments in quantum scale.

[44]

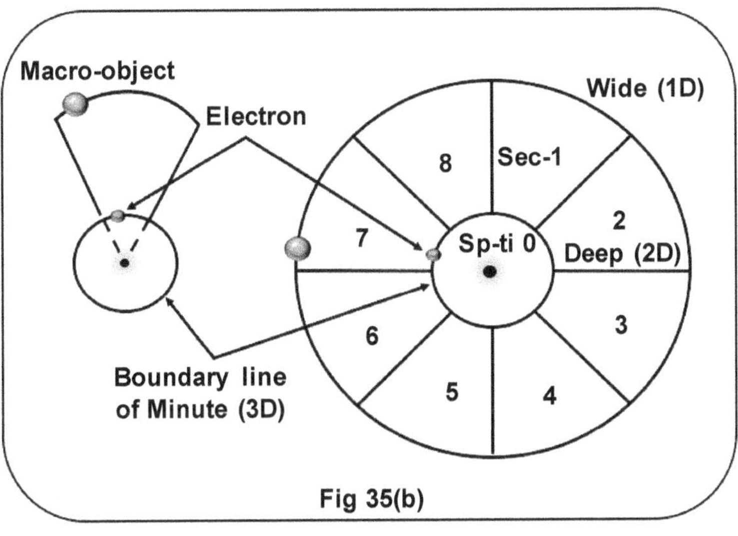

Fig 35(b)

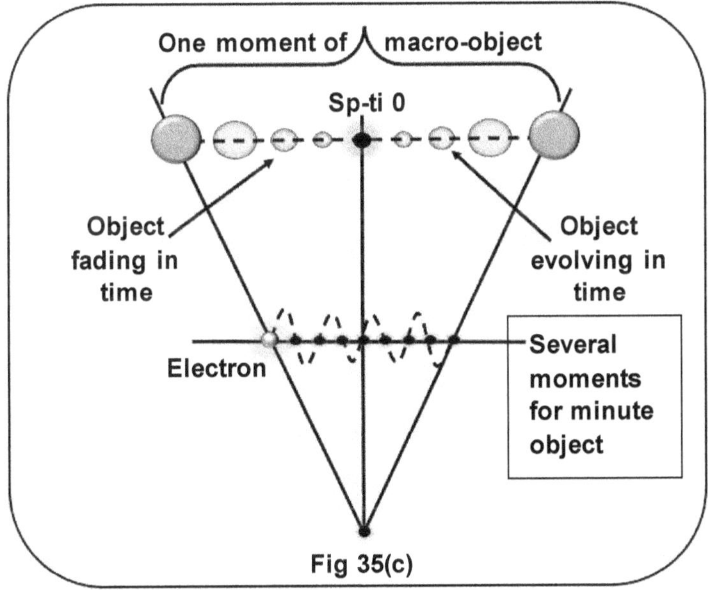

Fig 35(c)

Means, a quantum object such as an electron has more time to see a macro-object to evolve. If the object itself is made up of atoms and sub-atomic particles, which one of the electrons could fully watch the object evolving in space-time? The answer is, the deepest one in the dimensional cone is last one to remain and see the whole changes except its own disappearance in Sp-ti 0, to be noted.

c) Super position of a particle in terms of Space-time:

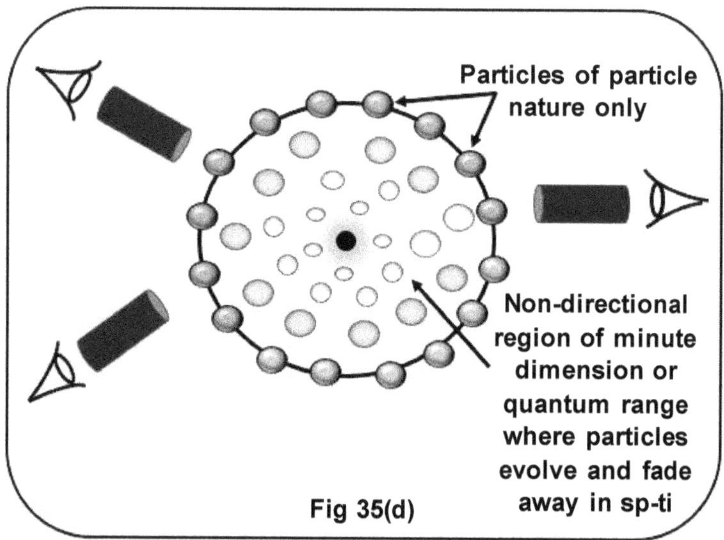

Fig 35(d)

The representation of super-position of a particle is same for both space and time as shown in Fig 35(d).

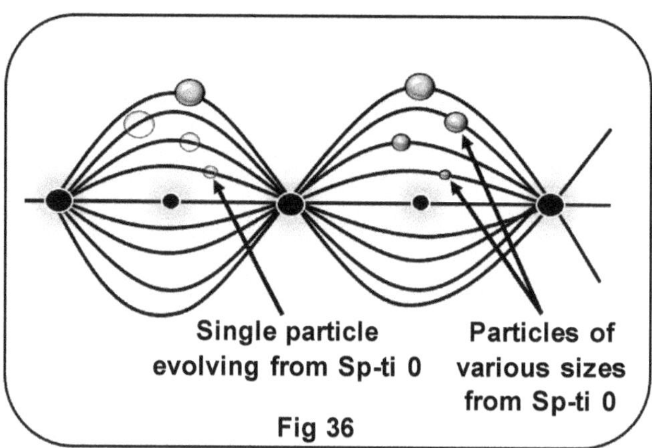

Fig 36

Multi-dimensional wave: Wave path of a particle and 3 dimensions in a single bead. Fig 33(b), could be used to show one electron evolving

[46]

from sp-ti 0, growing in size radially to reach wide path which is the boundary line of minute dimension.

The same diagram could be used for particles of various sizes, by splitting the diagram as follows.

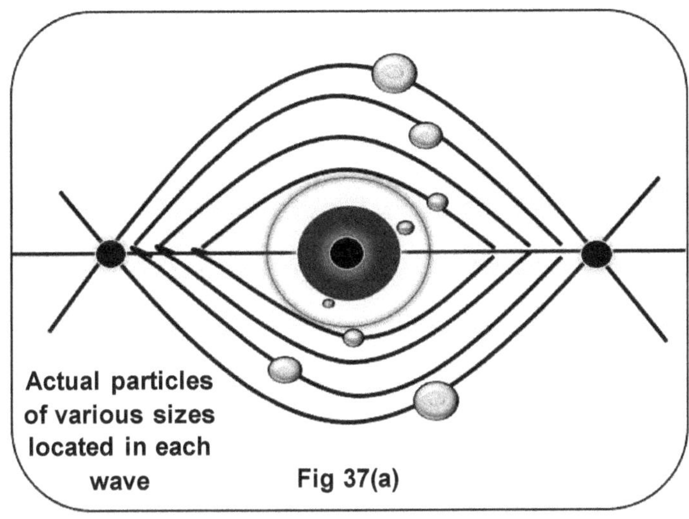

Fig 37(a)

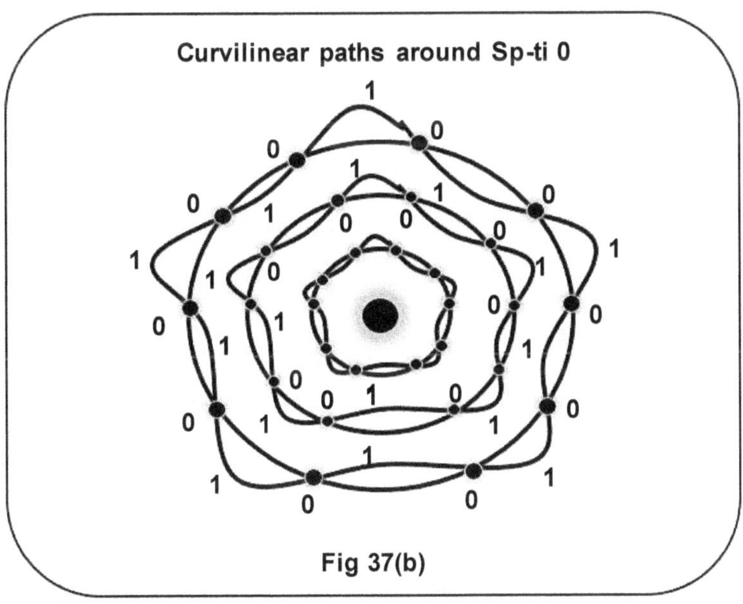

Fig 37(b)

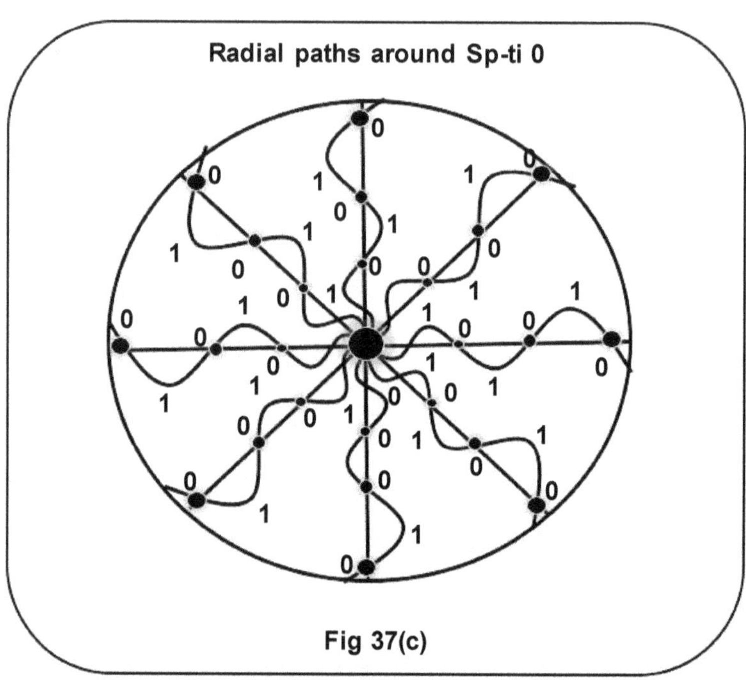

Fig 37(c)

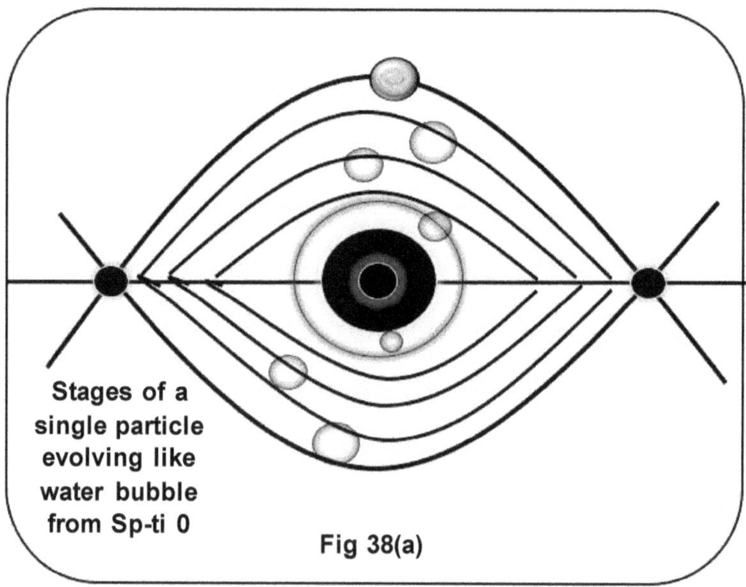

Fig 38(a)

[48]

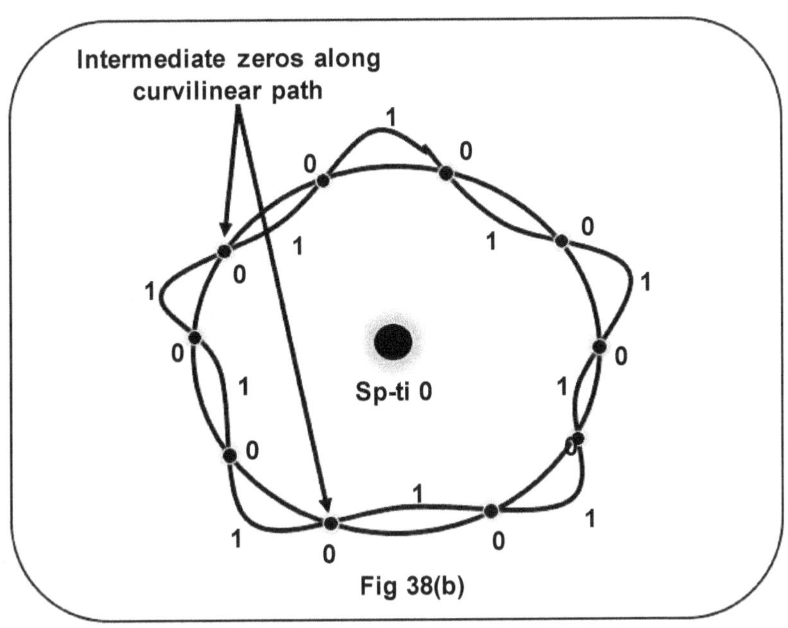

Fig 38(b)

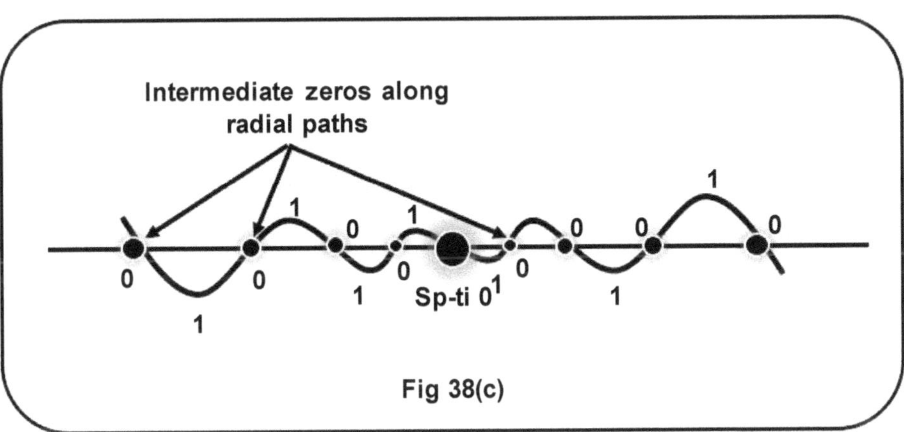

Fig 38(c)

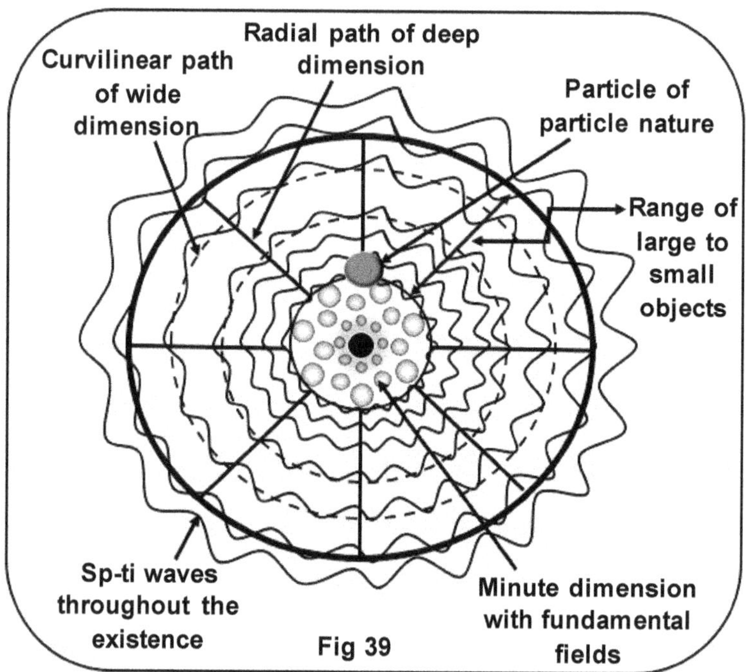

d) Quantum entanglement

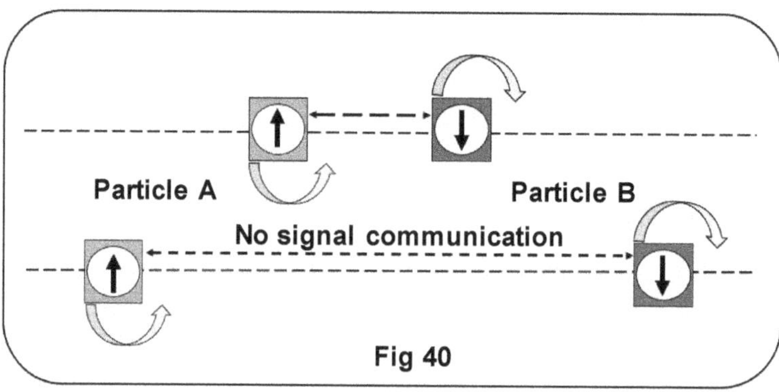

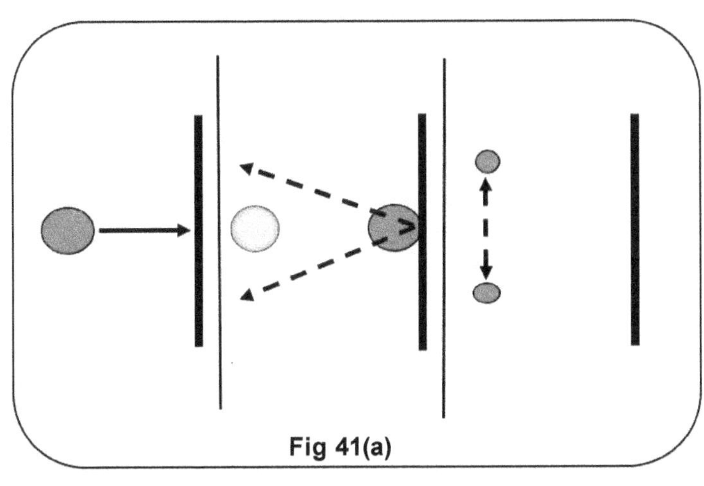

Fig 41(a)

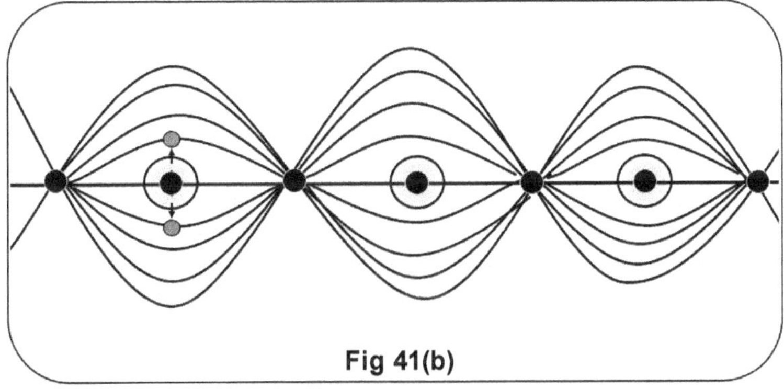

Fig 41(b)

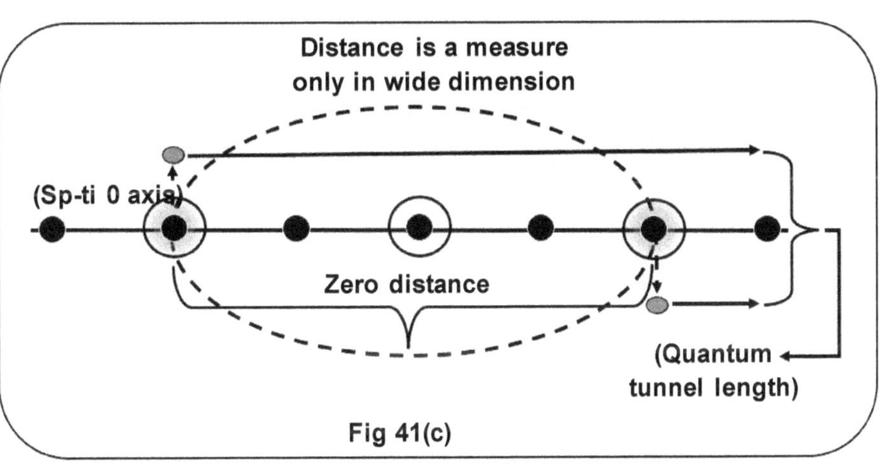

Fig 41(c)

[51]

9.0 FOURTH DIMENSION OF SPACE-TIME

1) Fourth dimension need not be a geometrical projection imagined with a 4D object (say) more like a cube in three dimensions.

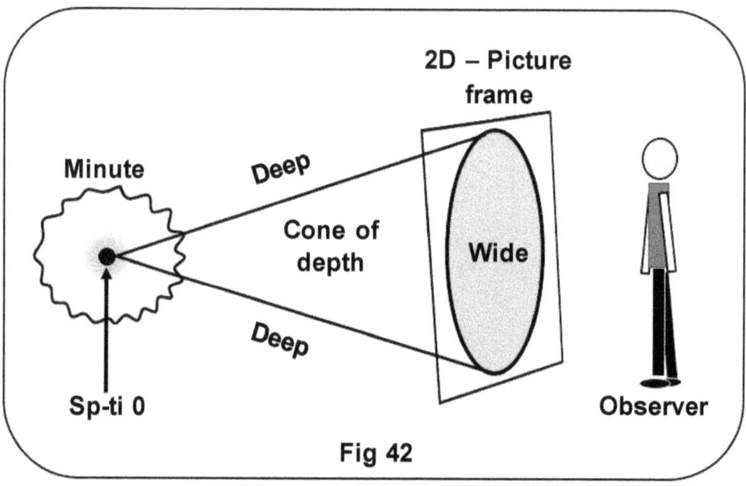

Fig 42

2) As we see the cone of depth in space-time, only the base is constituting the picture frame while depth is projected for our understanding, Fig 42. At no point the dimensions could exist independently like one without the other.

3) The most special aspect about 4D is, it could contain the other three lower dimensions one within the other. Considering a cube of wide dimension means, it contains the cube of deep dimension which in turn contains minute dimension in it, as shown in Fig 43(a).

4) The cubic representation also has the challenge of showing the connections between two considered sp-ti cubes such that the inner dimensions cannot be linked externally, Fig 43(b).

In this case, one may wonder how the Sp-ti 0 axis is said to have zero distance between any two points in space-time medium as the Sp-ti 0s situated at the centers of the cubes, are further away than the dimensions itself. The quantum entanglement between two particles could be solved only by knowing the possibility of this inner connection.

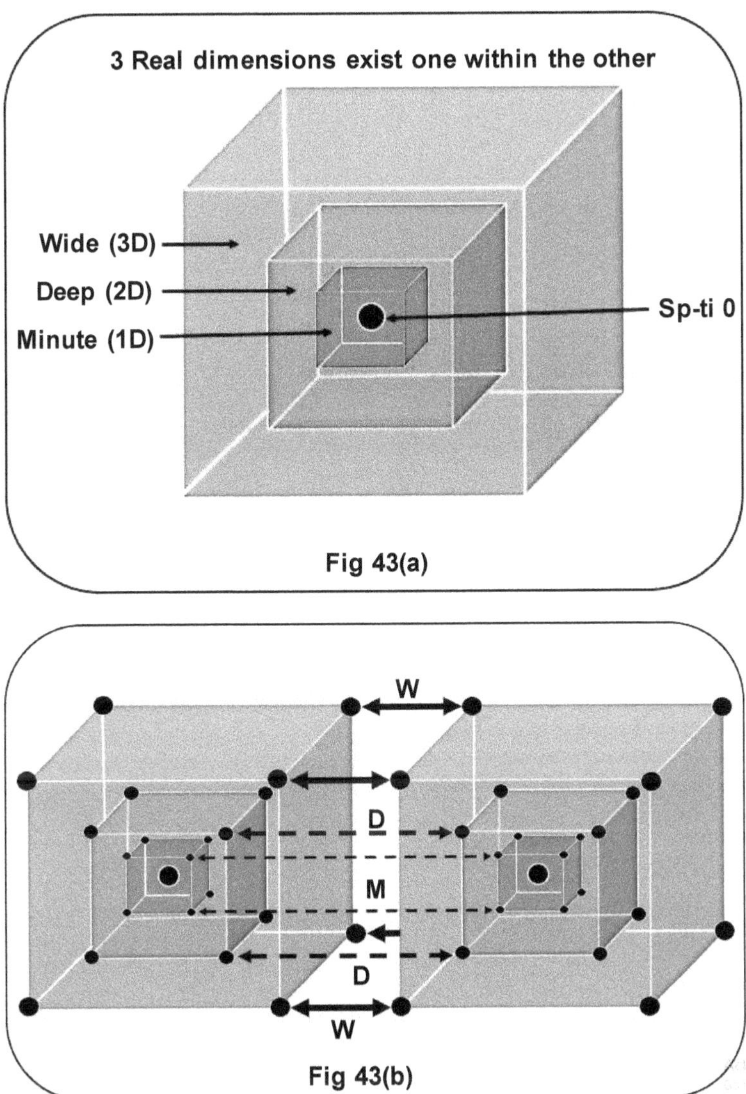

Now, as we know the fundamental fields and the Sp-ti medium are wave natures, the existence could be imagined to be full of waves whose simple representation is as shown, Fig 44(a). Previously we called the fundamental fields at the center of the representation as Sp-ti pond. Now, altogether along with Sp-ti waves, the medium is called as Sp-ti Ocean.

[53]

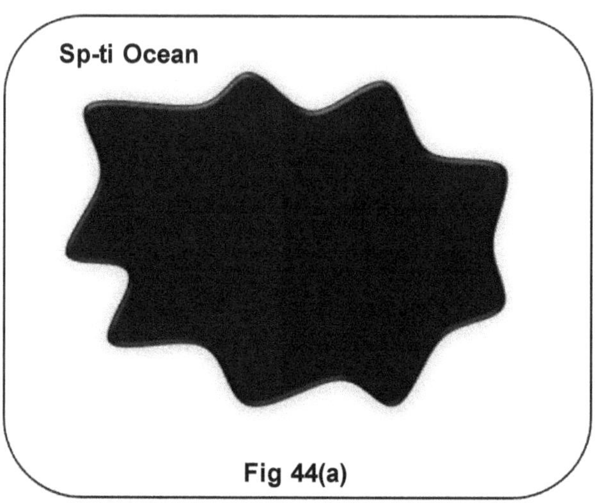

Fig 44(a)

We will have to solve the in & out duality of this shoreless ocean as well as reveal its nature in detail. For now, let us continue only with the wave shape of this dark ocean.

As we discussed before, the Sp-ti 0 points are distributed throughout the existence. The space-time medium without any dimensions at its bed, have the point of singularity in 0D, Fig 44(b).

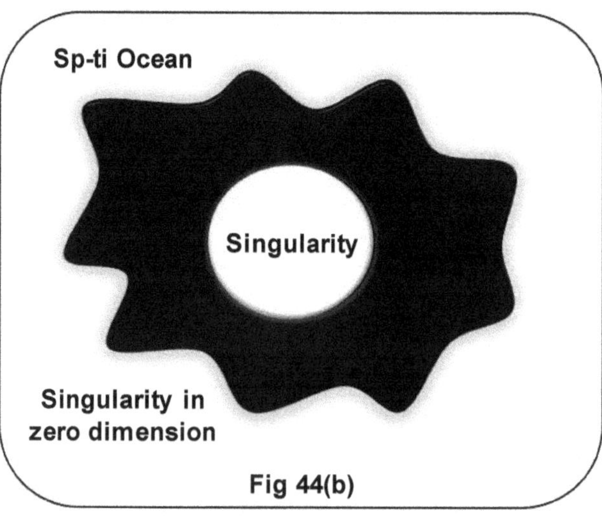

Fig 44(b)

The existing studies think that singularity is an unknown darkness with one way entry such as a blackhole. But it is not true, singularity is pure self-light source. Sp-ti 0 point discussed so far is also singular however, it is distributed from surface to depth of space-time medium whereas the singularity is the deepest point which is beyond the medium and the ever-existing nature.

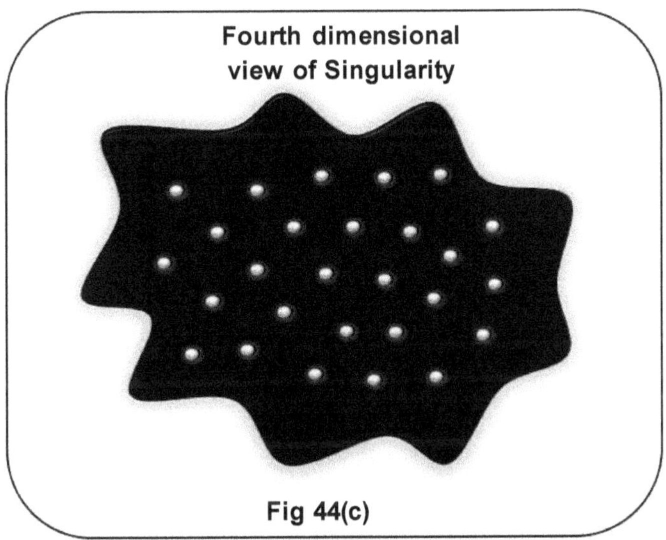

Fig 44(c)

Now, how to mark this point of singularity? Same like Sp-ti 0s, the singularity also could be shown as distributed points in Sp-ti Ocean, even if it is the singular deepest point though. What does it mean? Here comes the fourth dimension of space-time, Fig 44(c).

The zero dimension of singularity cannot have a wide variety of nature, colors, geometry, patterns, characteristics, features etc., and it exists only as nothing (observed by nobody). On the other hand, if it replicates itself with multiple points, it gives rise to life of complex attributes with differences. This difference between any two points is the basis for flow of life. The singularity in 0D is the unchanging, ever-existing and unobserved light source.

Fourth dimension is same as zero dimension when the whole existence is considered. Means, the whole observable differentiated appearances

[55]

called everything in 4D is same as single unobservable integrated appearance called nothing in 0D. So, the representation shows 0 and 4 to be same as 0 and 12 in a round clock, Fig 45.

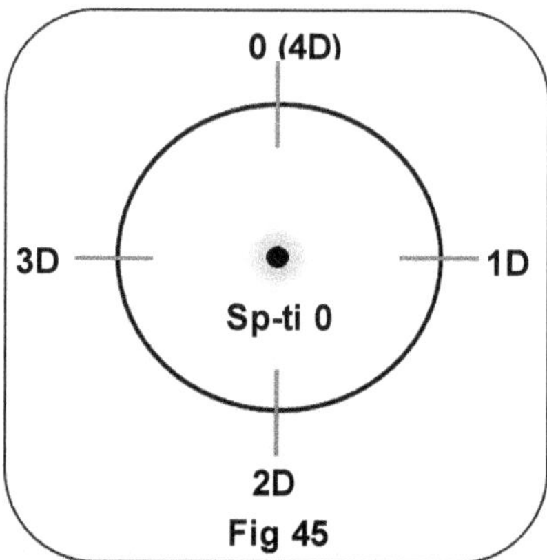

Fig 45

The Sp-ti ocean or pond contains the Sp-ti 0s same like water molecules however, it is unlike the ocean and pond we see in our world. There are three positions of sp-ti 0 such as boundary, base and core. In water bodies the molecules serve the base throughout the body of water and the boundary is associated with the shape of the container in which it could be poured or contained. There is no core point here.

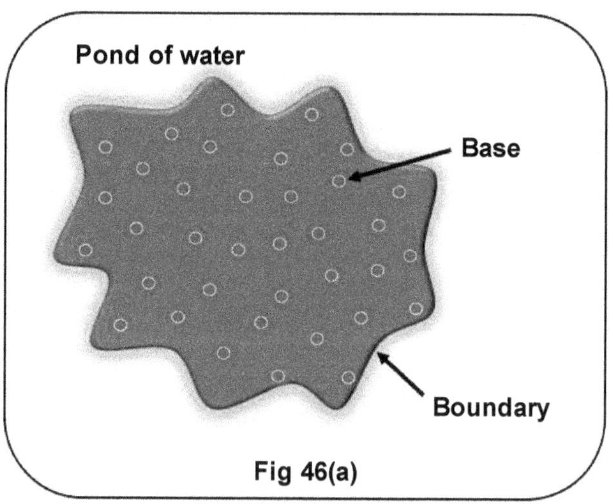

Fig 46(a)

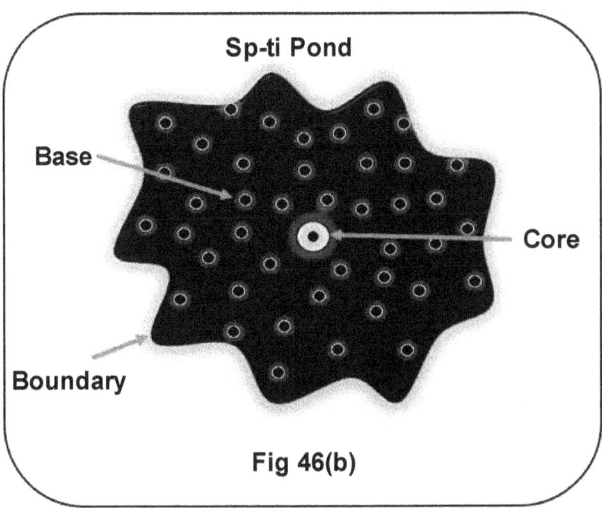

Fig 46(b)

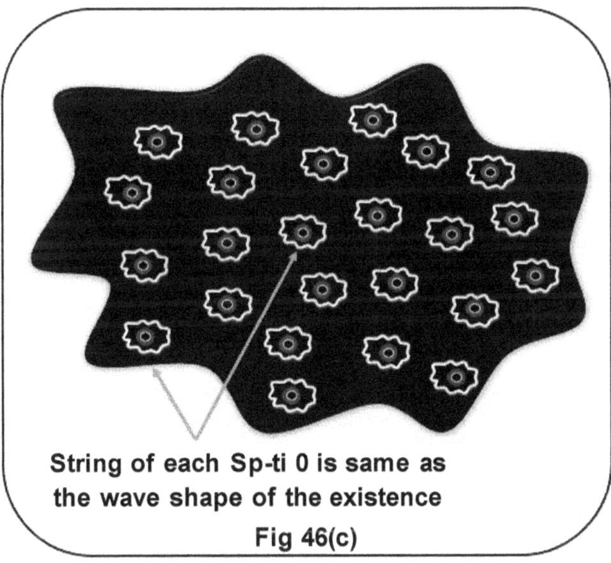

Fig 46(c)

Core position is within the quantum range, so applying the same, each Sp-ti 0 becomes a string Fig 46(c). Sp-ti Ocean is shoreless and four-dimensional, consisting of three aspects. The core point is yet difficult to imagine for the connection that constitute zero distance or no distance. To understand this point, let us break the darkness into bubbles with a center white dots or light spots before the evolution of Sp-ti medium itself.

[57]

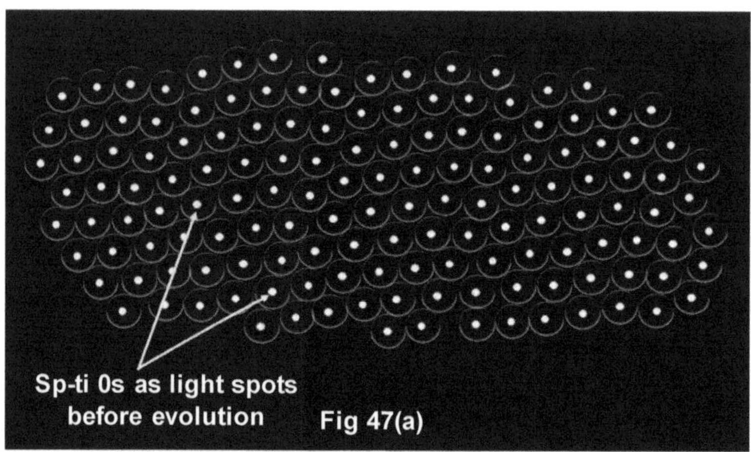

The conversion shown in Fig 47(b) is from 4D to 0D. But from 0D to 4D, it involves evolution through three real dimensions discussed so far in the order of 0-1-2-3-4.

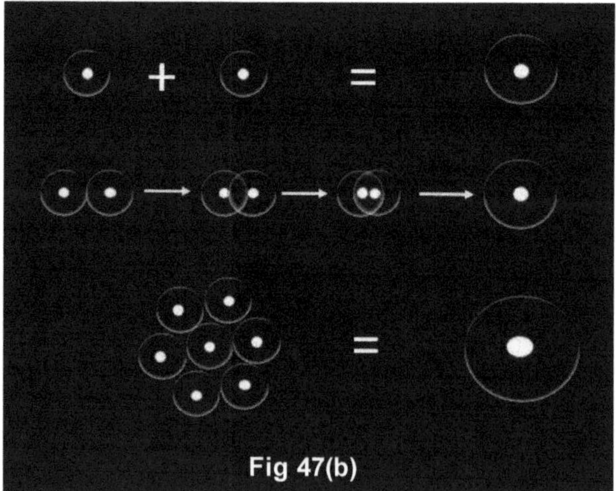

For our simple understanding, say 4D means the multiple reflection of Sp-ti 0 which is the singularity in 0D.

Fourth dimension is also a special kind that makes the previous three dimensions to exist indistinguishably. There is obviously a point that separates non-geometrical nature of space-time in reality from geometrical way of understanding, which is pertaining to human mind.

[58]

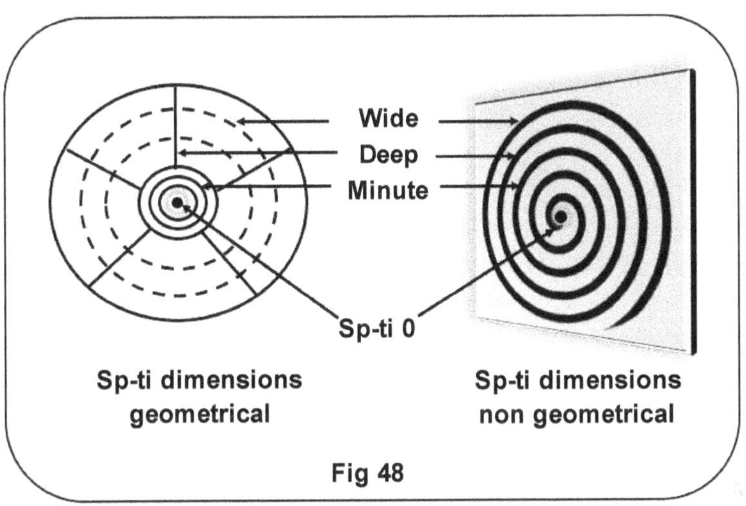

Fig 48

Applying the non-geometrical dimensions for each Sp-ti 0 as follows,

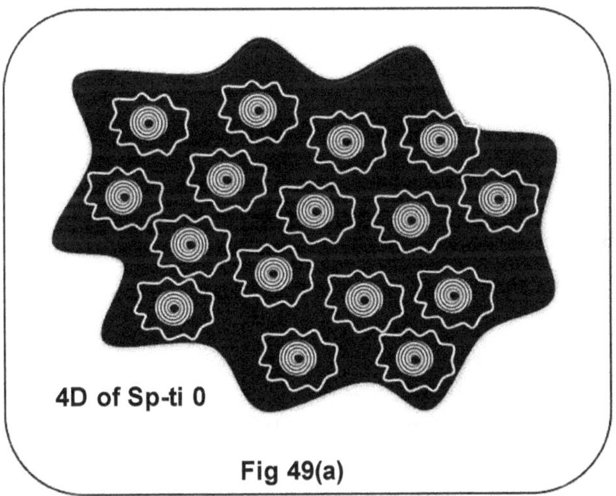

Fig 49(a)

The strings contain the spiral coils (real dimensions as non-geometrical aspects). From Fig 49(a), clearly beyond the quantum range both in 4D and 0D there is a spiral ending point of space-time which is same as the beginning point of evolution of space-time. So, the whole existence with the real dimensions at 0D could be represented as shown in Fig 49(b).

[59]

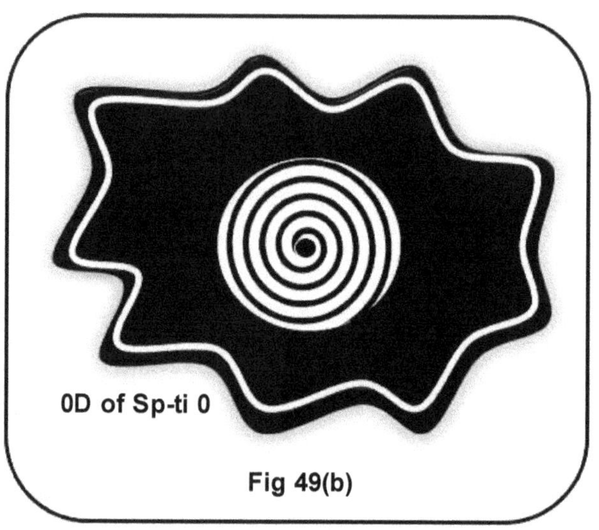

Fig 49(b)

10.0 REAL DIMENSIONS OF SPACE-TIME

(Non-geometrical aspects)

Earlier, we said that the maximum possible imagination about the Universe could only be spherically expanding or contracting which in turn has a duality of in & out. Anyone could imagine and raise the question of what is beyond the boundary of the Universe we live. This could be solved with fourth dimension.

4D has the following specialties – summarized,

- Containing the other three real dimensions.
- 3 Dimensions to exist one within the other.
- Three dimensions to be spirally indistinguishable.
- 3 Dimensions does not exist one without the other.

Now, what is more special about 4D is, it could solve the in & out duality of the existence, by the way it arranges wide, deep and minute aspects in

[60]

the form of dimensional rings, which is apart from Sp-ti grid configuration, Fig 50.

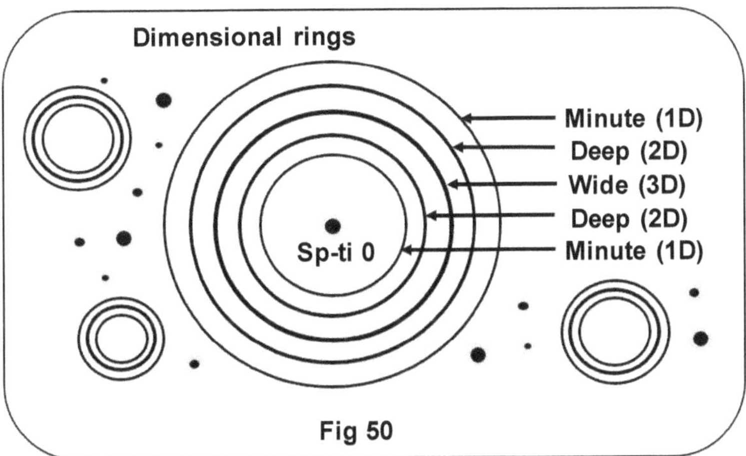

Fig 50

Fig 50, appears to be a representation of dimensions in concentric circles but it is not so, the deep and minute dimensions are on either side of wide dimensions. How come this could solve the in & out duality needs more details about boundary, base and core dimensions which are also more or less the same but non-geometrical aspects corresponding to wide, deep and minute dimensions.

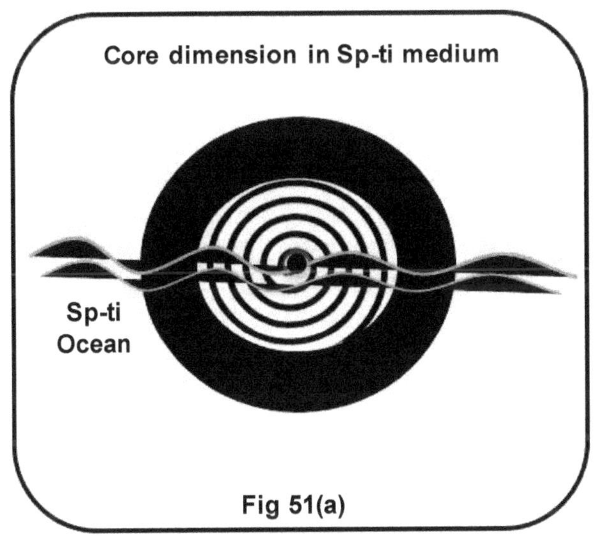

Fig 51(a)

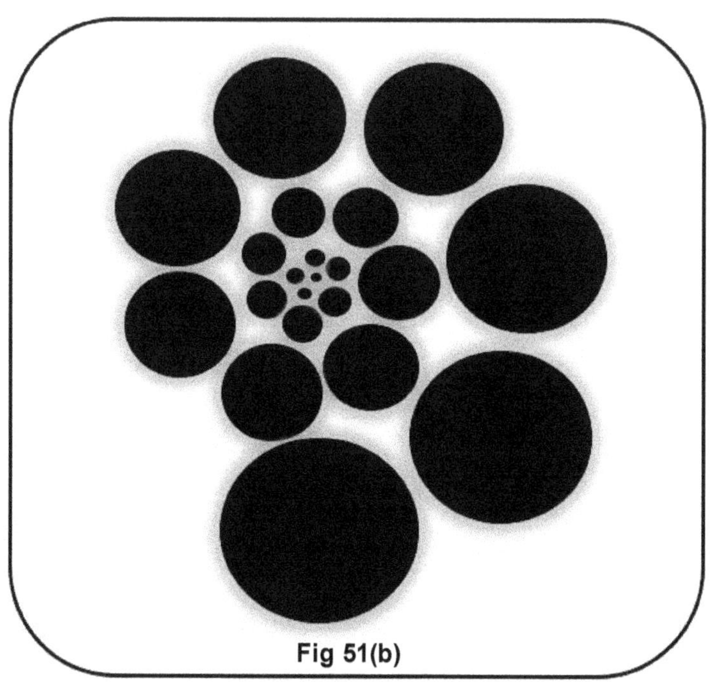

Fig 51(b)

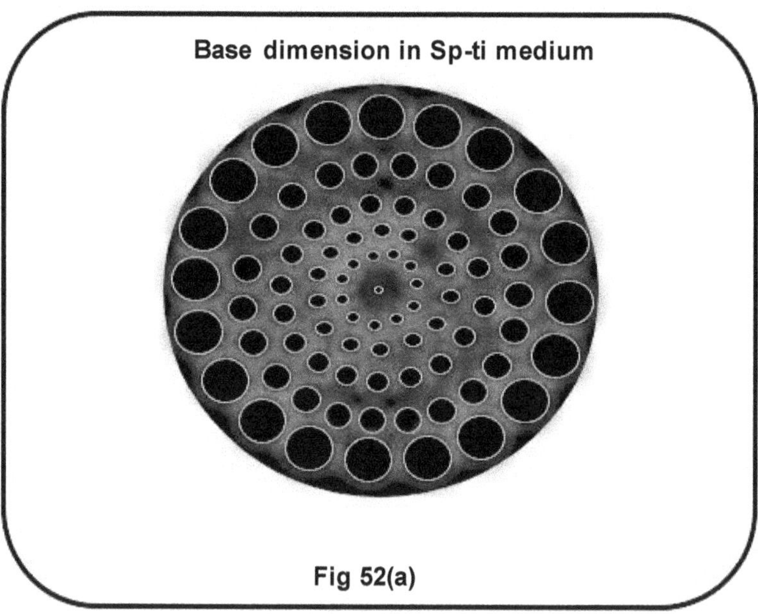

Fig 52(a)

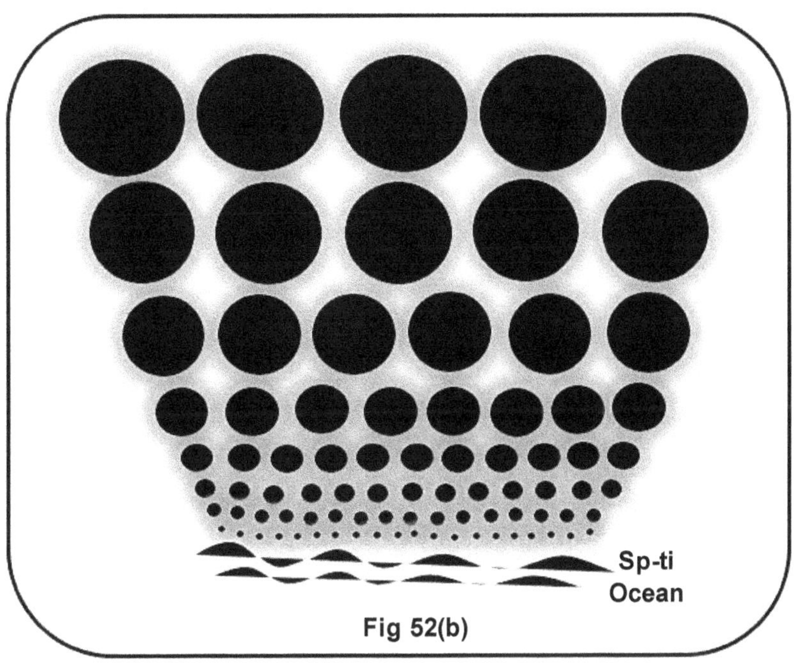

Fig 52(b)

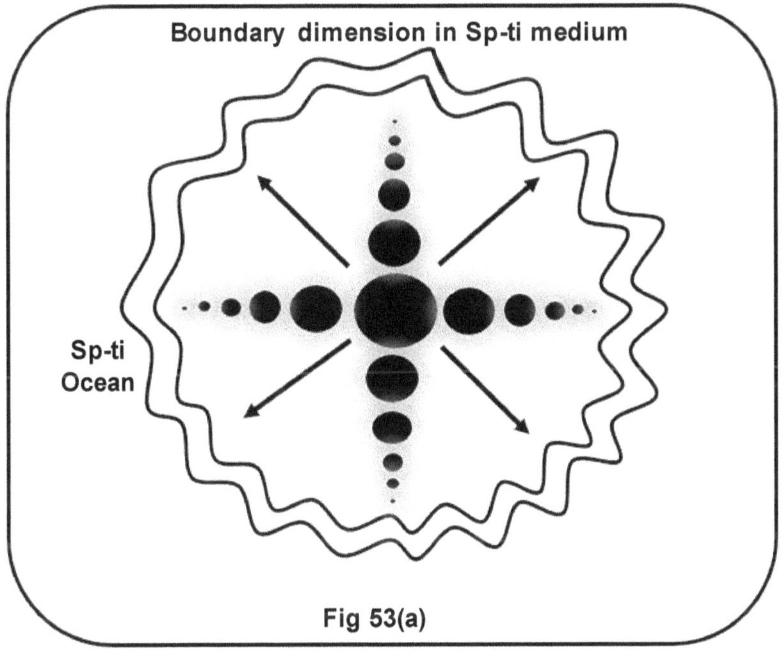

Fig 53(a)

[63]

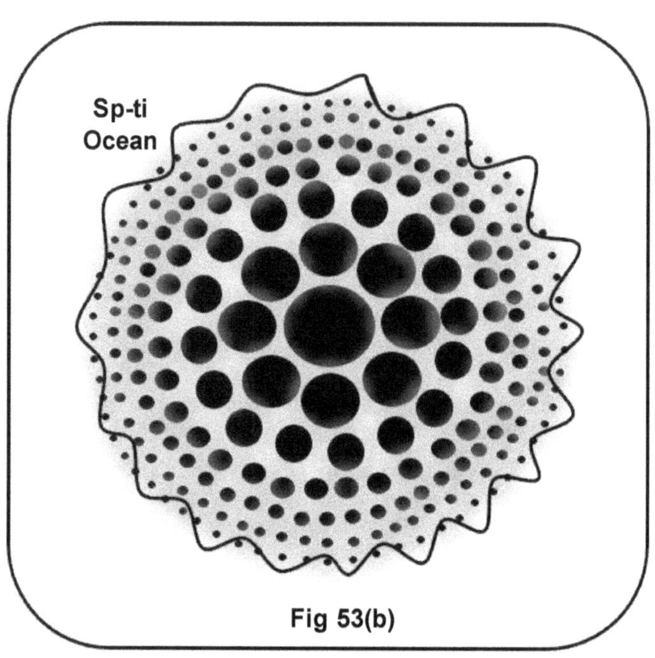

Fig 53(b)

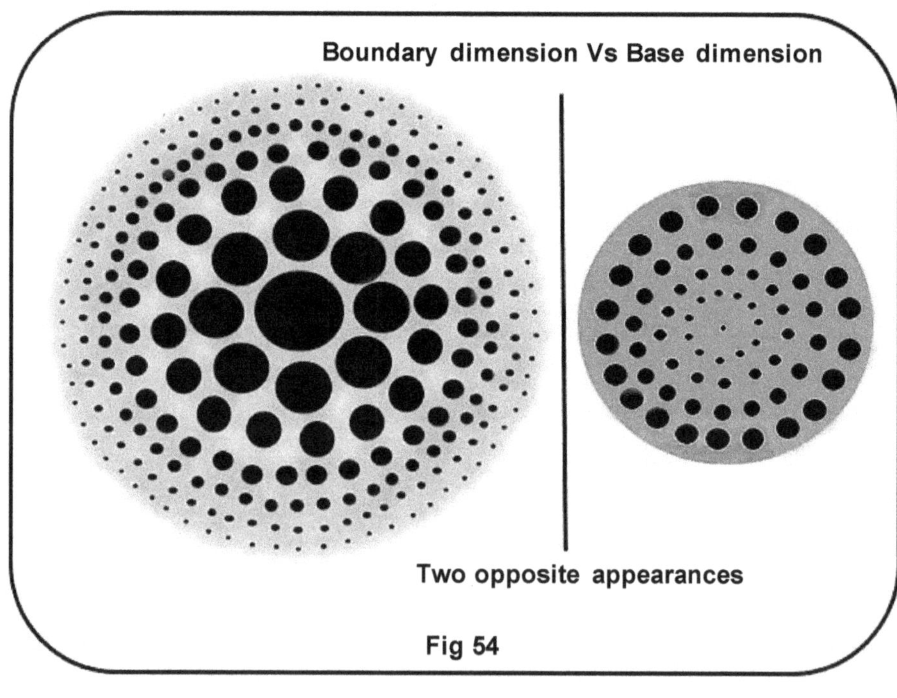

Fig 54

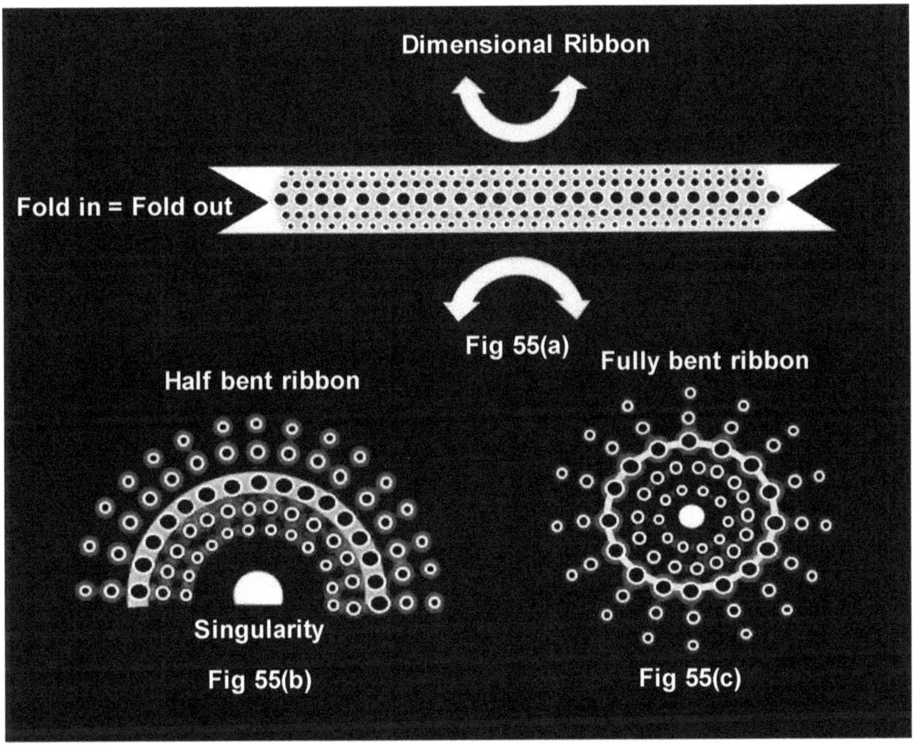

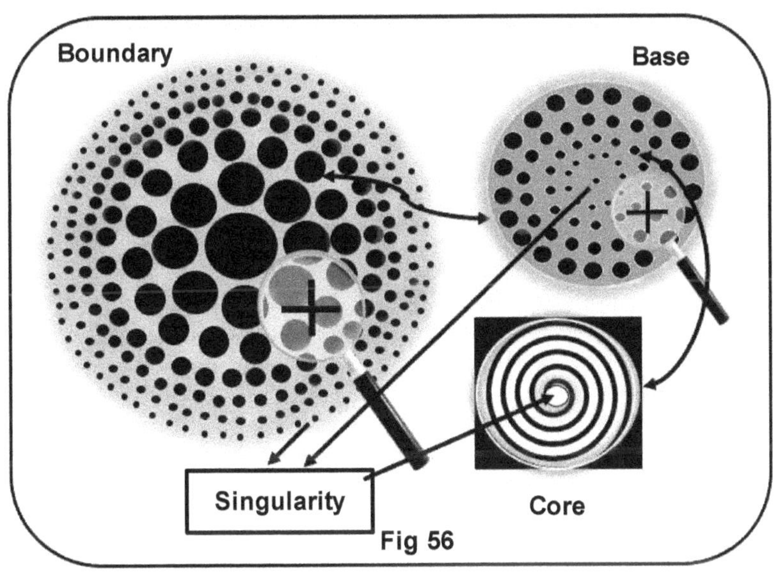

Dimensional Ribbon
Fold in = Fold out
Fig 55(a)
Half bent ribbon
Fully bent ribbon
Singularity
Fig 55(b)
Fig 55(c)
Boundary
Base
Singularity
Core
Fig 56

From 4D, every point of boundary dimension (3D) consist of base dimension (2D) and every point of base (2D) contains core dimension (1D) and finally the core (1D) leads to singularity (0D) as shown in Fig 56 & 58.

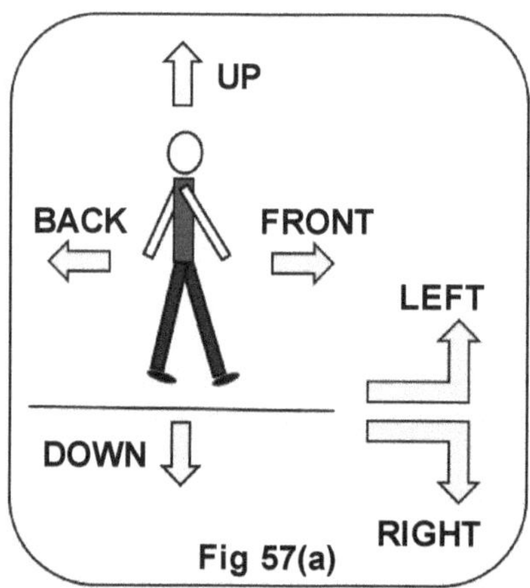

Fig 57(a)

Human consciousness is the reference zero for all dualities. Means human mind / perspective is the cause for all dualities.

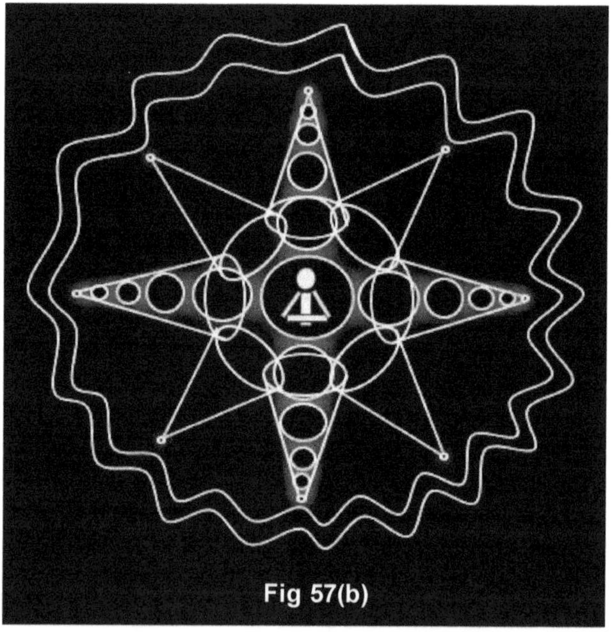

Fig 57(b)

Human consciousness sees a cone of depth in all the directions as shown in Fig 57(b), however there are two kinds of cone with boundary and base dimensions as a dual nature (opposite) with ribbon folding.

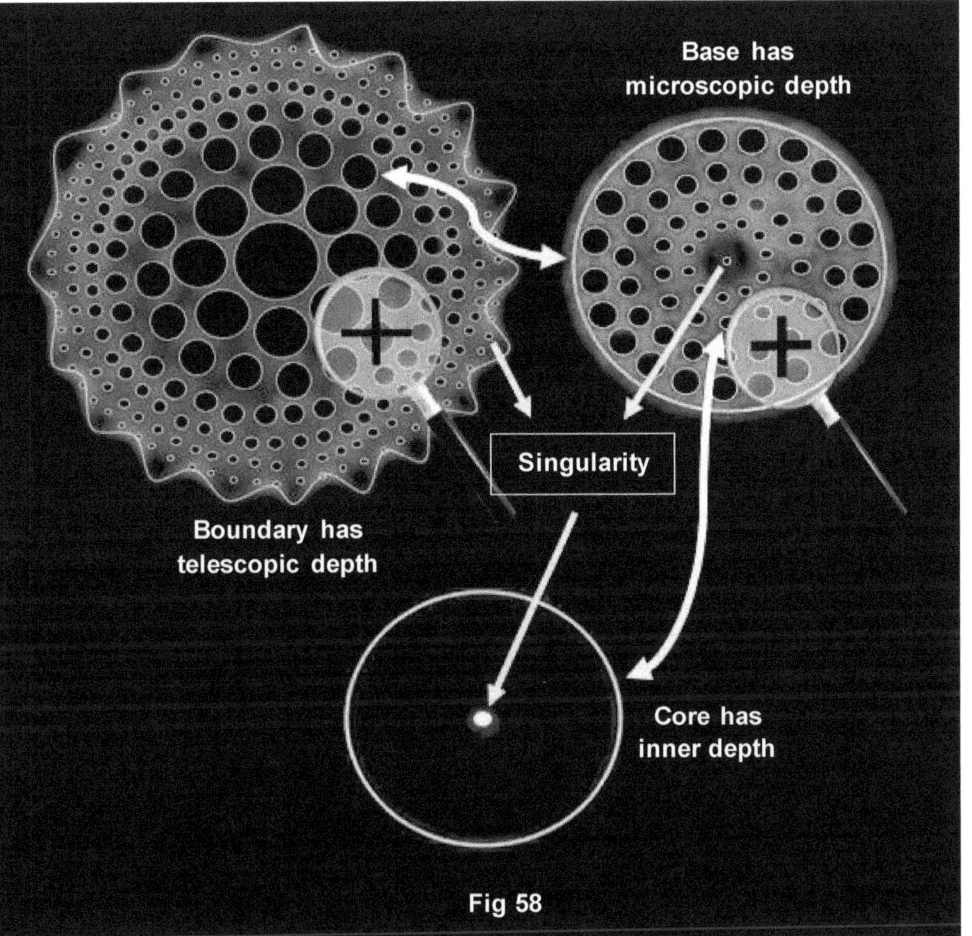

Fig 58

- Space-time is deep for a human view in anyway.
- The observer himself could not see the shape of the cones in both the views such as telescopic and microscopic depth.
- Analyzing space-time scale with speed factor of an object, is possible with telescopic cone. But the size factor does not help, as volume of the objects are occupied in microscopic cone.

[67]

- Any object in sp-ti frame would fall within these two cones for human vision.

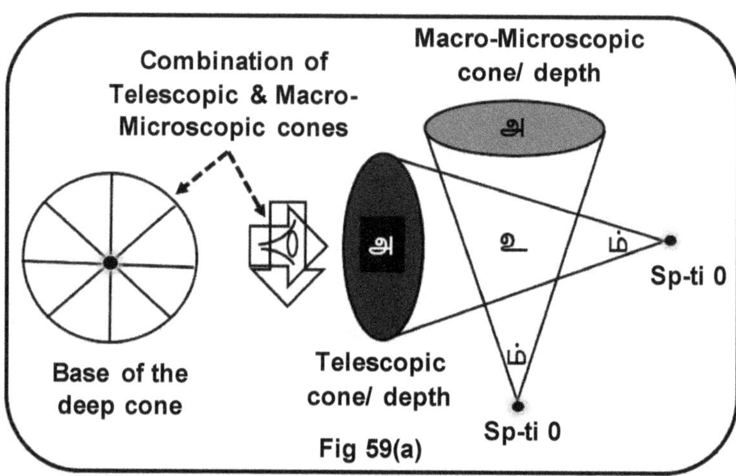

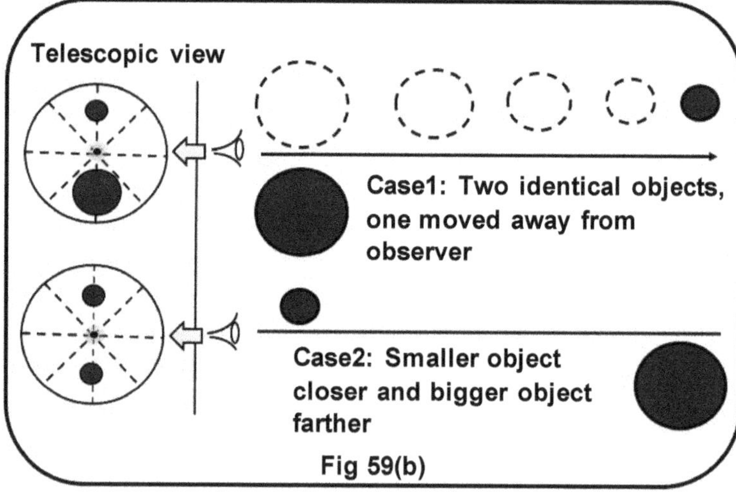

Conclusion for telescopic view: No object is farther or closer in space-time, it is all about how the objects are projected to human perspective by nature. The difference in scale arises only due to the measurement called as **distance**.

Now, moving on to macro-microscopic cone, the depth is shown perpendicular to telescopic cone. It is unlike the previous case, the size

[68]

of the two considered objects differs even without the distance factor, Fig 60.

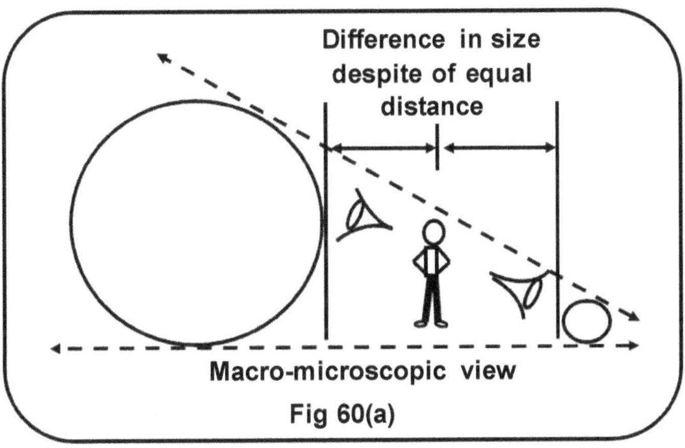

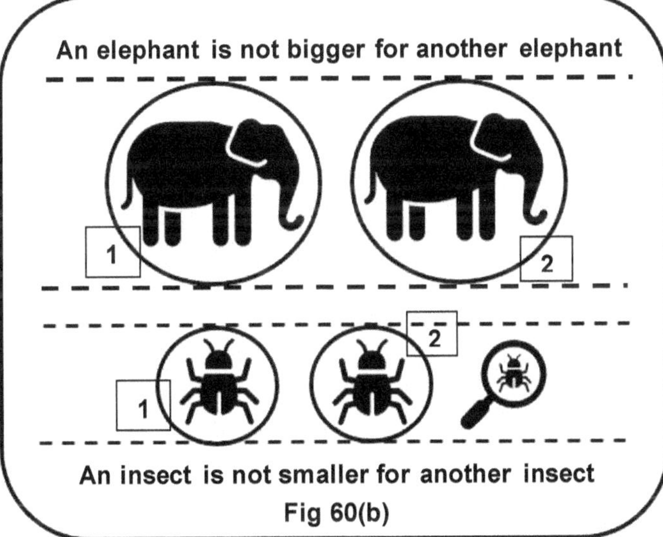

Note: It shall not be confused as a baby elephant is smaller for its parent elephants. Here, the size refers to variation in sp-ti scale itself that, to see the body parts of an insect, human require a zooming lens which is not the case for another insect at same scale.

Conclusion for microscopic view: No object is smaller or bigger, it is all about how objects are projected in life for human perspective. The

[69]

difference in scale arises only due to the measurement factor called as **size**.

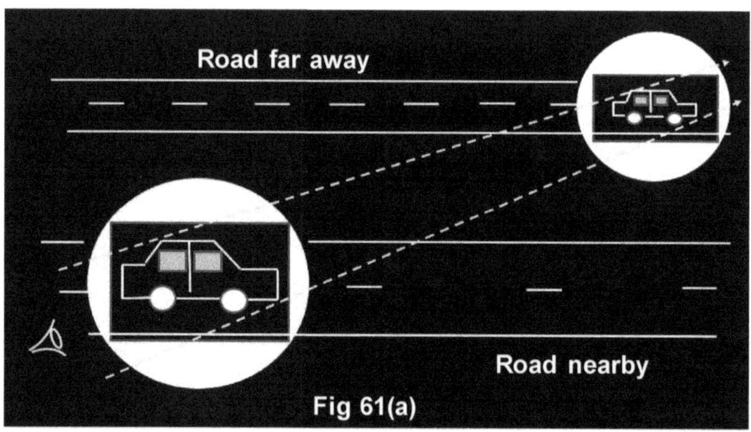

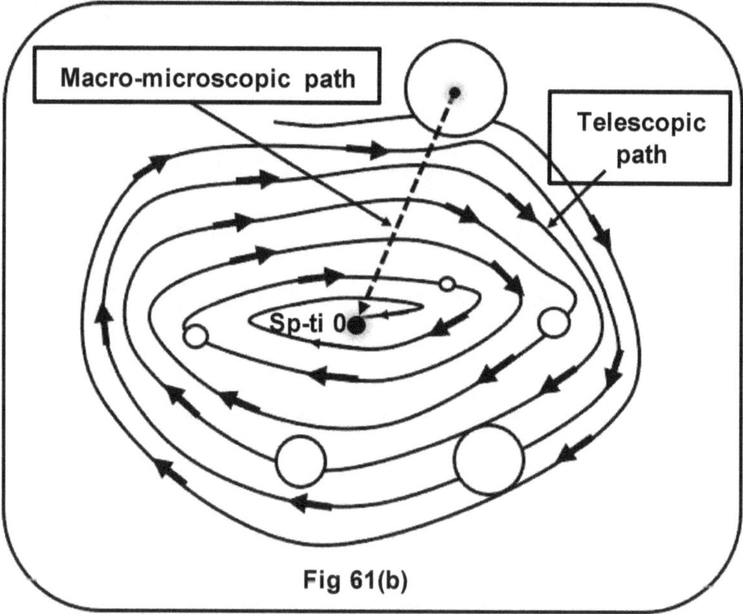

So, eliminating the measurements such as size and distance, the telescopic depth could meet the macro-microscopic depth towards Sp-ti 0 as shown in Fig 61(b). These kinds of ideas, one could not imagine for its utility in real life or local reality. However, this is how the dimensions travels, to go through all possible routes of existence and some way or the other it is required in formulating the theory of singularity. Fig 62 shows, how human consciousness see the duality of space-time in which the singularity is in 4D (beyond dimensions & unreachable) while the abode of God ever-exists as pure light in 0D (No dimensions & unreachable).

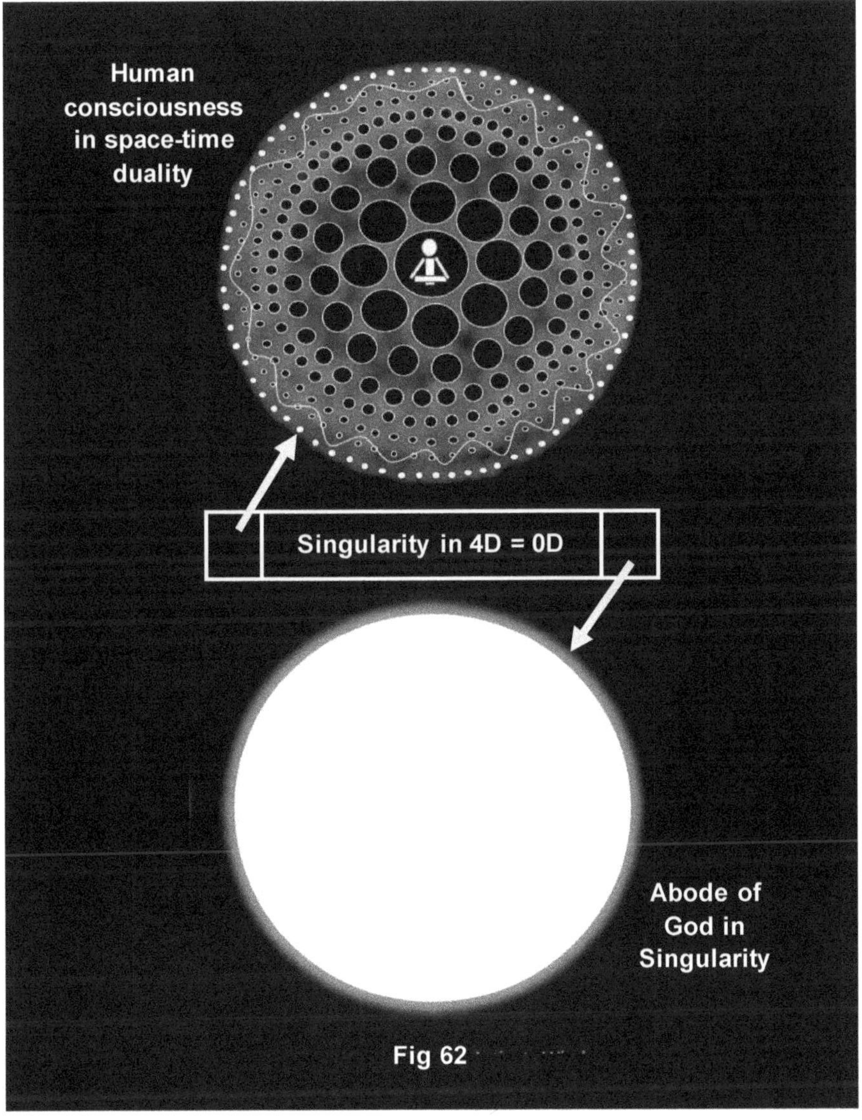

Fig 62

11.0 GRAVITATION – HISTORY & EXISTING STUDY

i) History: Sir Isaac Newton thought of gravitation with objects falling on to the earth, for example apple falling to the ground from the tree. He described it to be Earth's gravitational pull over the objects and that is the reason behind the objects sticking to the earth.

Later, he thought of why the moon at a height is not falling into the earth. Moon and Earth are thought to have a mutual force governed by the formula,

Gravitational Force $F = G* m1m2/d^2$

The force is equal to the Gravitational constant multiplied by product of the two considered masses m1 and m2 divided by the square of the distance between them.

So, gravitation required masses of two objects and also distance between them, to be the factors affecting gravitational force.

The Newton's thought of gravitation though worked for most of the part, it faced some lagging when it came to the orbit of Mercury around the Sun whose working is not as intended by him. It preceded the estimated path.

Then 250 years later, Sir Albert Einstein discovered space-time to be a single entity and behaves like a fabric, over which the objects such as Earth, moon and sun have caused curvature. The bending in the sp-ti fabric by the heavy objects is responsible for nearby objects either to fall into it or revolve around, if situated beyond certain distance.

This imagination worked for all the macroscopic objects considered with this bending effect more accurate than Newton's idea. He derived gravitation to be change in the geometry of space-time fabric (gravitational field) equated to the mass and energy density causing this change. In simple terms, **"Space-time tells matter how to move and matter tells space-time how to curve"**. [Ref: Google pages]

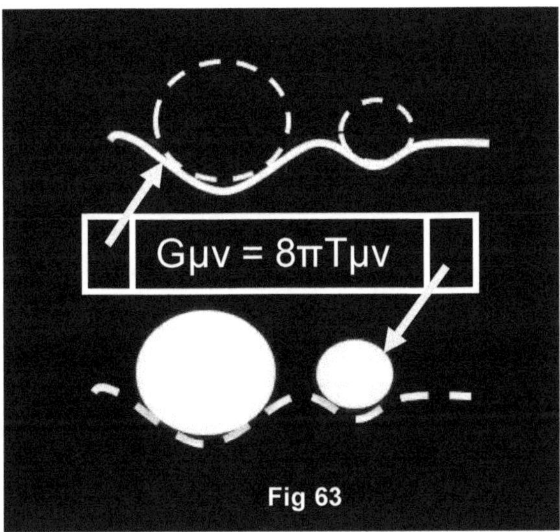

However, this time unlike Newton's gravity it required mass of only one object and no distance factor.

Now, again where did Einstein's assumption of gravitation also failed is, the gravity at quantum scale whose working could not be explained same as the curvature caused in space-time fabric by one object influencing the secondary object near to it (at macro-scale). The following diagrams shows how those earlier assumptions about gravitation are near to reality and contributions of the former scientists still remained an incomplete study and a mystery.

The study of gravitation has reached an intermediate level and its origin and terminating points are unknown in existing studies. We track the roots of gravitation and before that we visualize this intermediate point where the further analysis of gravitation is ceased and unable to reach quantum gravity.

ii) Local Gravitation (existing study):

Refer to Fig 29 & 30 and let us continue the discussion of object and the sp-ti medium. So, the bending of sp-ti lines with volume of the object is the more basic type, pertaining to length of the sp-ti lines.

Now, the second type of bending is due to the mass density of the object which is about the no. of bending sp-ti lines within the object. The number increases with increase in density.

[73]

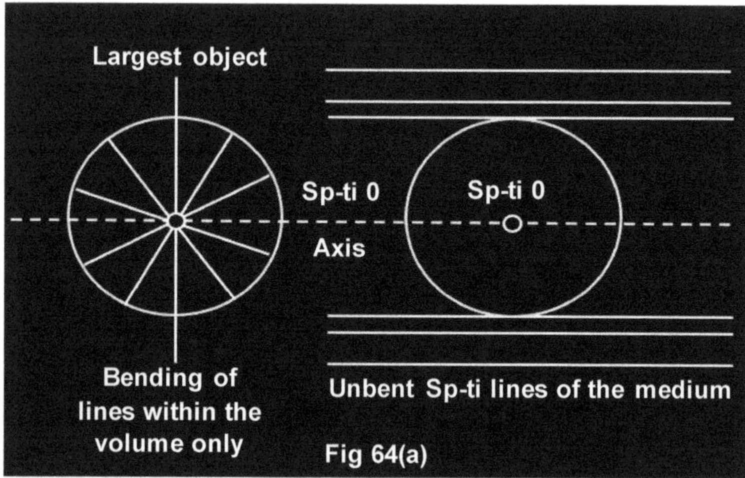

What happens beyond certain limit? When the available space-time inside the volume becomes less it starts consuming mobile space-time available in the sp-ti bubble and for further increase in density, the object starts bending the sp-ti lines of the medium externally.

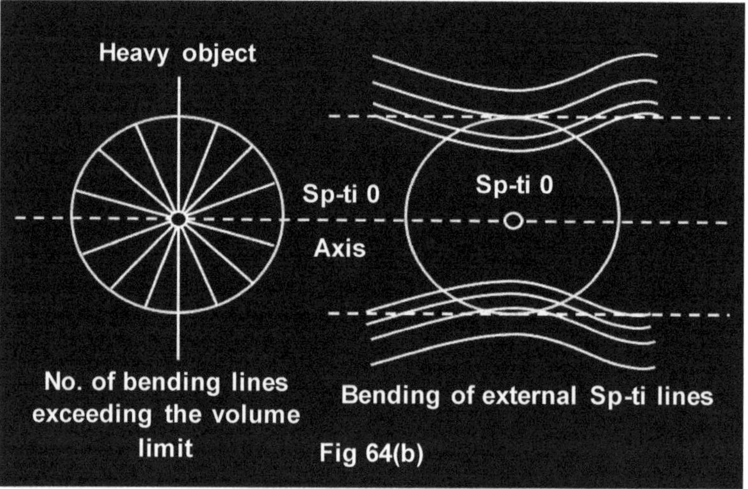

As it is said, heavy objects are bending the space-time with its mass density then there must an obvious point, where the space-time fabric is unbent by the object of certain density, Fig 64(a). To understand this, conventional single line representation of space-time fabric is insufficient. So, we are considering a pair of lines with symmetry that shows the variations clearly.

iii) New-interpretation of Gravitation:

We see the curvature of single line caused by the object to appear like sagging in space-time fabric. However, with double line representation, it shows that the space-time fabric is actually bitten by the object. Also, the unbent double line means a flat space-time medium without heavy objects or in other words, the objects within this tolerance limit does not bend space-time grid lines of the medium. This dual line with certain limits could be termed as **"Sp-ti tolerance"**.

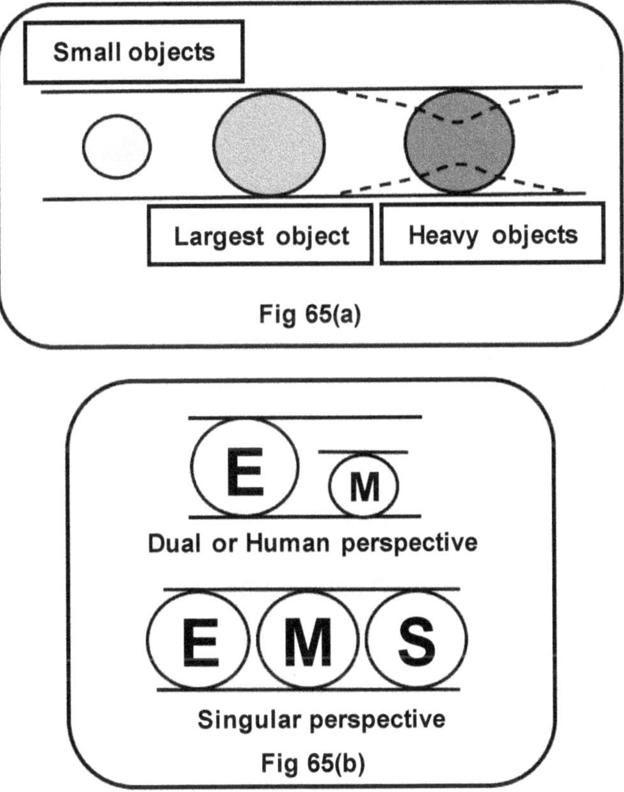

Fig 65(a)

Fig 65(b)

Now, for further analysis there is a crucial technique to be applied. We know the heavy objects such as Moon, Earth and Sun are in different sizes. Clearly, the bending of sp-ti lines of the medium is only due to the mass density of the object.

[75]

So, for our representation the size factor has no significance and could be eliminated such that all the objects are shown with circles of same size and the difference is indicated only with the amount of bending pertaining to their densities, Fig 65(c).

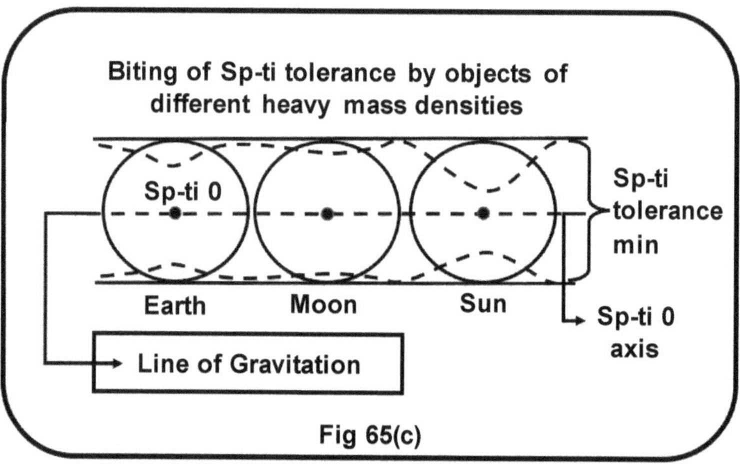

Fig 65(c)

Fig 65(c) shows that the bending of sp-ti line differing with mass densities of Earth, Moon and Sun. This is the minimum point from where the Sp-ti tolerance starts reducing. To see the maximum limit of this Sp-ti tolerance, we need another way of representation [Fig 65(d)], so that it is possible to know the maximum utilization of the tolerance by certain object. Whereas black holes are beyond this limit.

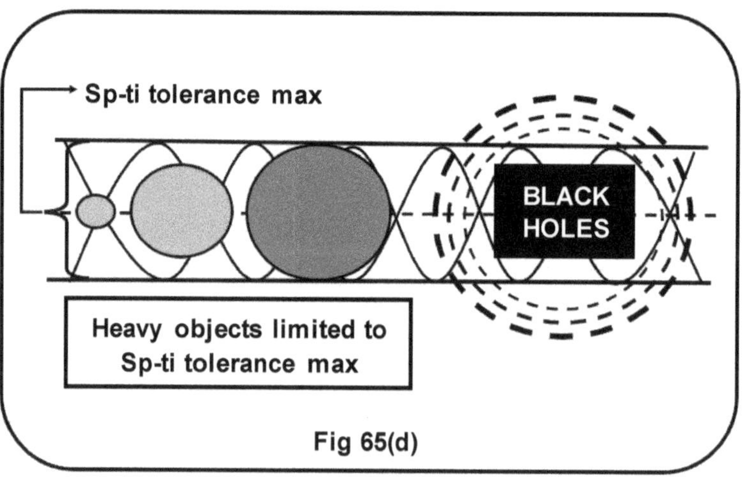

Fig 65(d)

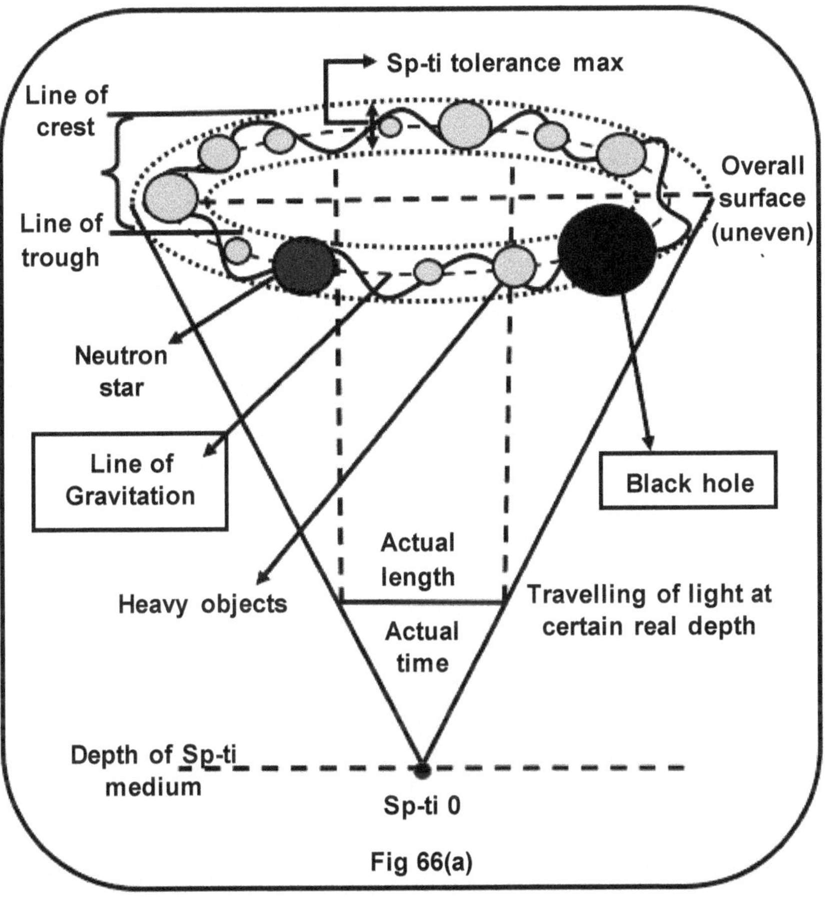

Time dilation 1: Observed with variation (curvature caused) in Sp-ti tolerance max due to heavy objects. This bending of space-time line forms ridges. Thus, here the time dilation is the indication of surface and depth in terms of crests and troughs on the overall surface of the Sp-ti medium, Fig 66(a).

Time dilation 2: Observation made on the surface of space-time we live, which is actually a projection from the depth where the light is travelling, Fig 66(b). Thus, in this case time dilation is the indication of surface and depth of the entire space-time medium.

[77]

Conclusion: In both the cases time dilation is accounted for difference in up & down and surface & depth levels. It shall not be imagined for time travel with relative speed which is a further significance while it has already served its purpose and done with it. How relative speed is also a misconception shall be seen in the fore coming topics.

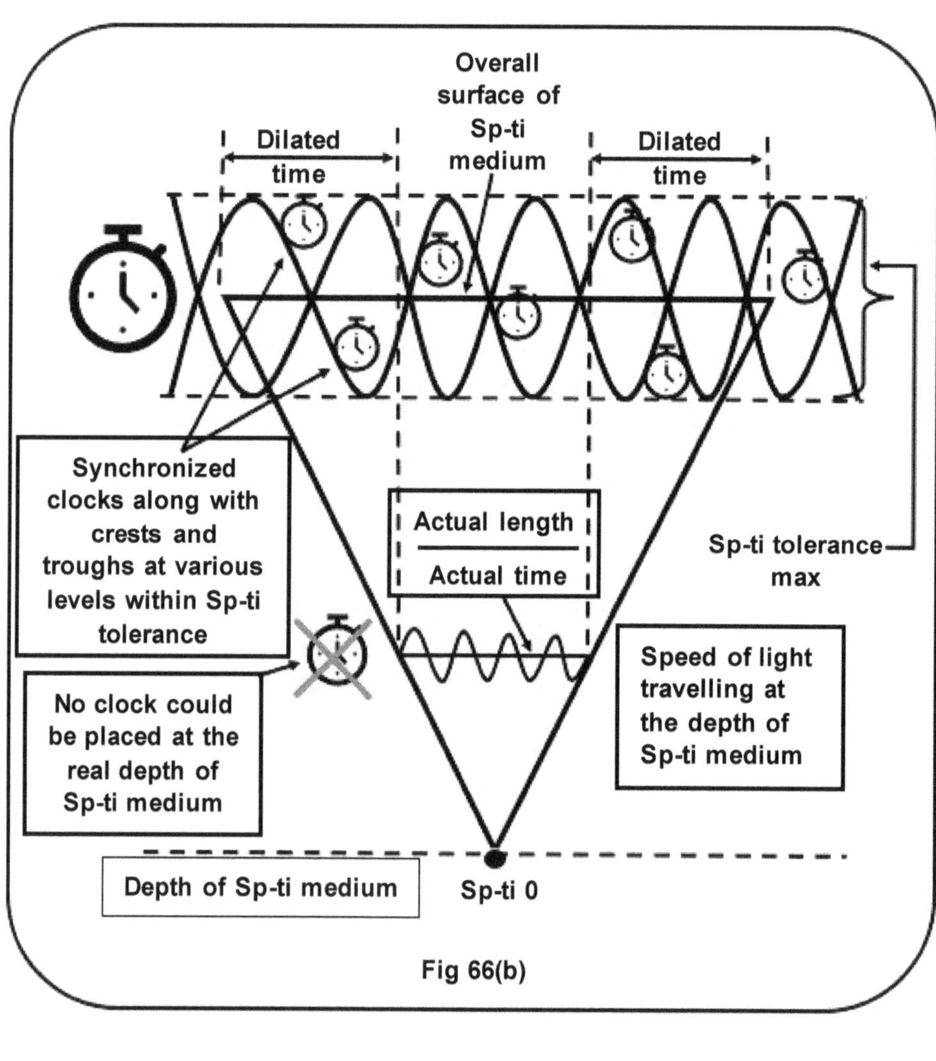

Fig 66(b)

12.0 GRAVITATION - NEW STUDY; PART-1

Existing researches says when two black holes collide with each other, there is a ripples formation in space-time. These ripples are called as gravitational waves. Only mild ripples are received so far, huge ones could cause severe destruction. However, in theory of singularity, the line of gravitation is traced from surface to depth (start to end), at no point it is a wave. The ripples or waves are actually the nature of the medium itself. Space-time usually have standing waves at its ocean surface which does not move on the sides, as there is no shore in the sp-ti ocean and also, nothing other than black holes could cause these changes in the Sp-ti medium. All the evolved objects are floating in spacious vacuum whose surface level is far away from this ripple formation happening at the depth.

When heavy objects like two black holes are colliding with each other, could cause the waves move away from the point of this merging process. So, it is the sp-ti waves of the medium and not the gravitation, which is a fourth dimensional aspect.

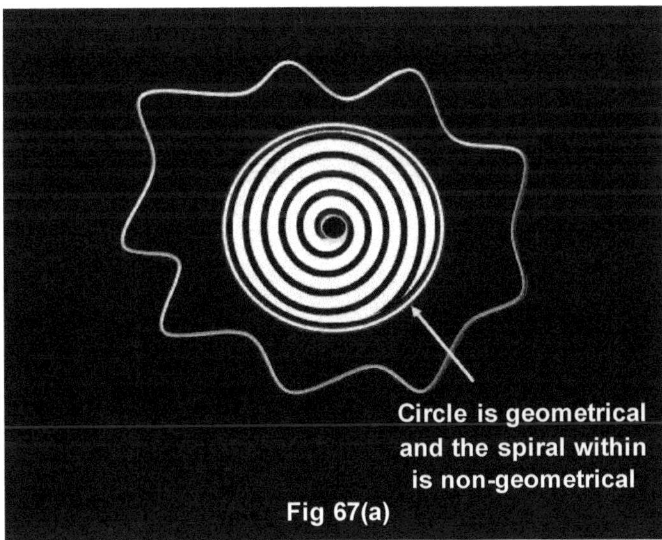

Fig 67(a)

The spiral point of the existence beyond certain limit give lead to dual aspects called Gravitation-Orbitation. It is the parent duality of space-time medium itself. It could be distinguished such that Gravitation-Orbitation is a circular web network whereas space-time is square grid network. There is nothing like line or circle however, henceforth we assume gravitation to be a line and orbitation to be a circle, as shown in Fig 67(b) for our study. The spiral motion in the existence means continuous evolution which involves in creation as well as circulation of sp-ti medium between liquid and gaseous state of darkness.

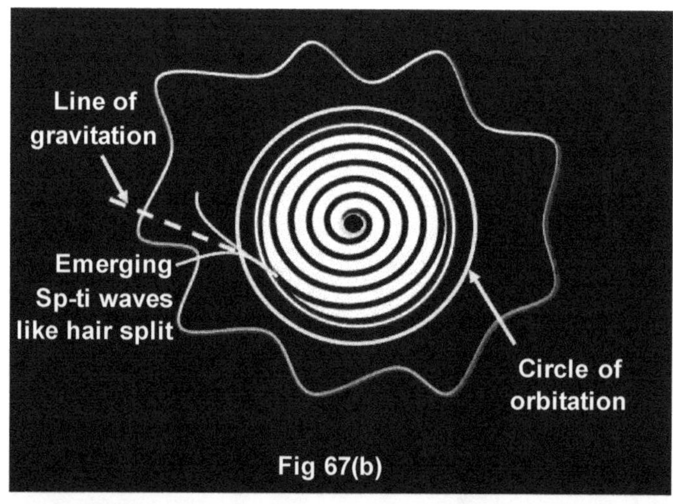

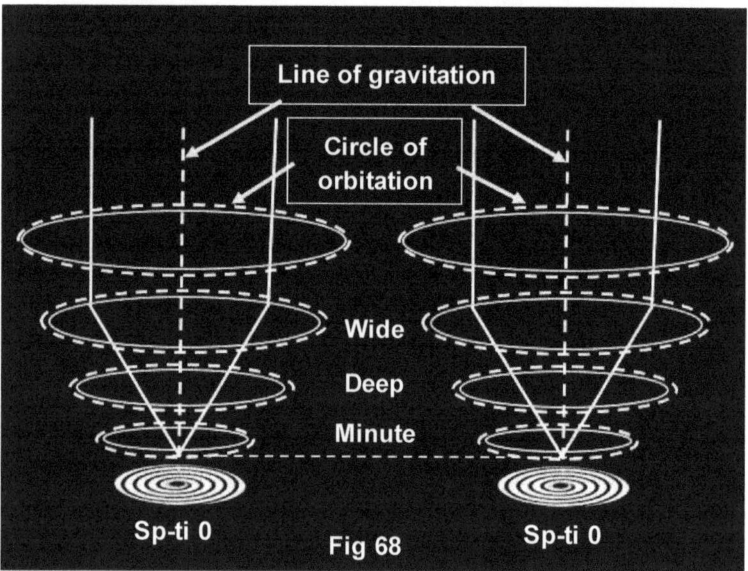

Throughout this book, the three real dimensions are represented in so many different ways for easy understanding and remembrance.

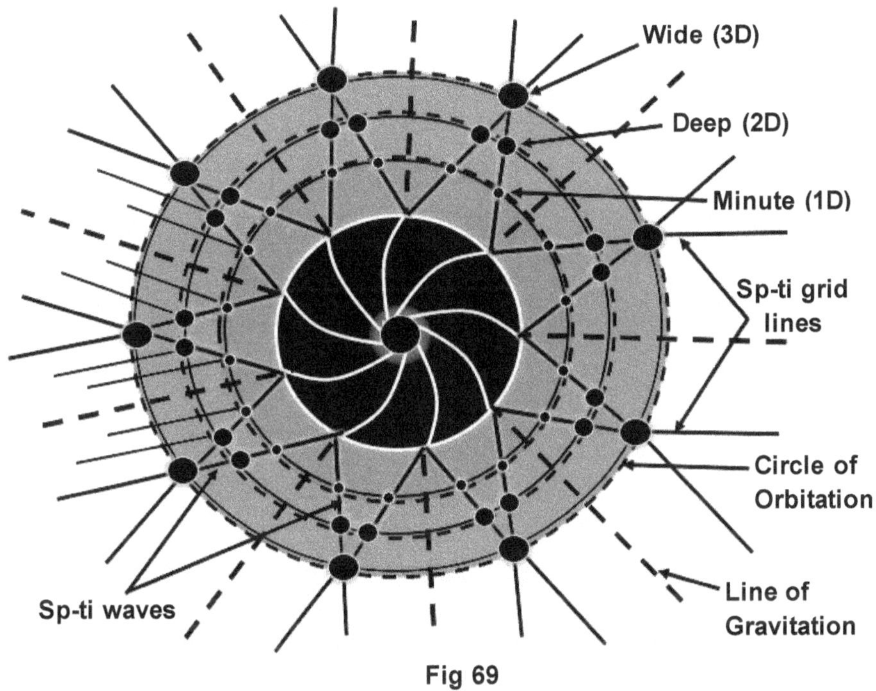

Fig 69

The two figures 69 and 70 could be clearly compared for different ways of representing, where the sp-ti waves have cone-like termination or emergence, within the dimensional rings. Whereas out of the rings, it becomes parallel lines that constitute sp-ti grid in the medium. The impeller associated with black holes and point of creation has opposite faces of fan rotation.

It is the same energy utilized for dual purpose of creation with forward driving force for creation while pulling force due to resulting suction on the other side. These impellers could also be assumed to be separate for each action differently using two or more impellers also, as fourth dimension means multiple appearances of the same thing to serve multiple purposes.

[81]

As shown earlier, the sp-ti waves have male-female waves that mates to conceive the fundamental particle in sp-ti womb, though simply it could be assumed same like water bubbles that emerges to the surface of water.

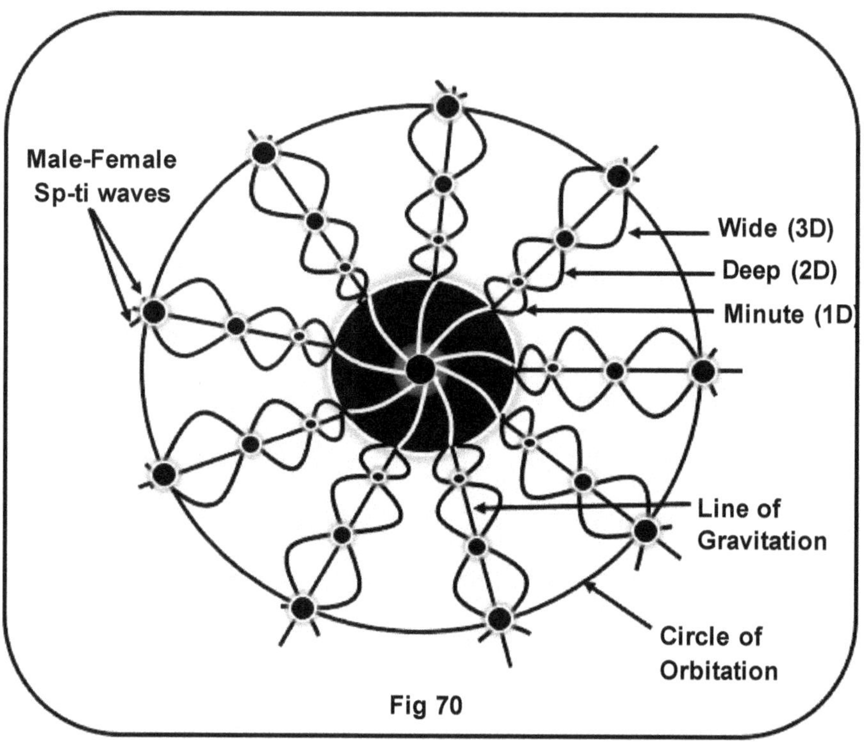

Fig 70

The line of gravitation and circle of orbitation are perpendicular to each other and develops into a web network prior to space-time. Along with this duality arises the sp-ti grid from depth to surface of sp-ti medium. The structure of single sp-ti 0 is shown in Fig 71, which also contains the three real dimensions that goes deeper and deeper. The purpose of this structure means that the entire sp-ti medium is made up of tiny black particles however, there is certain point where a sp-ti 0 is said to be significant and actively involves in the working of the Universe. Points tinier than these, serve the sp-ti medium itself.

The structure of single sp-ti 0 contains the merged line or circle of gravitation-orbitation to be indistinguishable, Fig 71 and 72(a). When the group of sp-ti 0s is considered, they form a spiral line in which the

[82]

sp-ti 0 points aligns itself in the manner of sp-ti 0 (deep) – sp-ti 0 (deeper) – sp-ti 0 (deepest) with a spiral motion. Multi-dimensionally, this spiral motion involves numerous spiral coils altogether starts spinning. This spinning is detached from gravitation-orbitation and work independently. This spinning could be like high-speed cutting wheel. The no. of wheels required to govern the motion of galaxies and solar systems is determined by the super nature and govern them at different speed rates, as anything is possible with 4D.

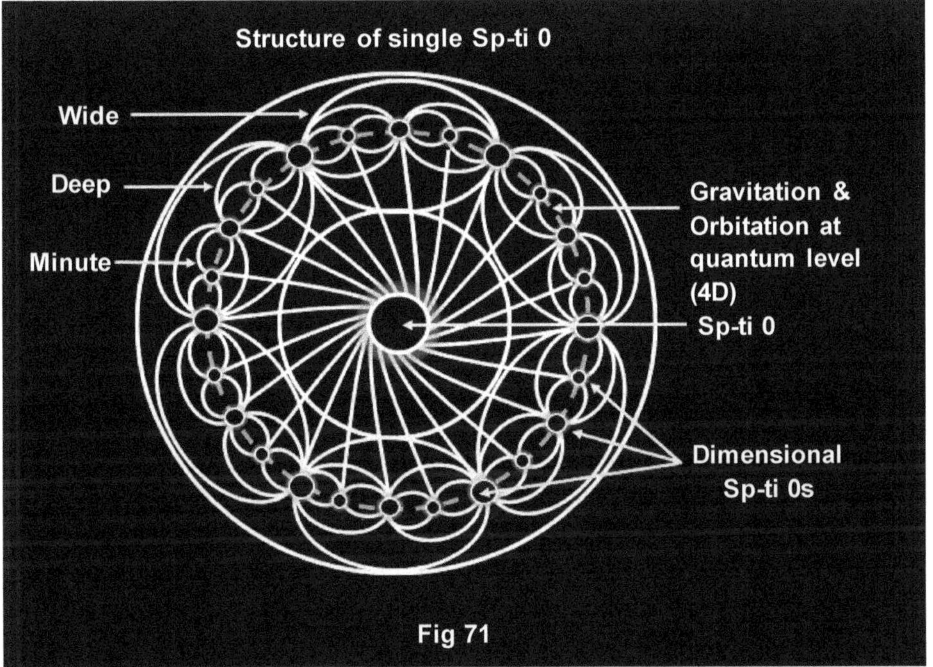

Fig 71

The line of gravitation and the circle of orbitation from one sp-ti 0 opens for another one, which requires a minimum space as shown in Fig 72 (b). The same extends for the third one which shows the actual working of gravitation-orbitation even deeper than the quantum range, which is only pertaining to the sp-ti medium even without the creation of objects.

So, the gravitation in existing studies have an understanding only with mass and distance factors of the objects. Our new study shows the gravitation at point level.

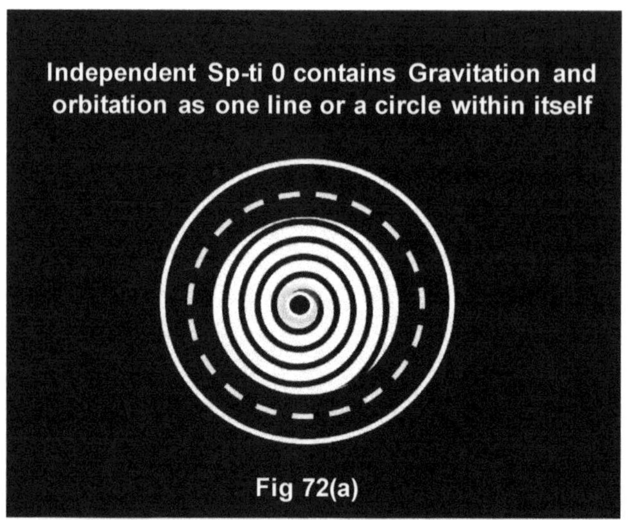

Fig 72(a)

Local gravity and local orbit are stronger than primal gravitation and great orbit in terms of attraction and revolution respectively, as shown in Fig 72(c).

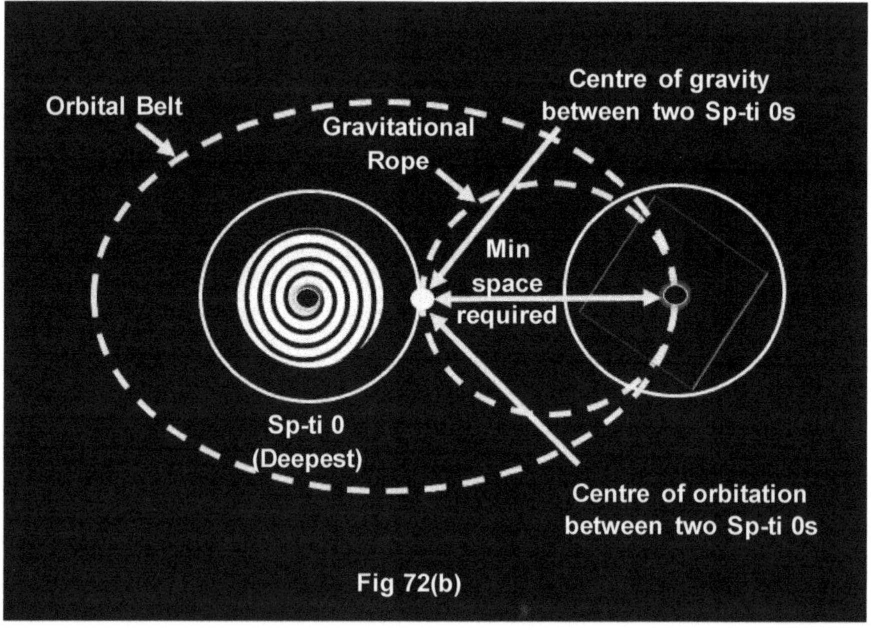

Fig 72(b)

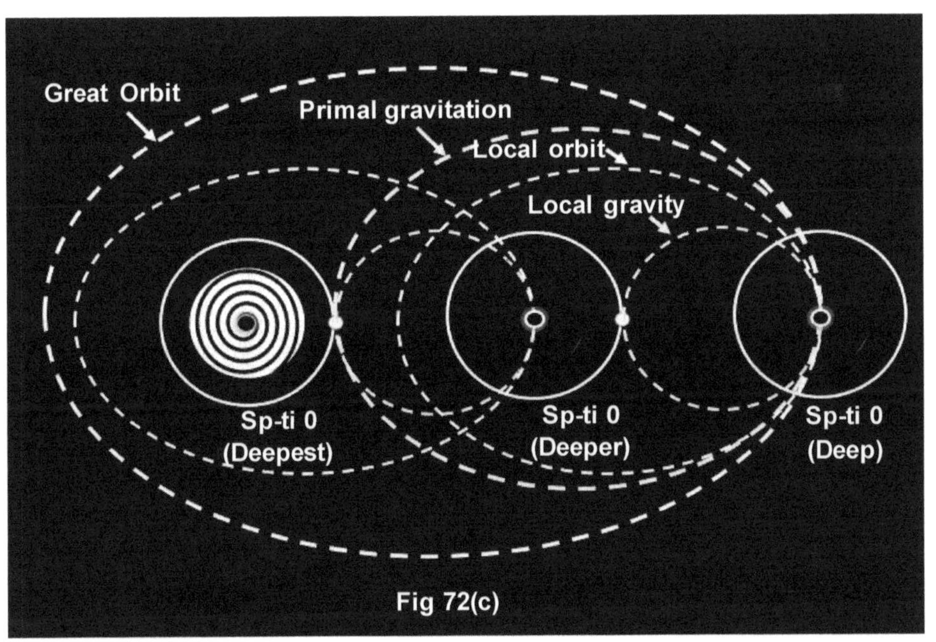

Fig 72(c)

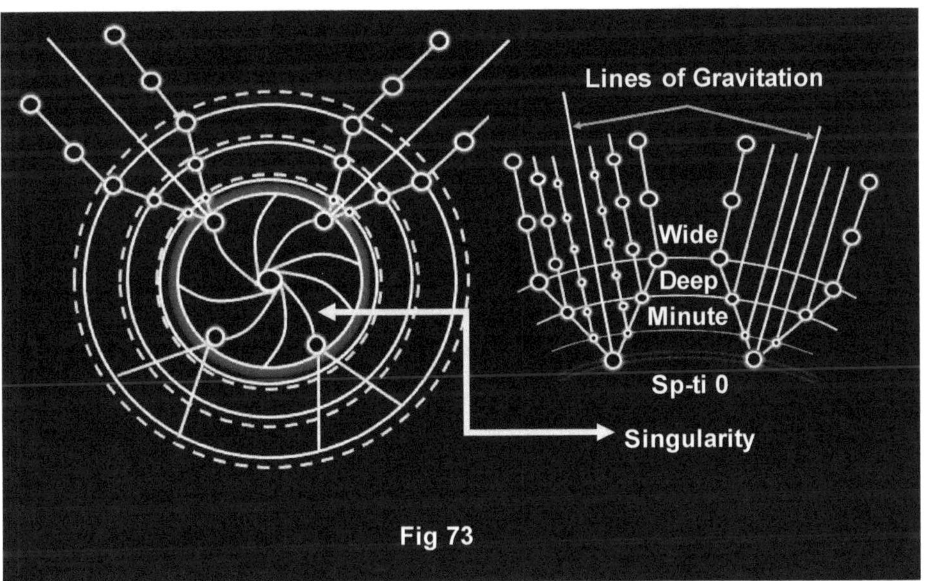

Fig 73

Dimensional Sp-ti 0s are more like liquid drops, about to detach from one another whereas spacious Sp-ti 0s are blown and expanded to constitute sp-ti grid.

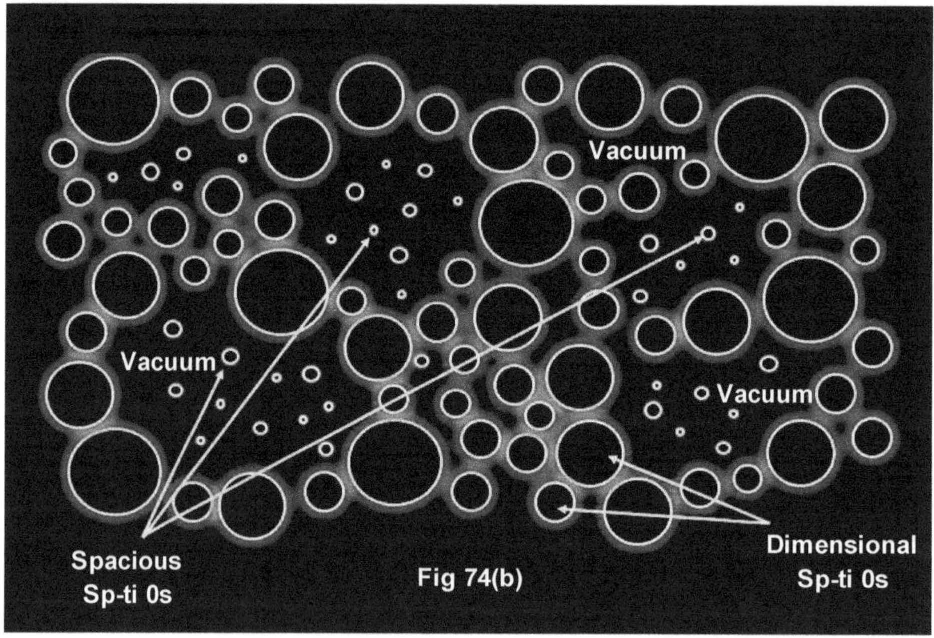

[86]

Line of
Gravitation
Sp-ti waves
Wide
Deep
Minute
Non-Geometrical
Geometrical
Fig 75

Line of
Gravitation
Sp-ti grid
Line of
Orbitation
Point of
creation
Point of Sp-ti medium
Point of
destruction
Fig 76

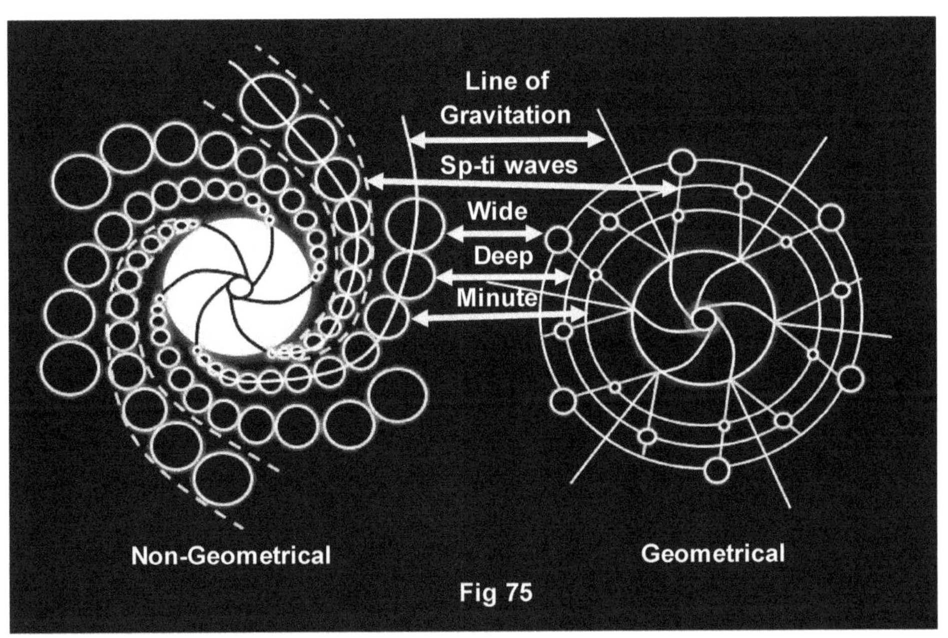

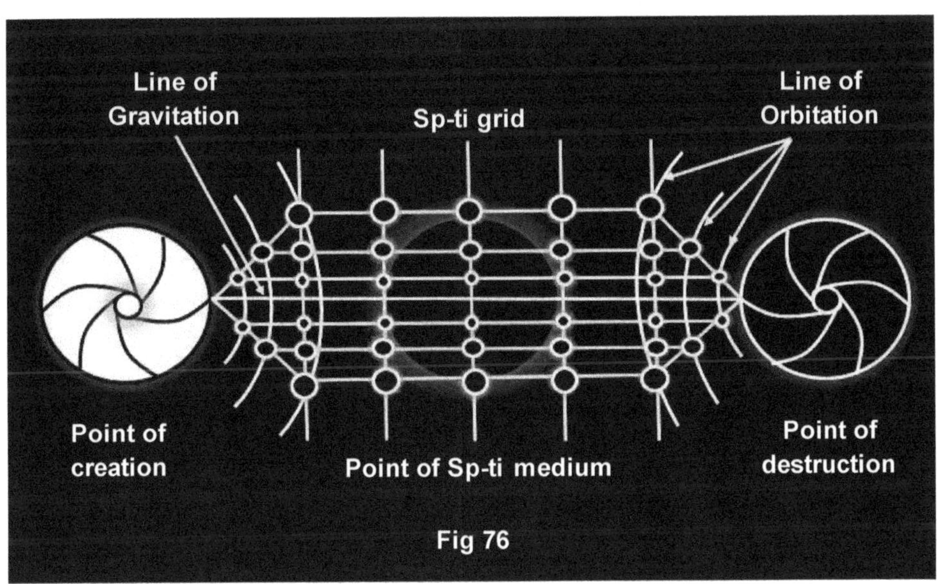

[87]

13.0 EVOLUTION OF SPACE-TIME

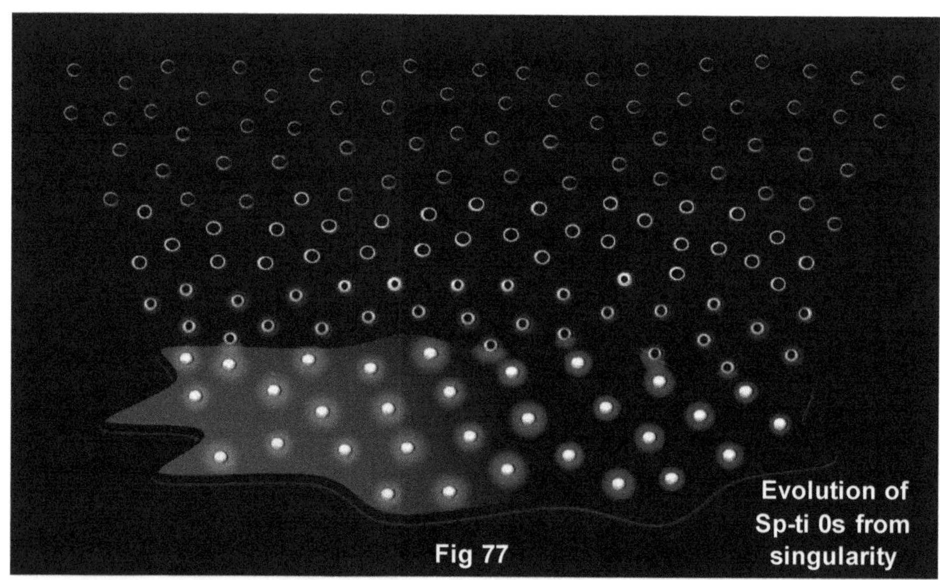

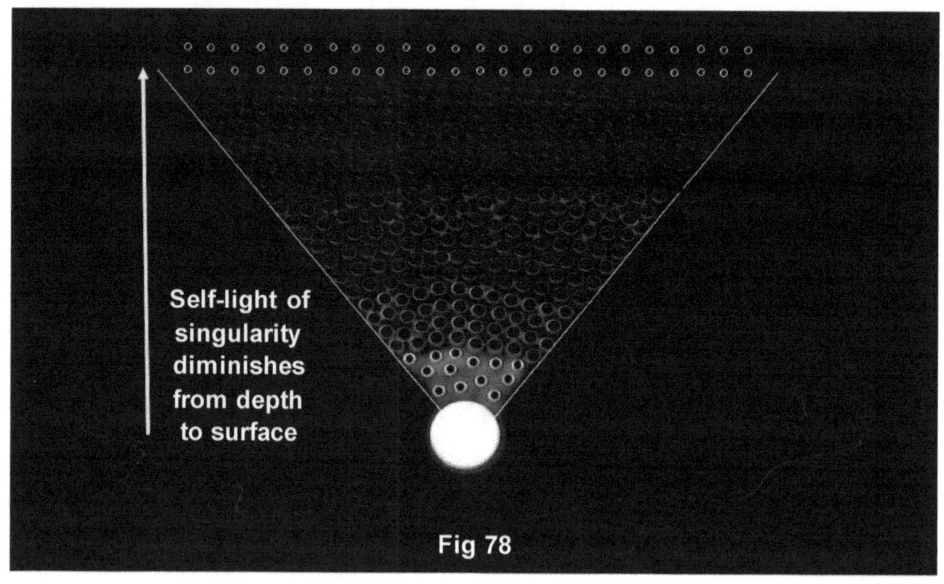

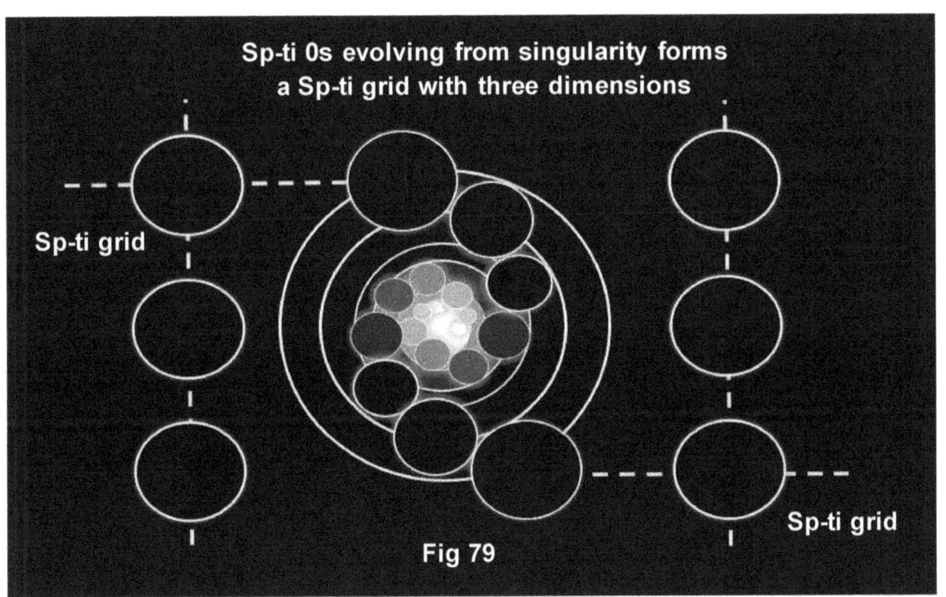

Fig 79

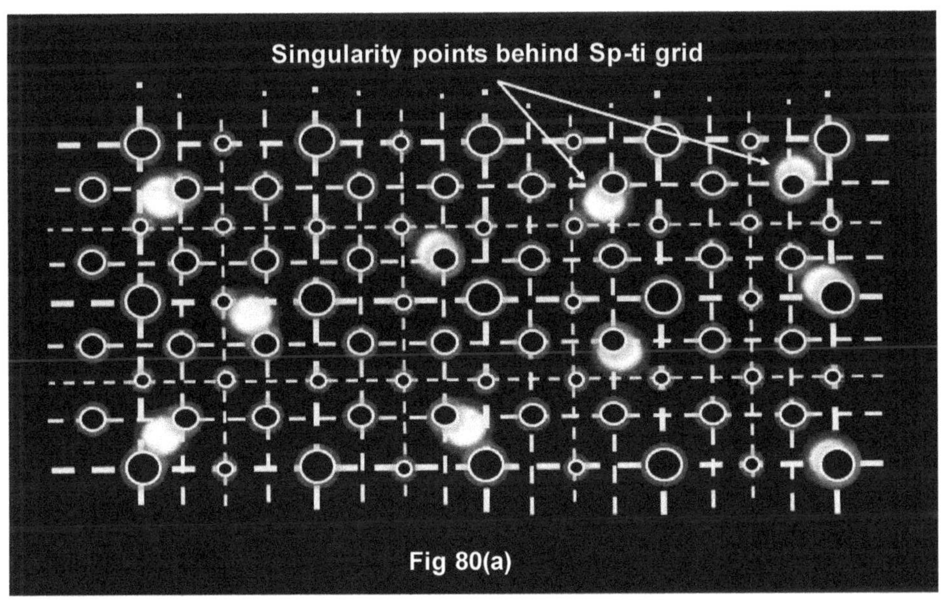

Fig 80(a)

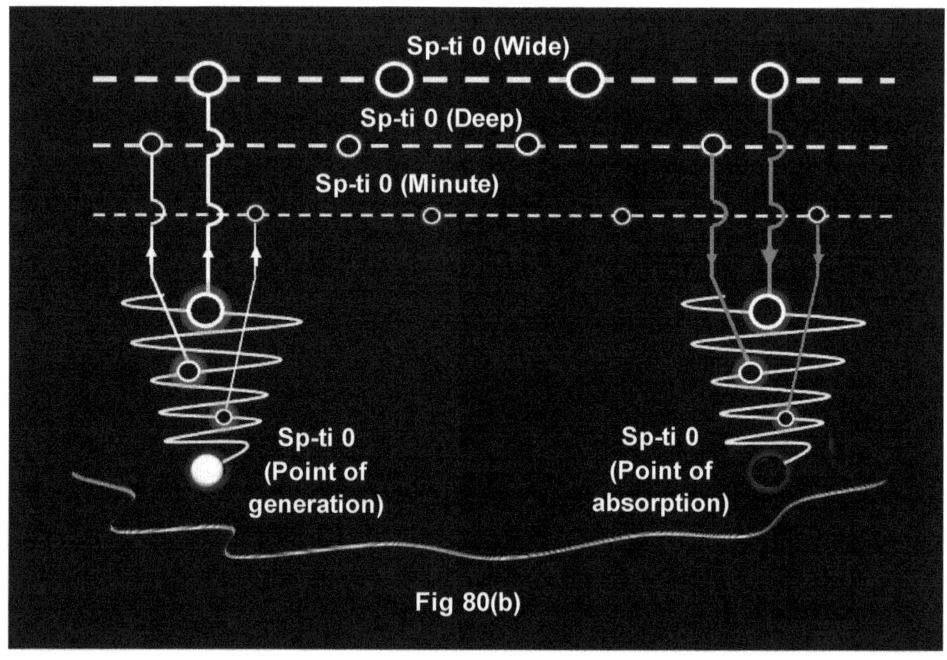

Fig 80(b)

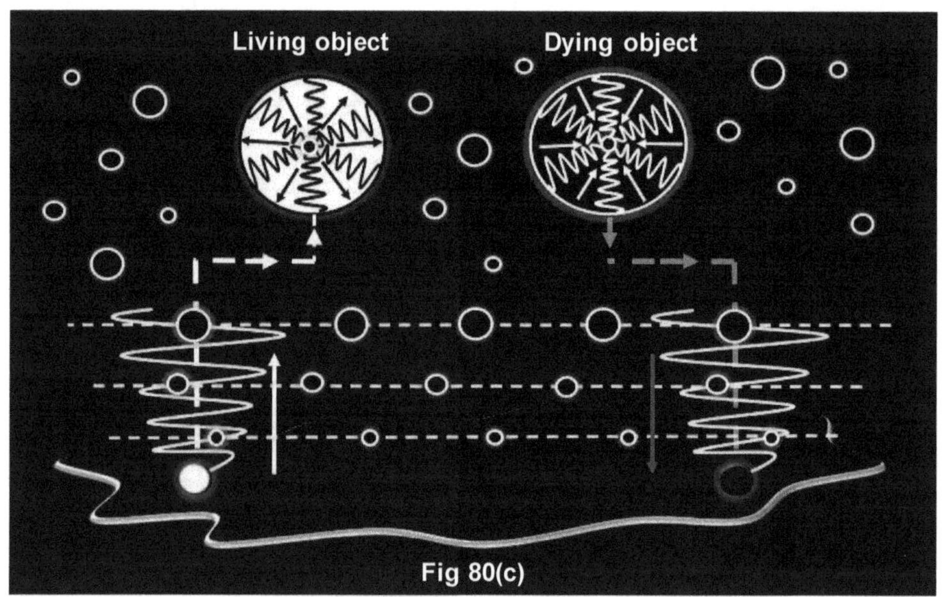

Fig 80(c)

[90]

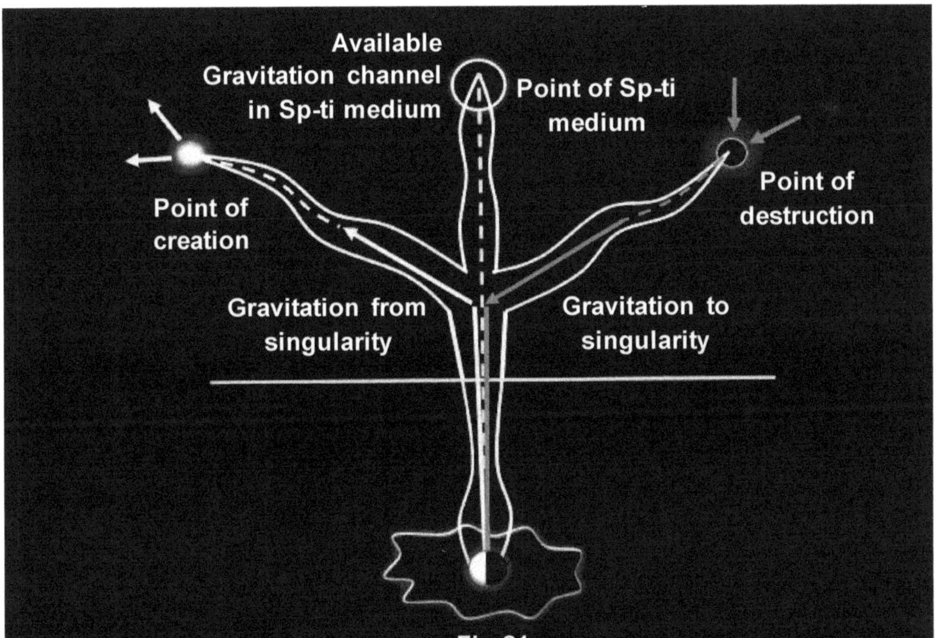

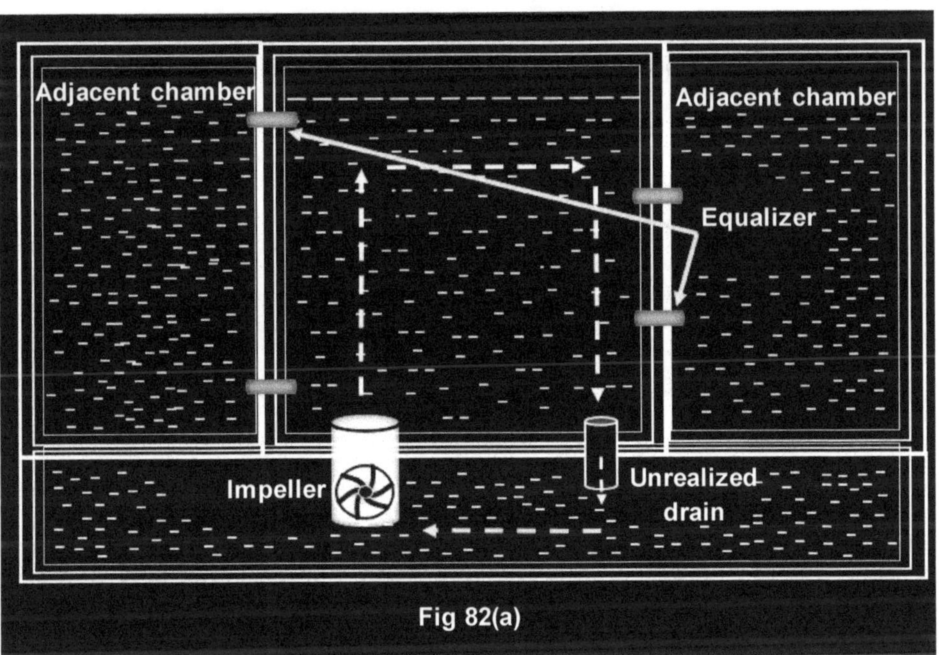

Fig 81

Fig 82(a)

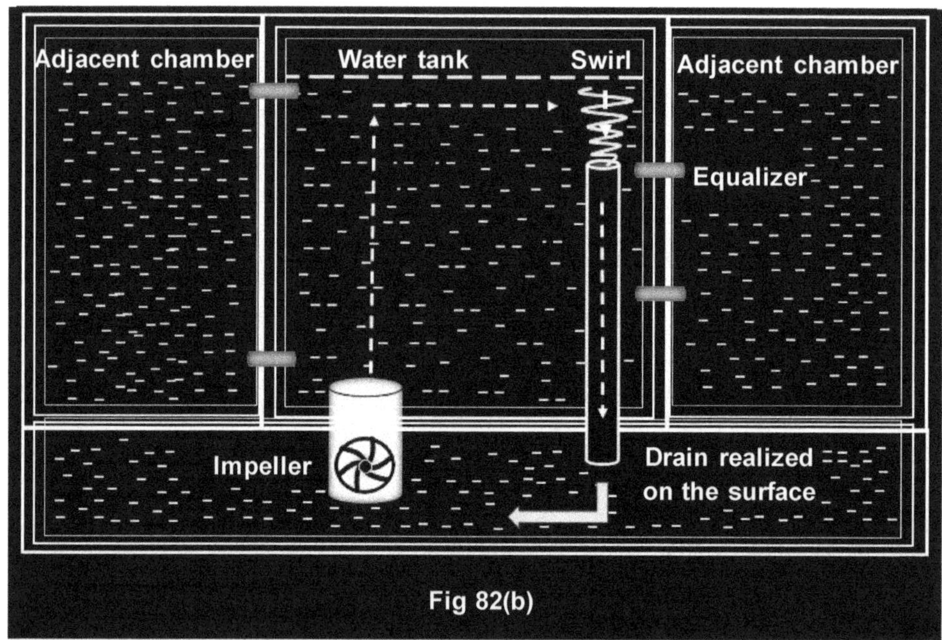

Closed water tank of fluid fountain mechanism

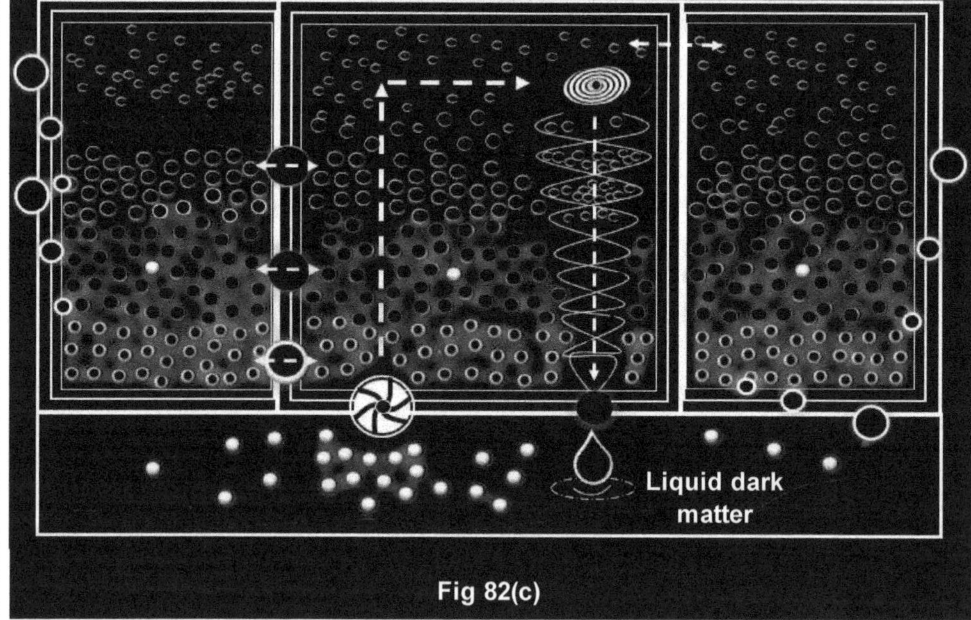

Sp-ti 0
Singularity
Closed quantum black holes
Open surface black holes
Fig 83

Bloomed lotus represents spacious Sp-ti 0s called as vacuum
Sp-ti Pond
Pond
Multi-dimensional lotus of Sp-ti 0
Fig 84(a)

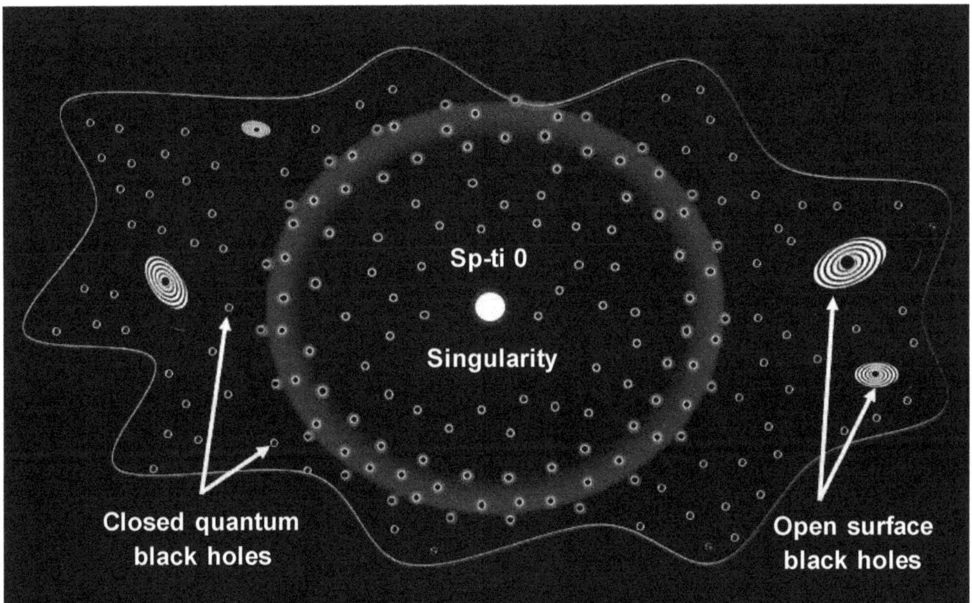

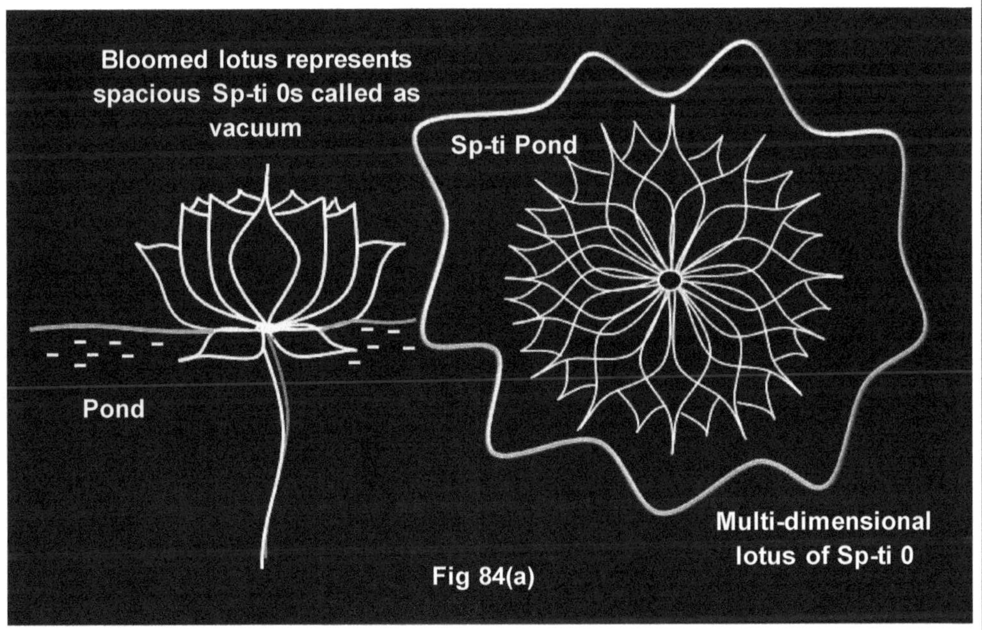

[93]

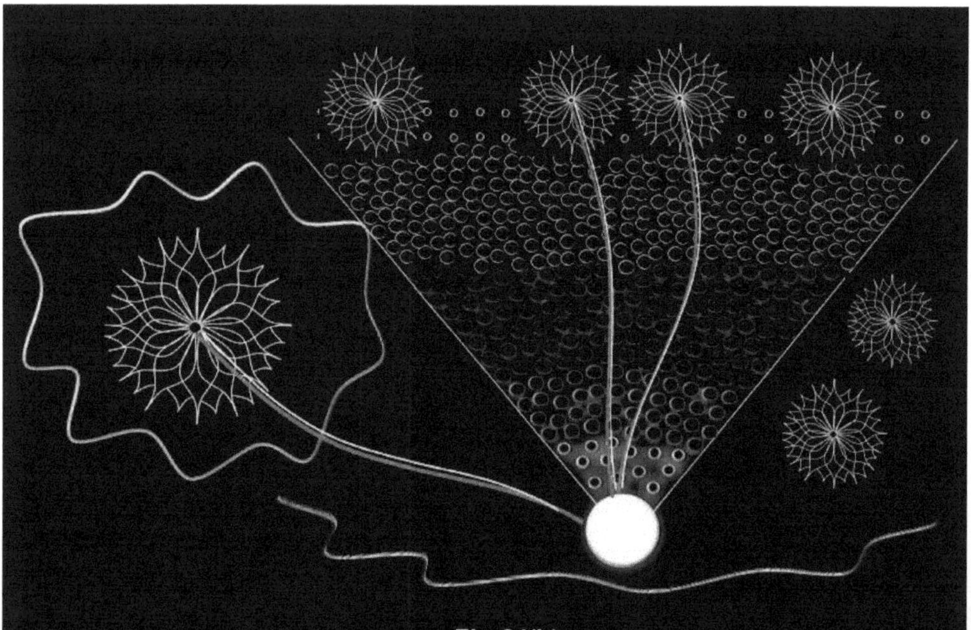

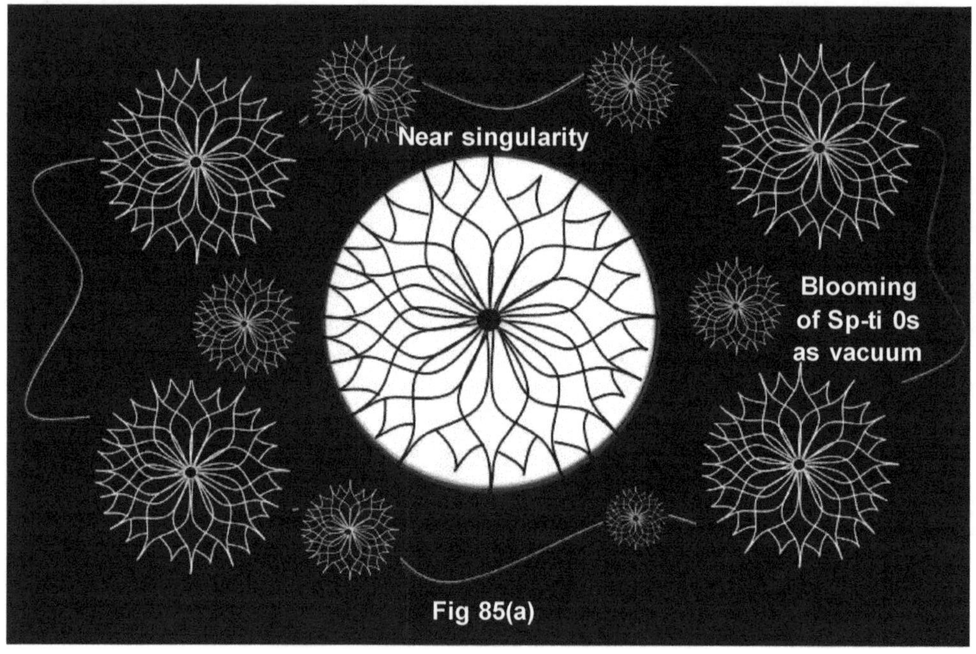

Fig 84(b)

Fig 85(a)

[94]

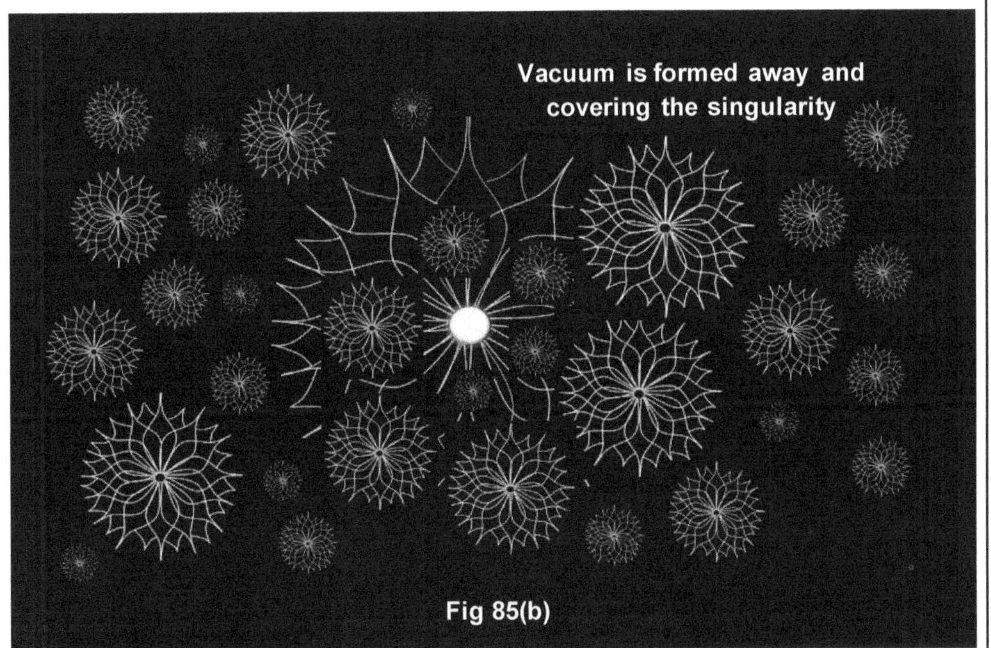

Fig 85(b)

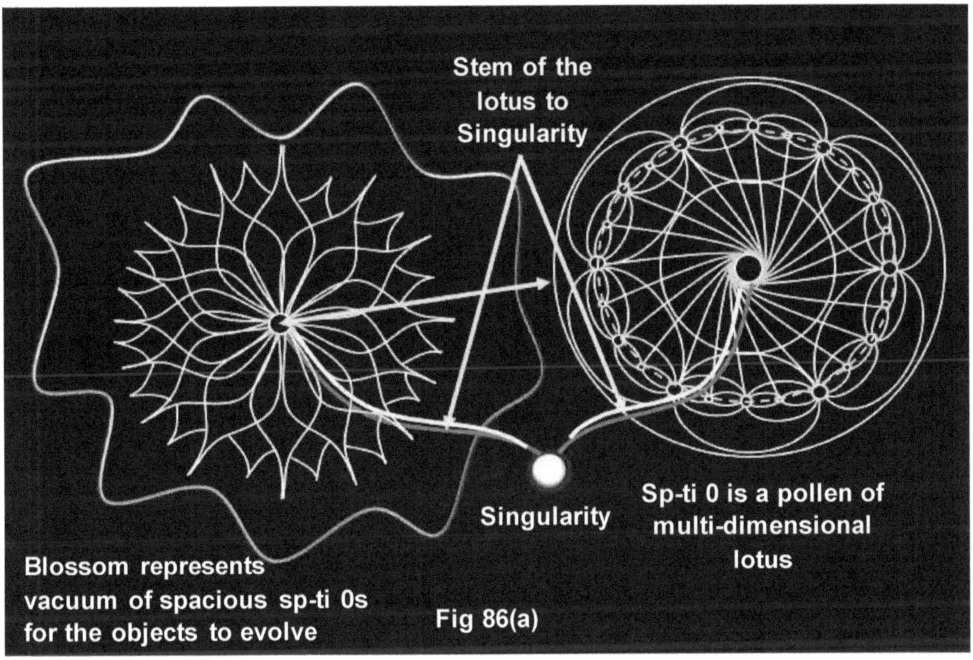

Fig 86(a)

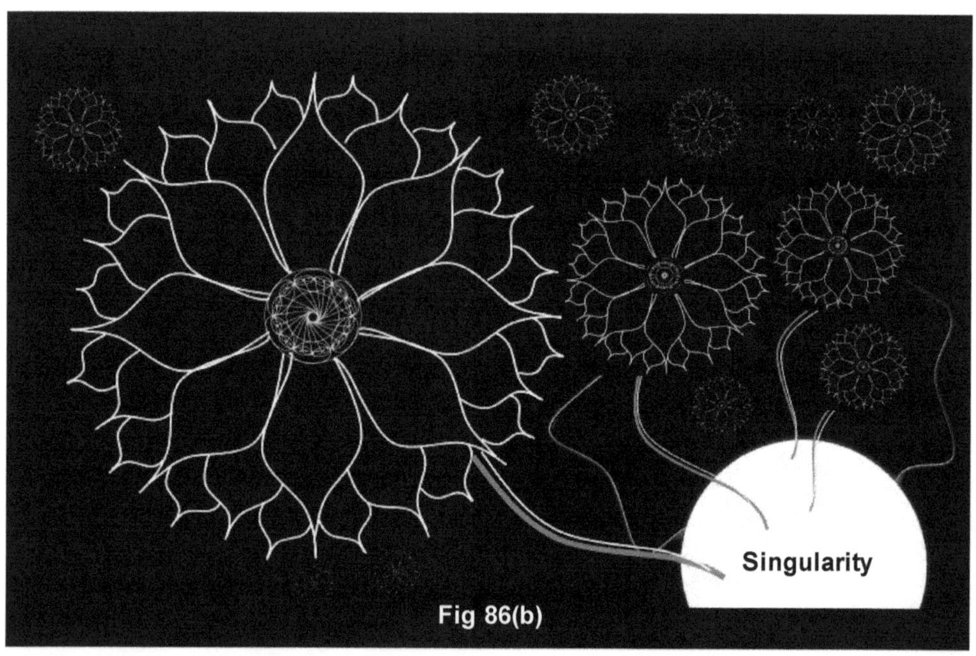

Fig 86(b)

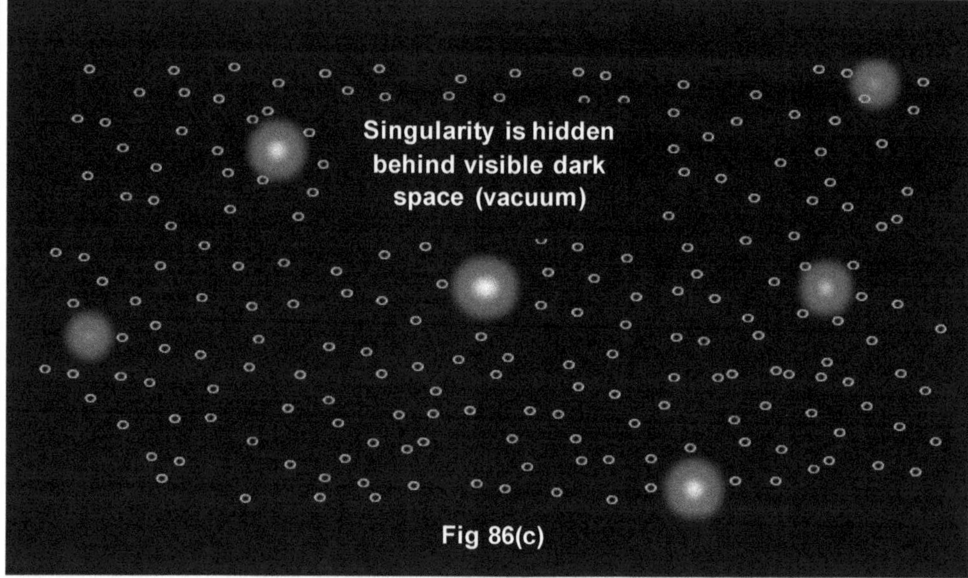

Fig 86(c)

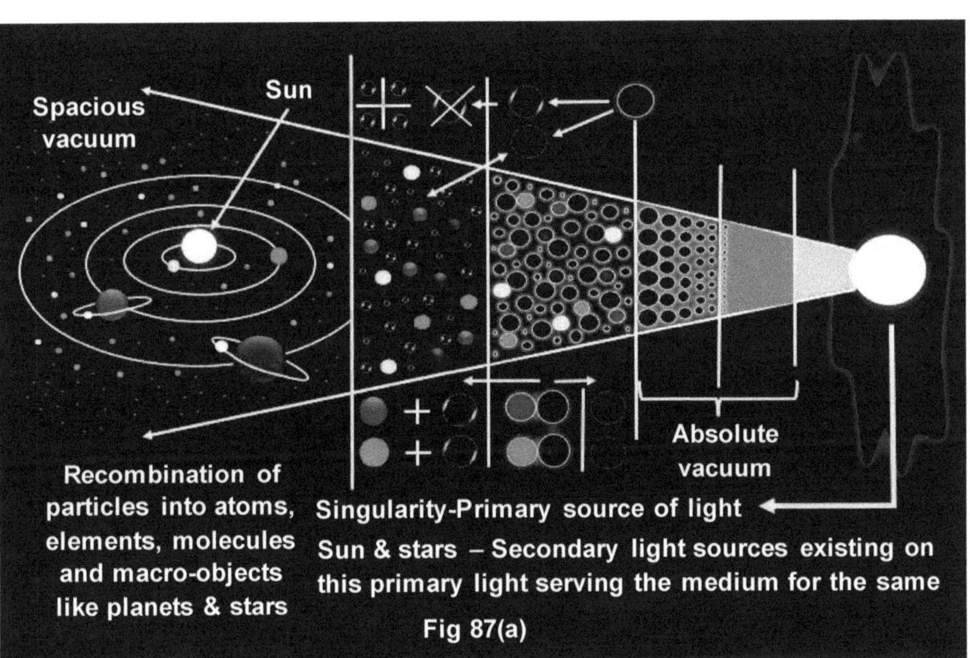

Fig 87(a)

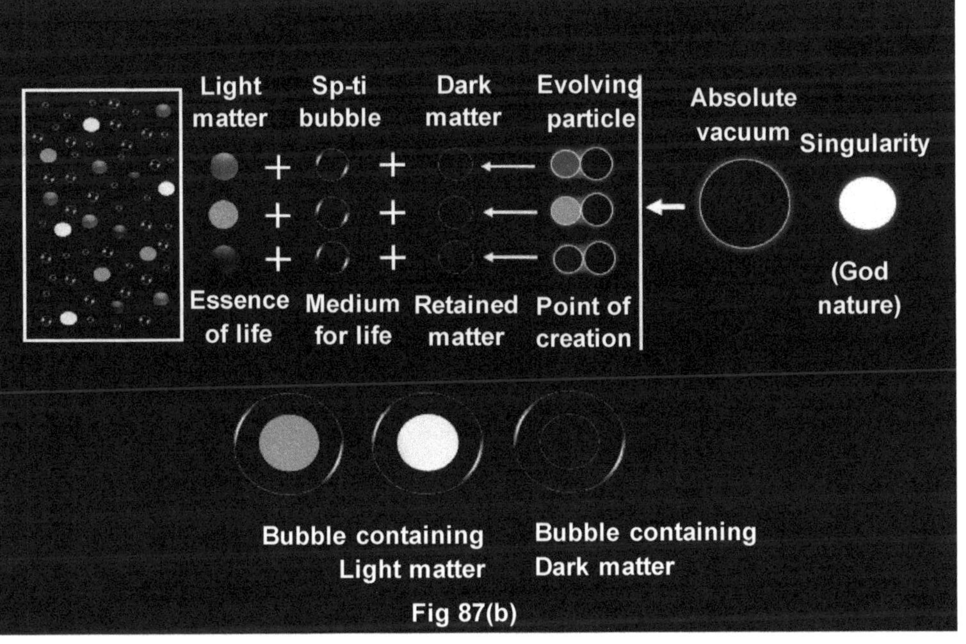

Fig 87(b)

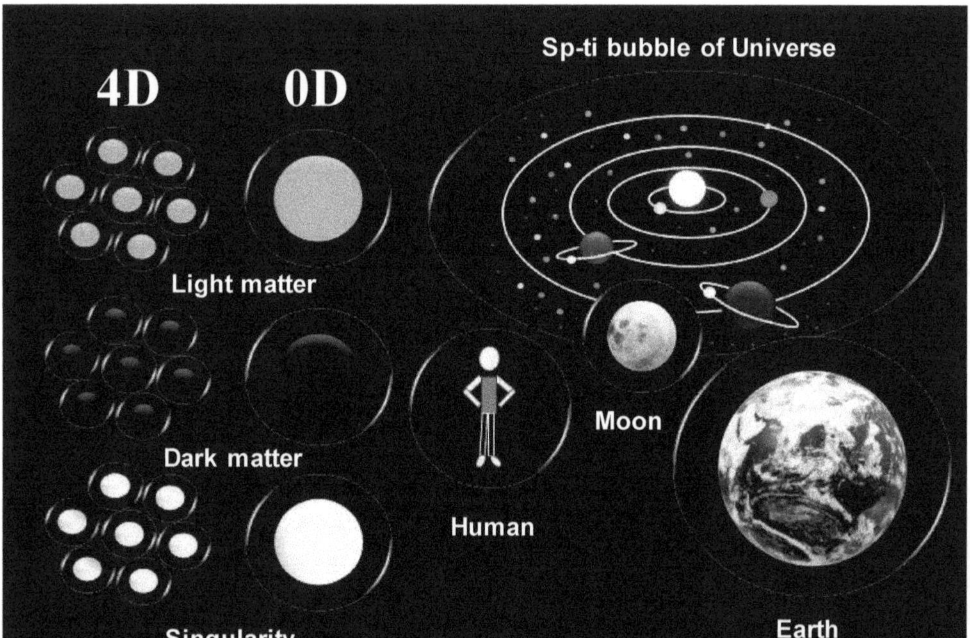

Fig 87(c)

Representation of light matter and dark matter of the existence only pertaining to color code and without any dimensions involved.

However, the sp-ti bubbles of objects grow with its size whereas the bubbles of dark matter (Sp-ti 0s) do not grow and forms the spacious medium for the objects for free motion, thus it could be represented as shown in Fig 88.

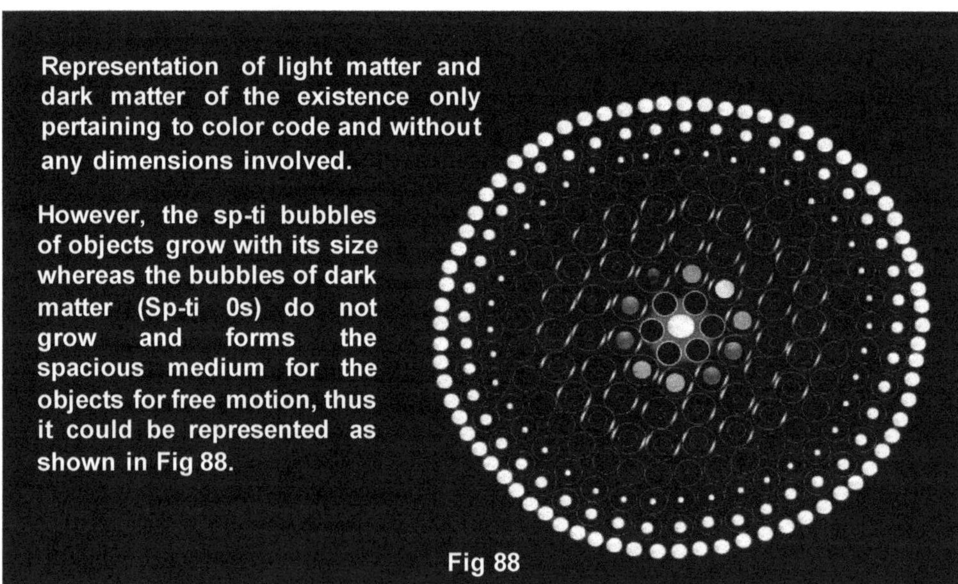

Fig 88

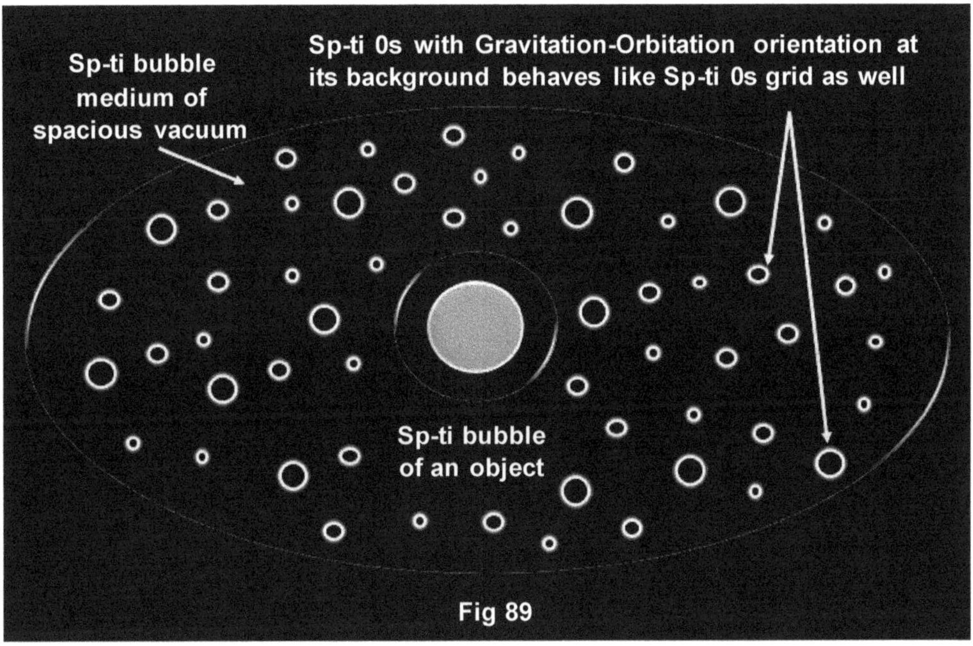

Fig 89

14.0 GRAVITATION; NEW STUDY PART-2

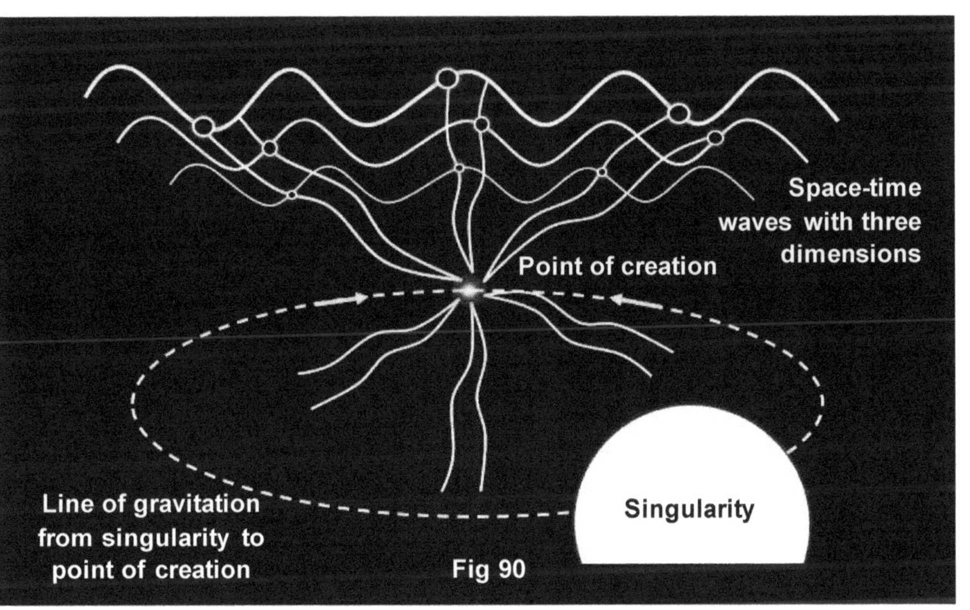

Fig 90

[99]

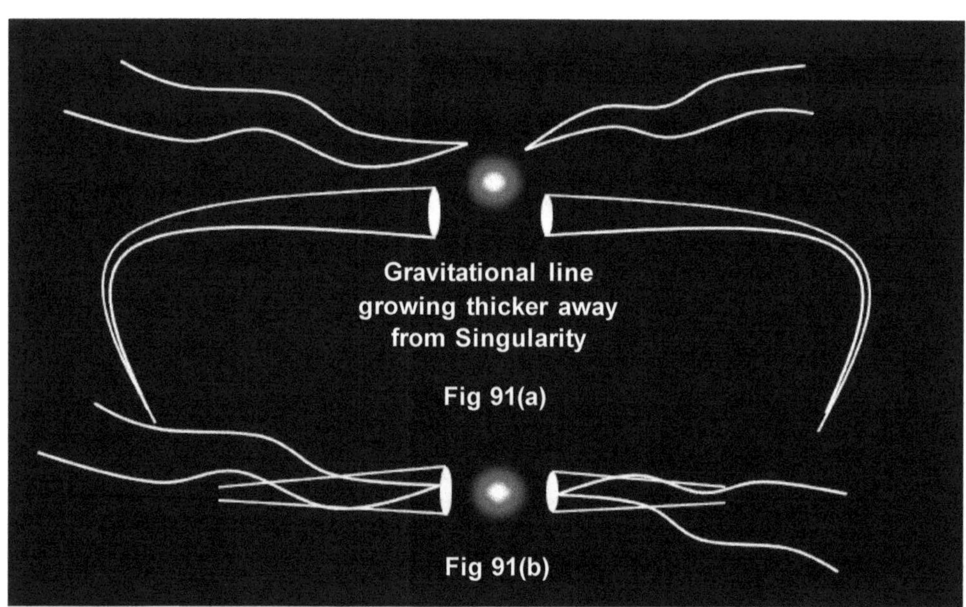

Gravitational line growing thicker away from Singularity

Fig 91(a)

Fig 91(b)

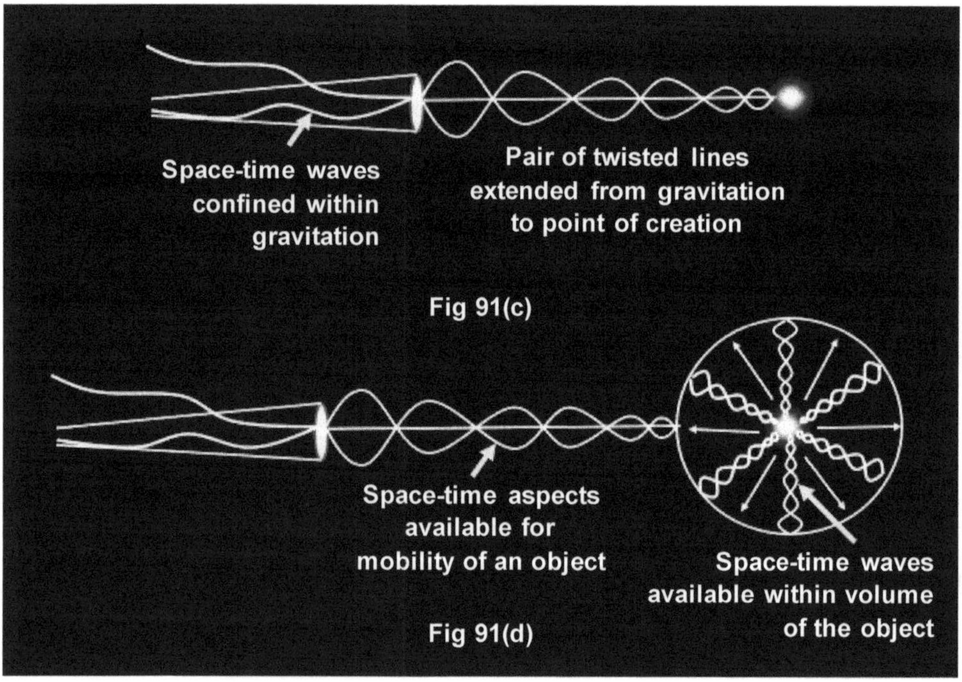

Space-time waves confined within gravitation

Pair of twisted lines extended from gravitation to point of creation

Fig 91(c)

Space-time aspects available for mobility of an object

Space-time waves available within volume of the object

Fig 91(d)

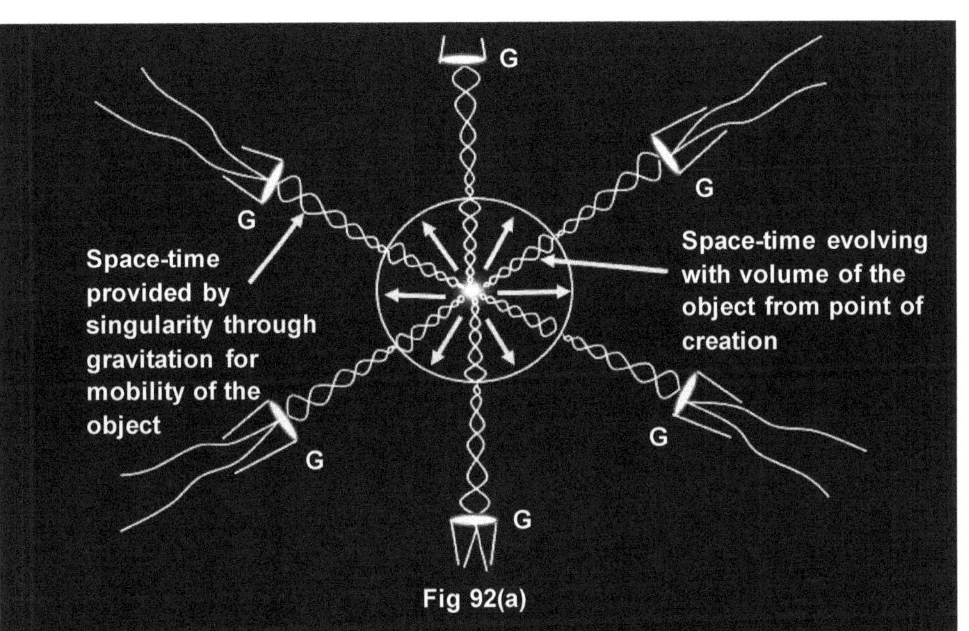

Fig 92(a)

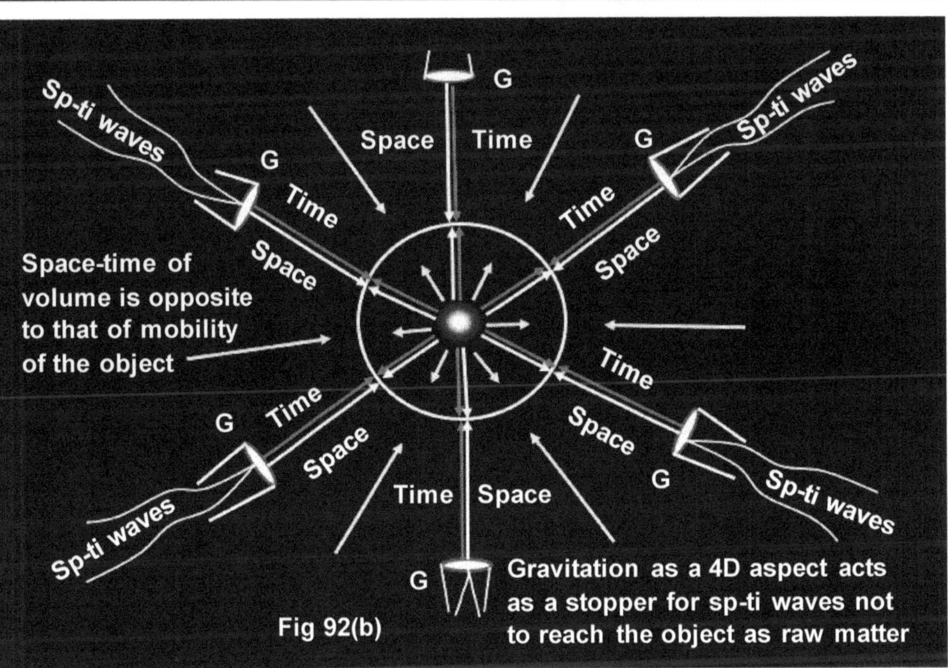

Fig 92(b)

[101]

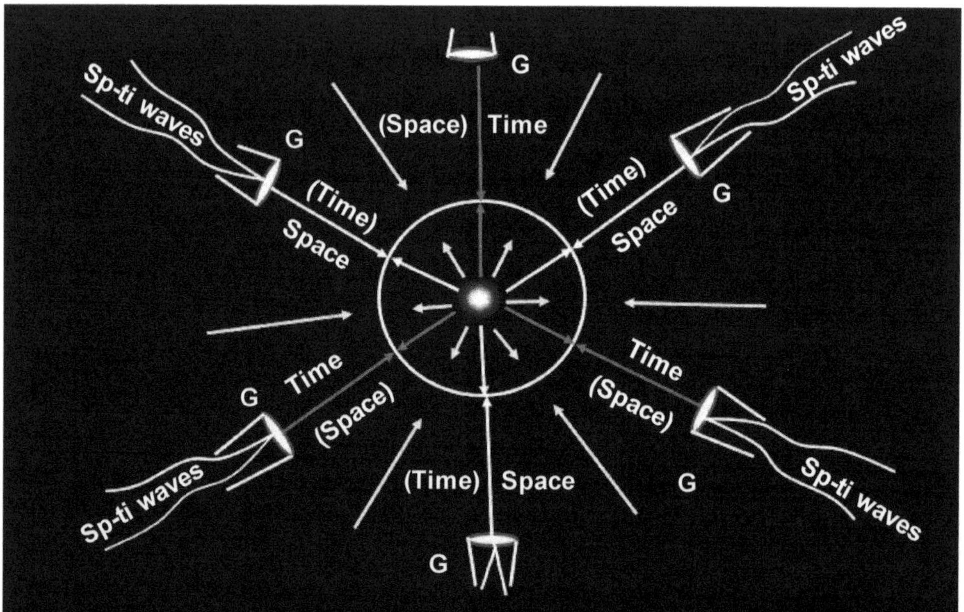

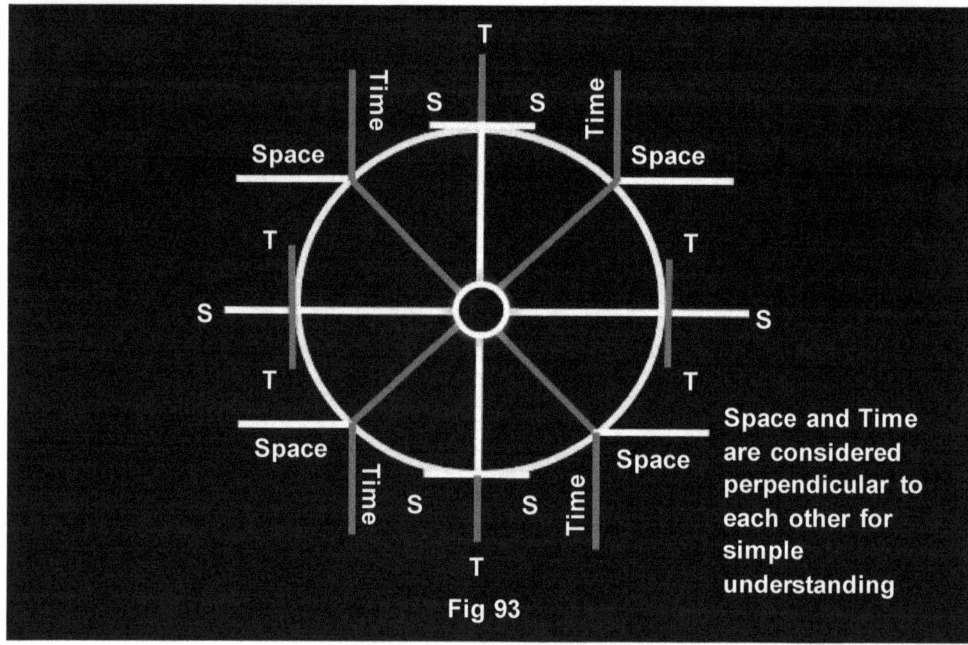

Sp-ti waves
G
(Space) Time
(Time)
Space
Sp-ti waves
G
(Time)
Space
G Time
(Space)
(Time) Space
G
Sp-ti waves
Time
(Space)
G
Sp-ti waves
Fig 92(c)

T
Time
S S
Time
Space
Space
T
T
S
S
T
T
Space
Space
Time
S S
Time
T
Space and Time
are considered
perpendicular to
each other for
simple
understanding
Fig 93

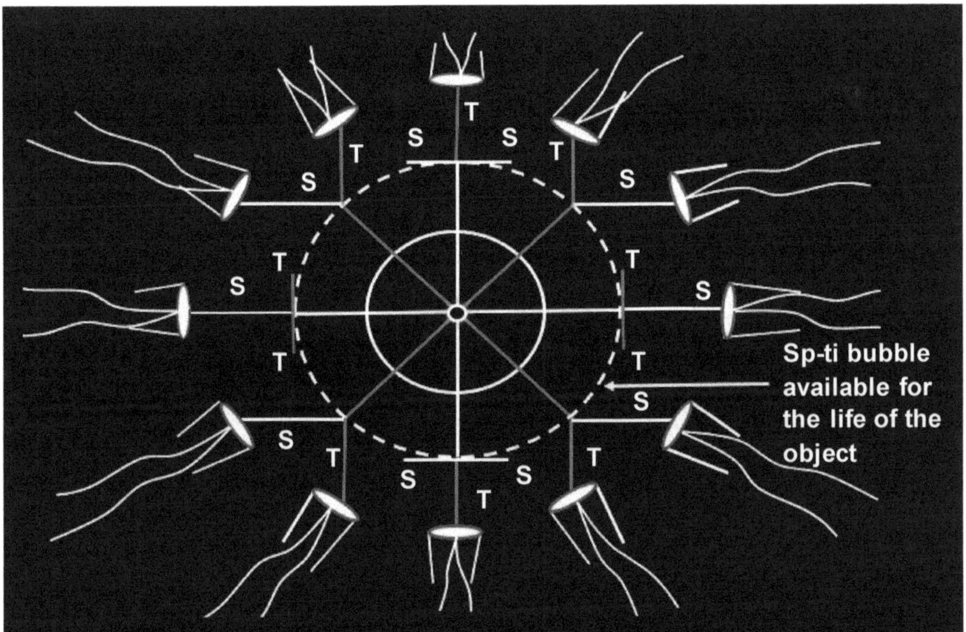

Fig 94

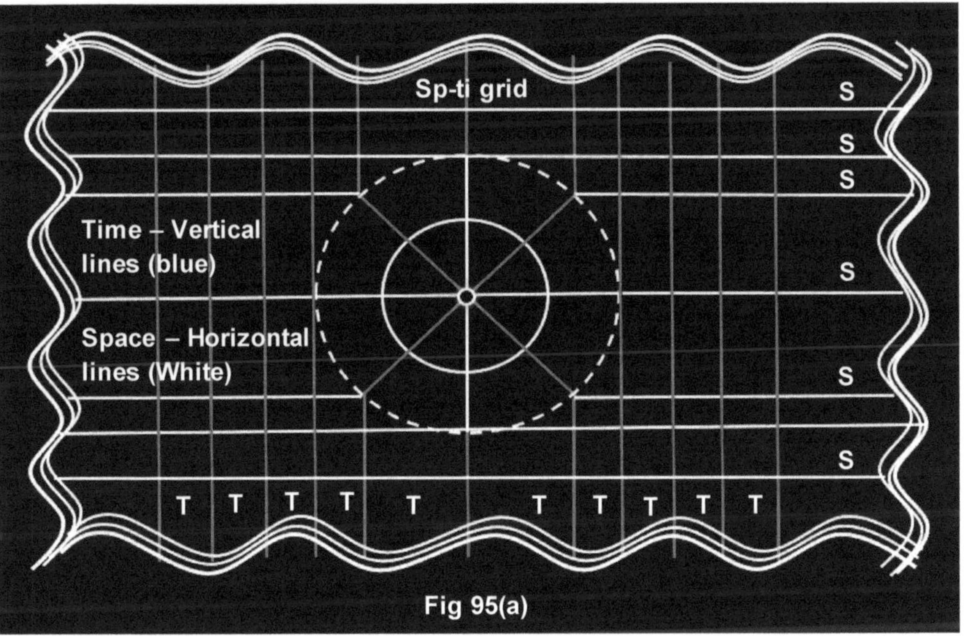

Fig 95(a)

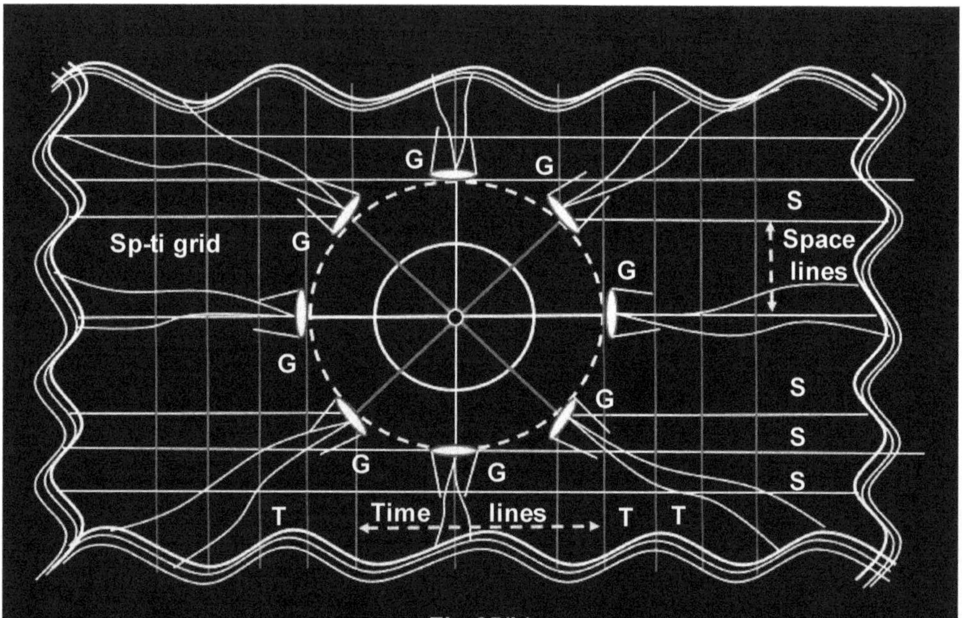

Fig 95(b)

Gravitational boundary filter – "Ring-surround stoppers"

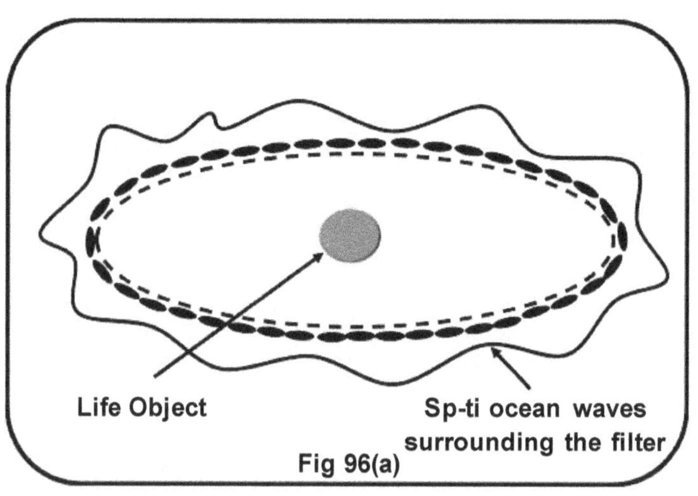

Fig 96(a)

Gravitational base filter – "Mat-spread stoppers"

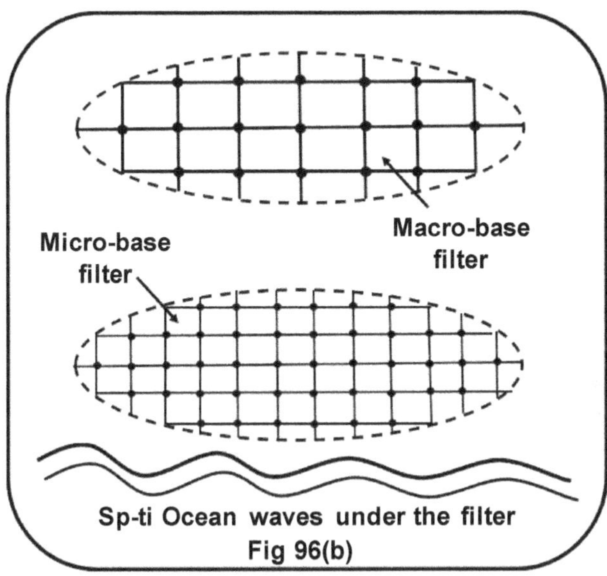

Gravitational core filter – "Needle-point stoppers"

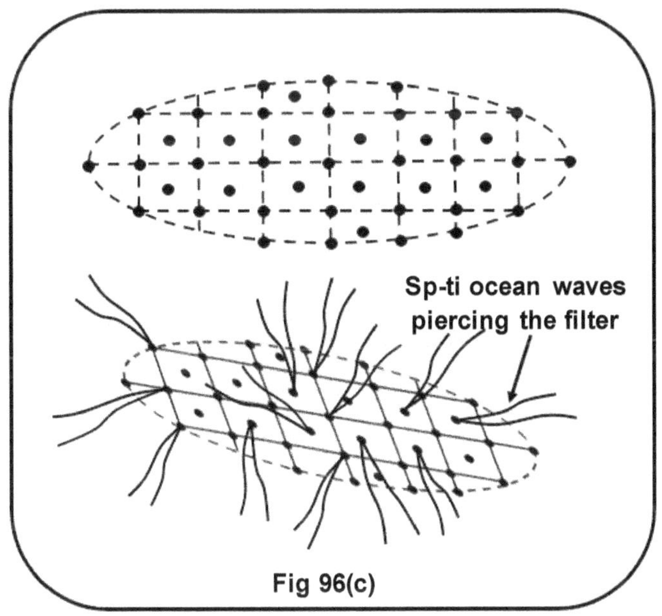

[105]

Three types of gravitational filters are shown in Fig 96. These filters are responsible to stop the raw nature of dark liquid matter and prevent its entry into the evolved objects in three different ways. These filters are very minute knowledge about space-time that one may think whether these details are even required for our study. The core knowledge of the existence takes us deeper and deeper integrating towards singularity.

To destruct our Universe, it does not even require a fraction of second as it would dissolve in the liquid medium of Dark Ocean same like a spoon of sugar put in a vessel of water. Life of Universe is obviously somebody's consideration to exist with a measured distance, away from ultimate reality. There is a point that separates the local reality called life, whose direction is destined opposite to singularity. Hence theory of singularity makes us feel uncomfortable as it demands us to leave the attachments that holds oneself down to earth. However, once if drifted in its way, it is blissful.

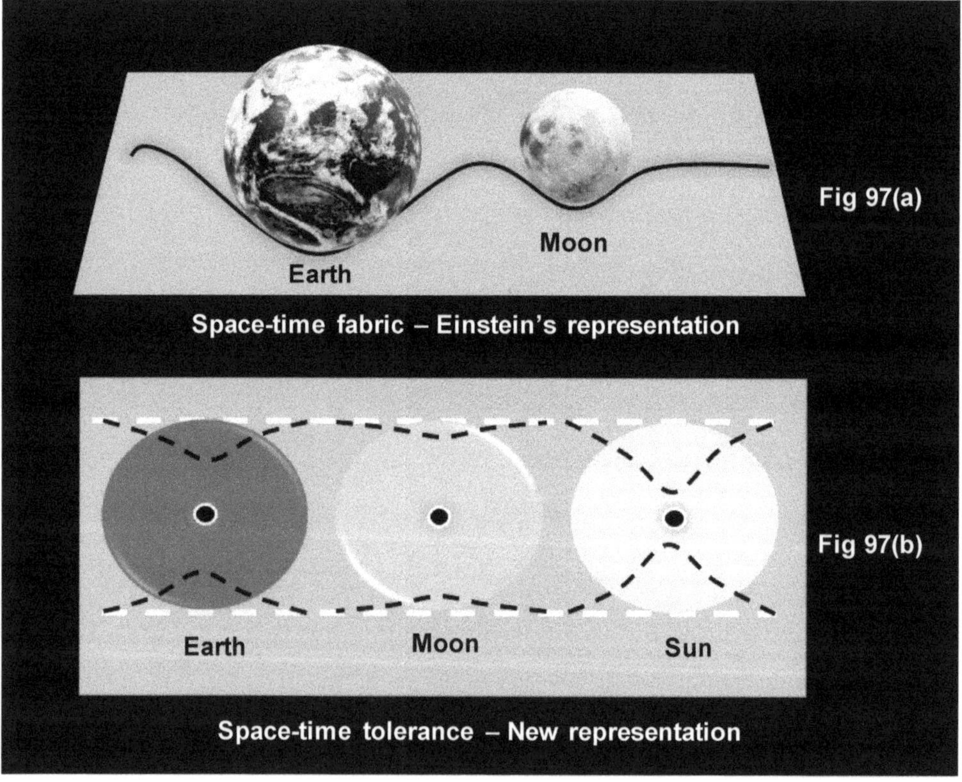

Space-time fabric – Einstein's representation

Space-time tolerance – New representation

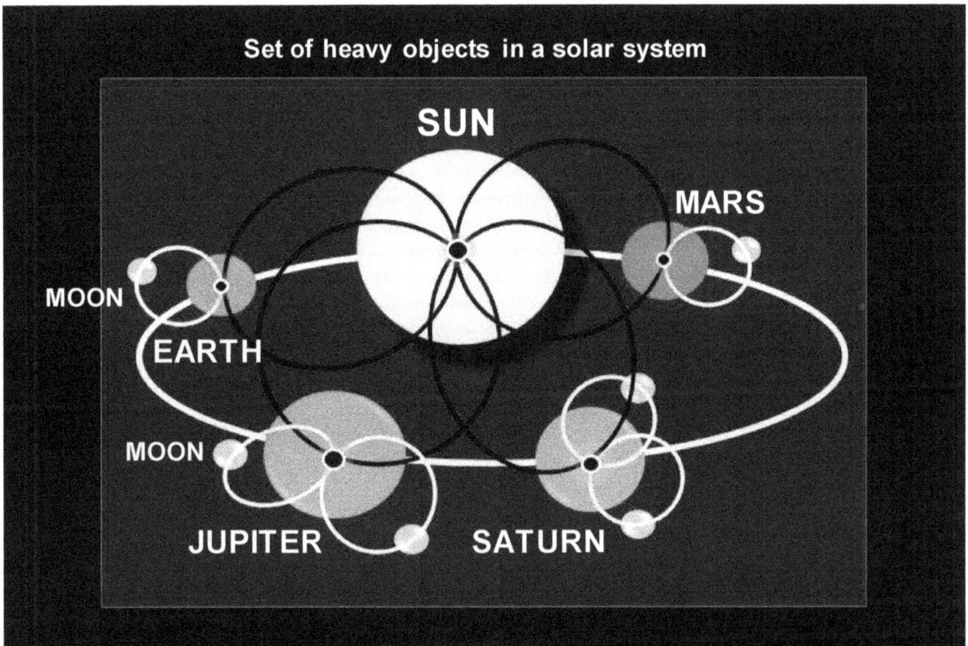

Fig 97(c)

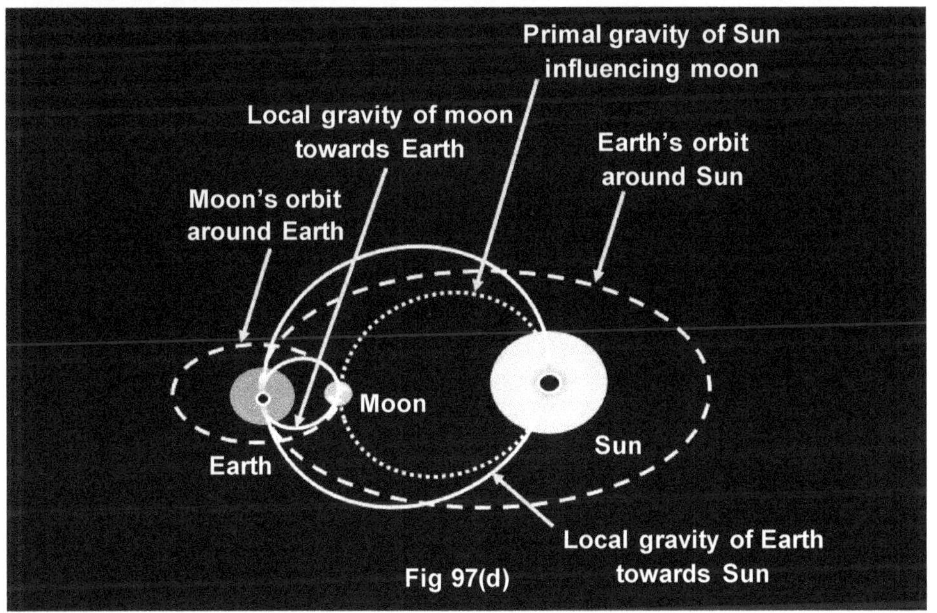

Fig 97(d)

Line of gravitation
irrespective of size, mass
and density of objects
Gravitational
stoppers
Gravitational
rope
Gravitational thread
or quantum gravity
Sp-ti pond of
fundamental
fields
Singularity
Dark Liquid
Ocean
Fig 98

Gravitation-Orbitation
web network
Fig 99

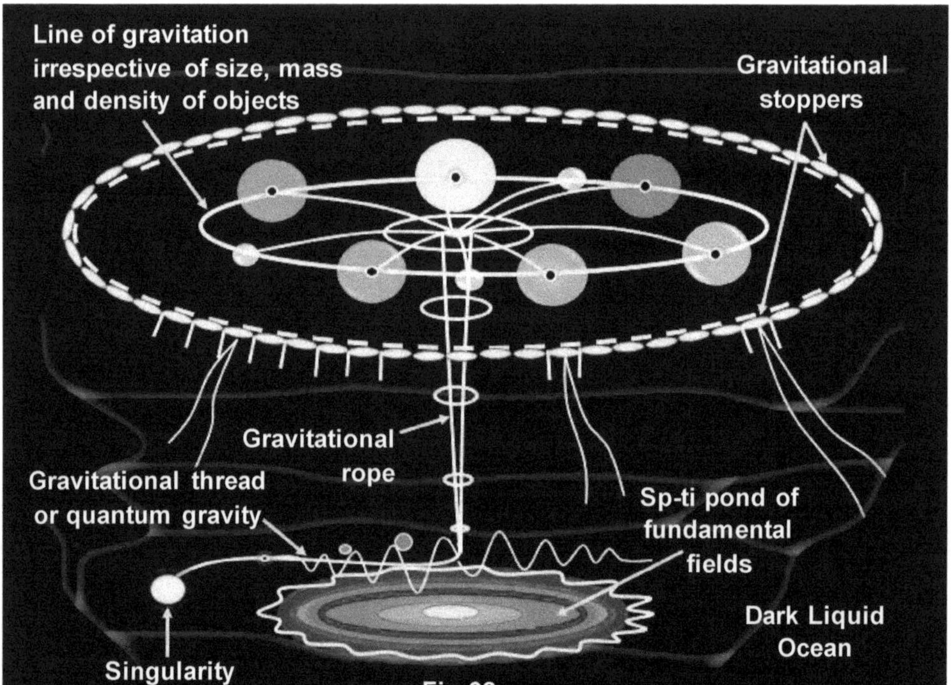

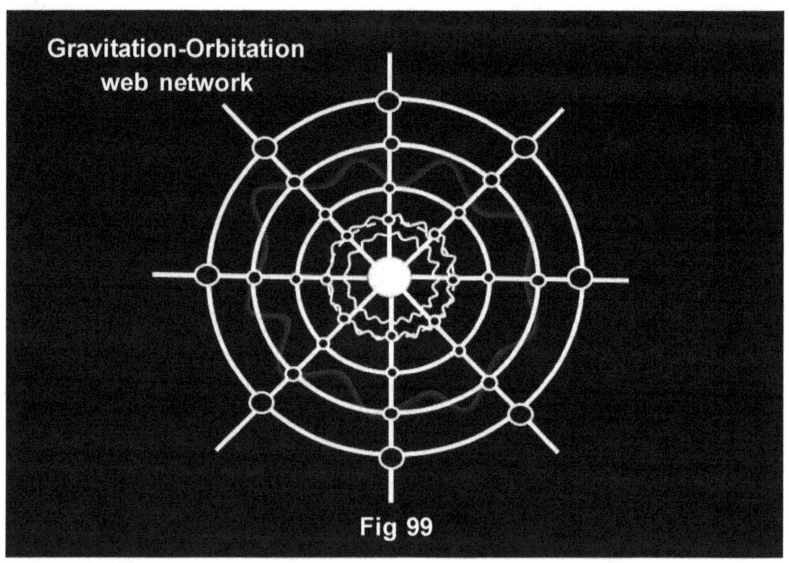

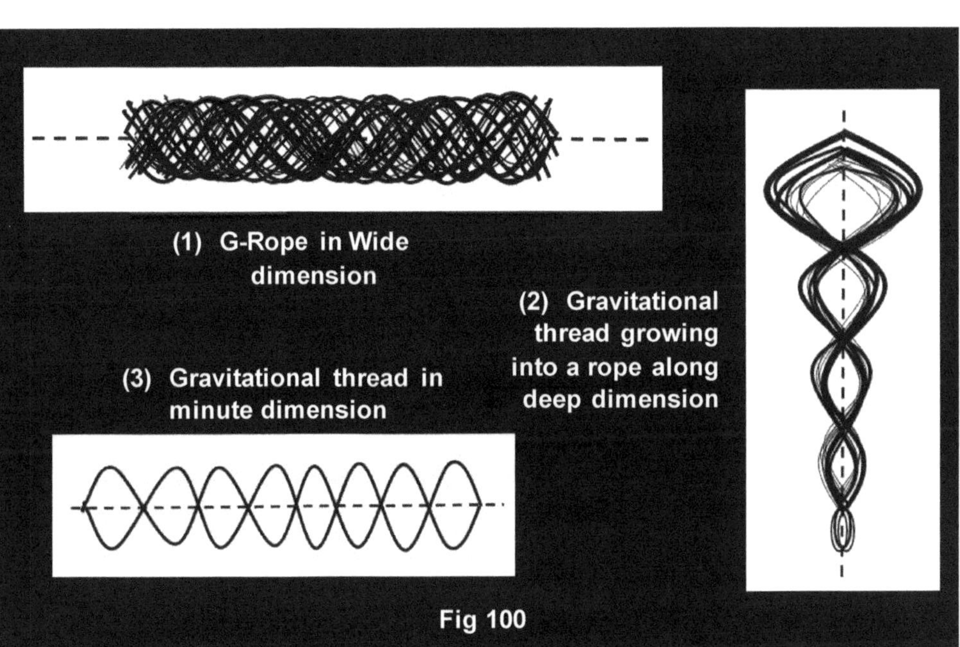

Fig 100

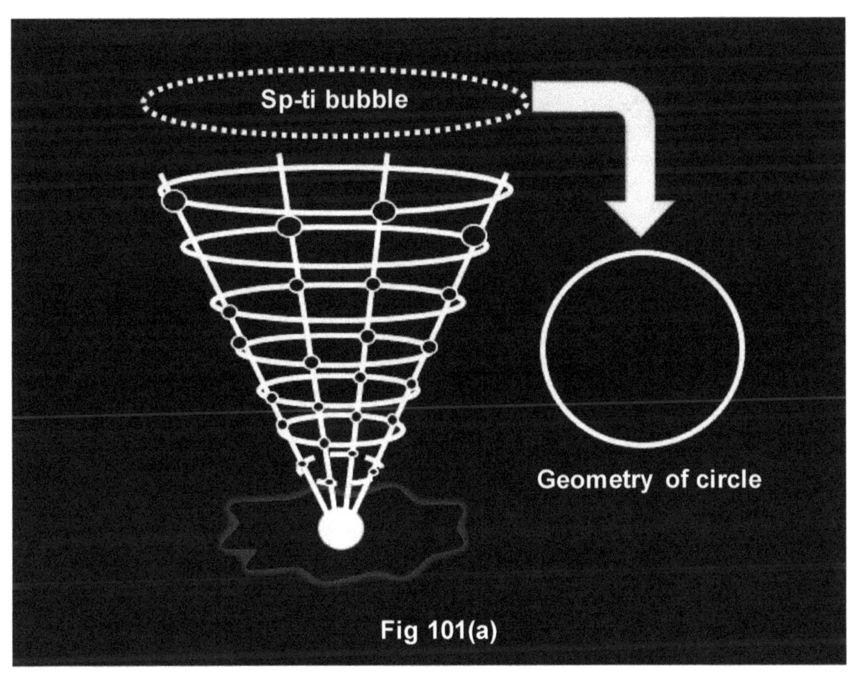

Fig 101(a)

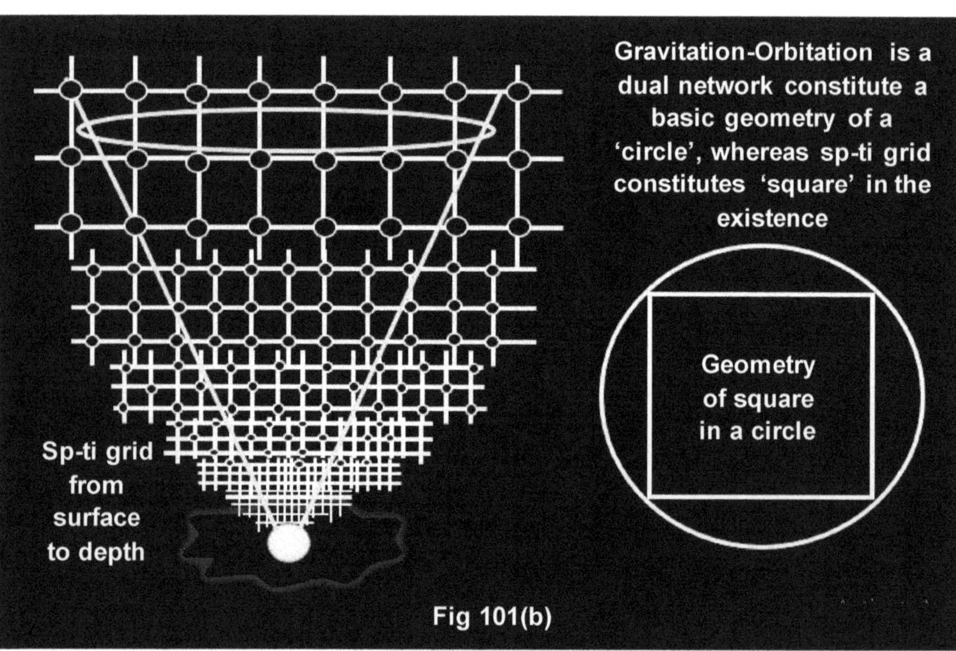

Fig 101(b)

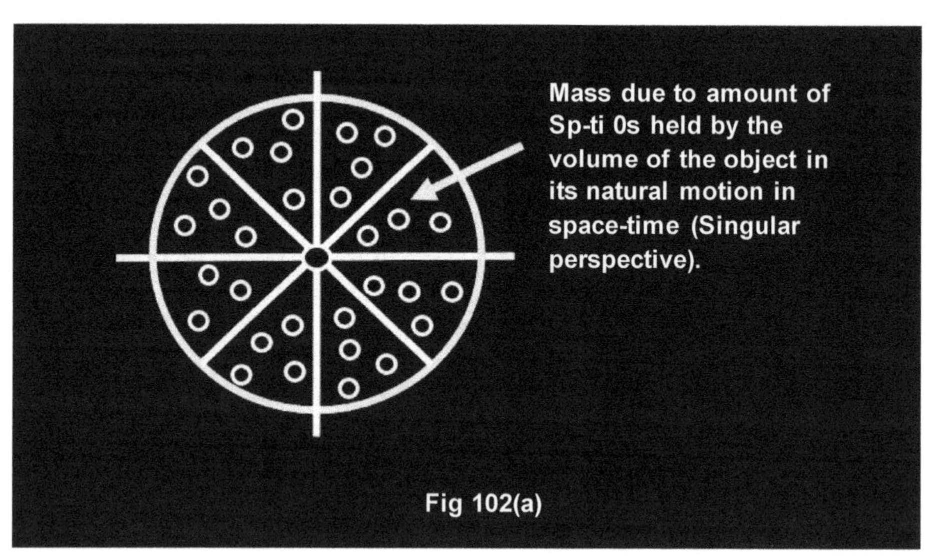

Fig 102(a)

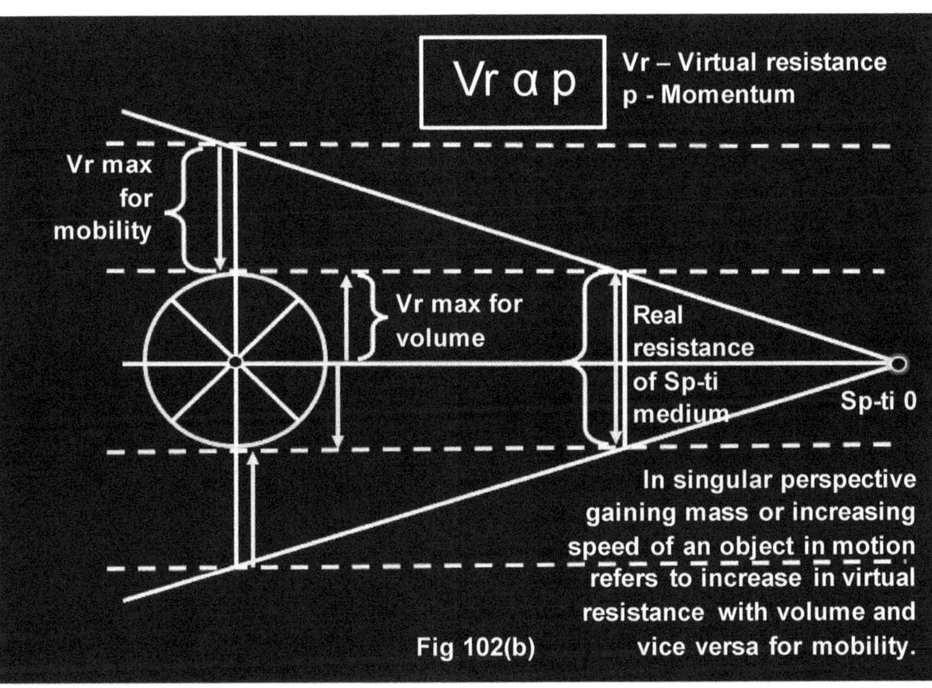

Vr α p
Vr – Virtual resistance
p - Momentum
Vr max for mobility
Vr max for volume
Real resistance of Sp-ti medium
Sp-ti 0
In singular perspective gaining mass or increasing speed of an object in motion refers to increase in virtual resistance with volume and vice versa for mobility.
Fig 102(b)

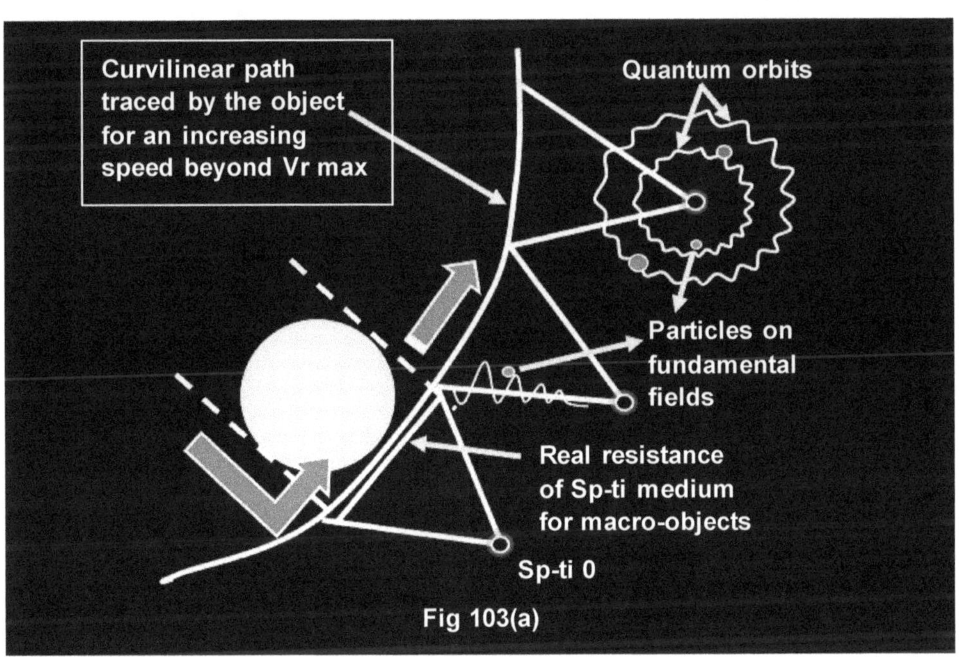

Curvilinear path traced by the object for an increasing speed beyond Vr max
Quantum orbits
Particles on fundamental fields
Real resistance of Sp-ti medium for macro-objects
Sp-ti 0
Fig 103(a)

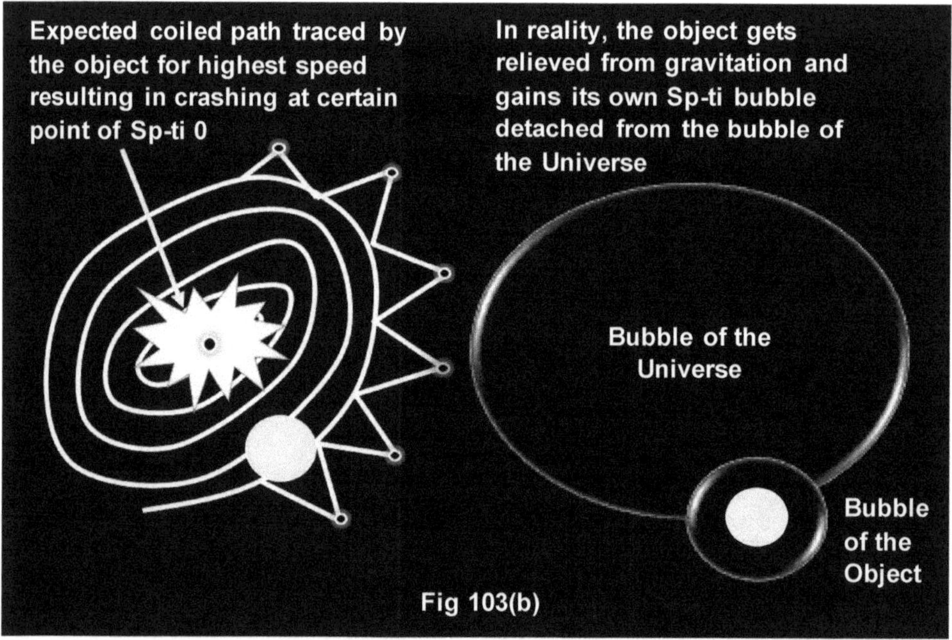

Fig 103(b)

The dimensional cone stops the object for further entry into it and offers a real resistance. Obviously, if the cone is a solid aspect, then the object has to deform or crush itself to reach the point of sp-ti 0. In reality the fluid nature of space-time medium allows the object to slide and slip away to trace a coiled path to reach the point of sp-ti 0 in another way. However, for further increase in speed, the object gets its own sp-ti bubble and get relieved from the bubble of the Universe. At this time, the object is said to be free from gravitation.

Fig 103(a) shows the particle on fundamental field wave with quantum gravity, the axis towards Sp-ti 0 as well as the quantum orbits around sp-ti 0, to be noted.

15.0 REAL CONE OF REAL DIMENSIONS

The three main real dimensions such as Core, Base and Boundary that differs with positions of Sp-ti 0 has to be further analyzed for hidden dualities. For example, we see base-boundary is an inseparable duality that, when there is plate-like base, obviously there must be an edge of this plate with a boundary.

However, considering a real cone of dimensions it is possible to separate the base-boundary dimensions. Overall base could be assumed as an inner cone whereas the boundary dimension is assumed to cover the base cone, which could be unfold as a wrapper, Fig 104(a & b).

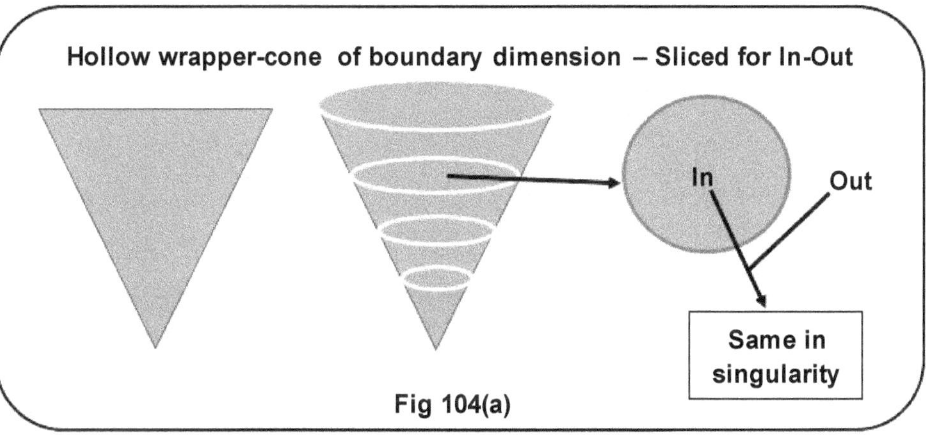

Fig 104(a)

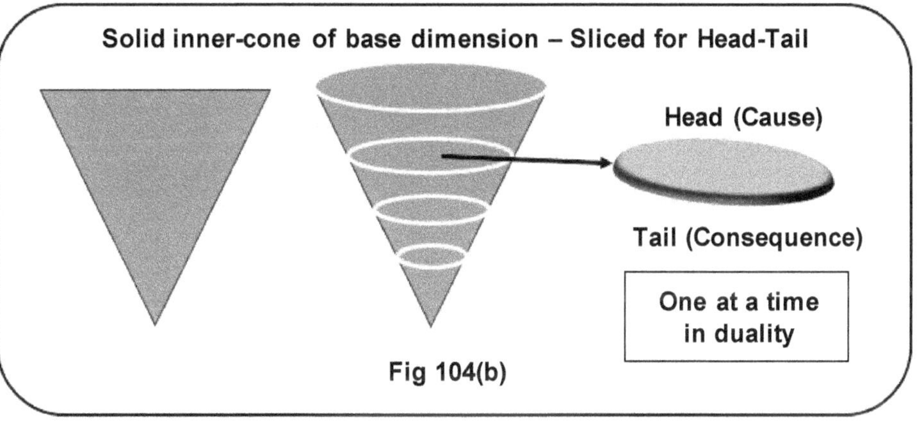

Fig 104(b)

Real cone is a combination of six new discovered dimensions curled-up beyond human vision and even imagination. These cones constitute the shape for space-time study indeed. And without these representations it is impossible to understand space-time as a whole-existence. Even if science and technology make observations with videos of outer space captured through powerful telescopes for thousands of years, mysteries remain the same and concepts would float in isolation. We will see how the cone of real dimensions contains the finite structure of Sp-ti.

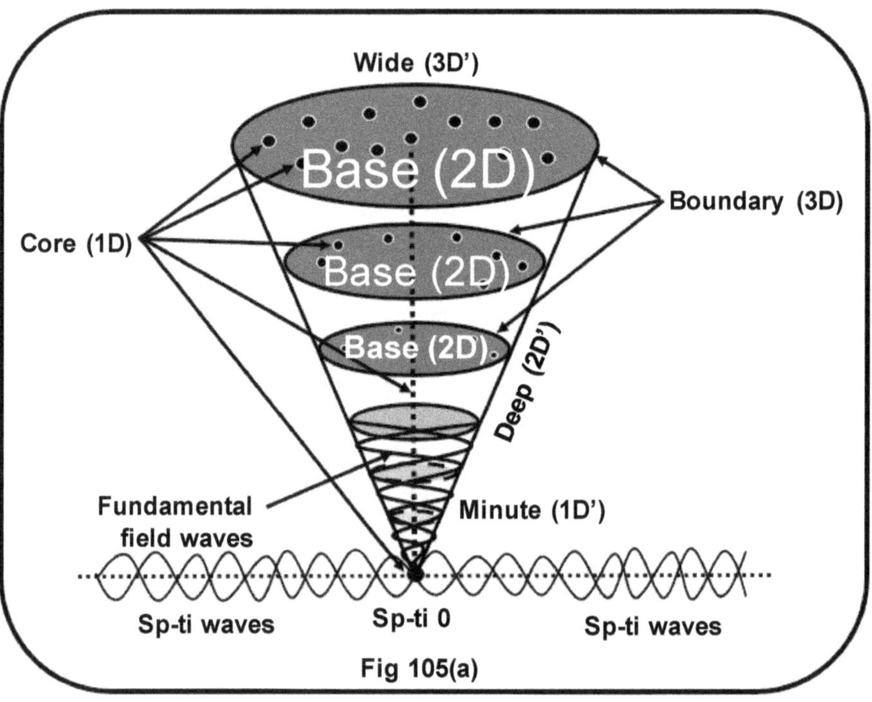

In Fig 105(a) sp-ti waves serving the medium is shown to be horizontal whereas the fundamental field responsible for evolution of fundamental particles is shown vertical. Core dimension is points everywhere.

Clearly, cones of base and boundary dimensions could be represented to have opposite faces, now let us see how the cone of core dimension shall be included. Core dimension is absolutely non-geometrical, Fig 105(b). If all the diagrams are shown with real appearances, nothing could be interpreted properly as it would be complicated with full of spiral coils.

[114]

The work of singularity mainly utilizes both geometrical and non-geometrical aspects as required and focused only in formulating the theory in all possible ways.

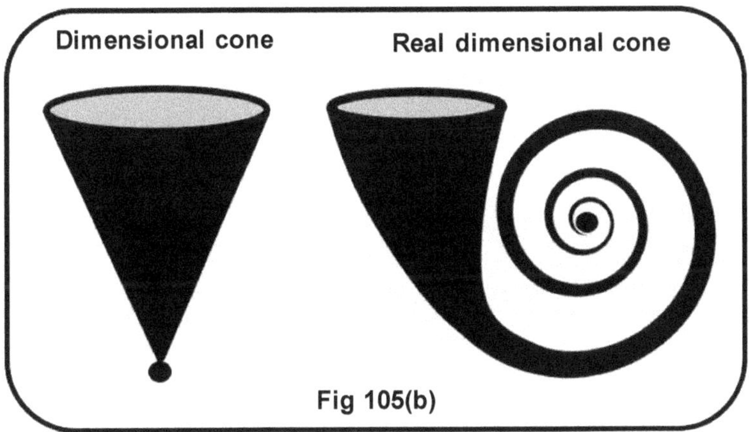

Applying the real cones with the combination of geometrical and non-geometrical aspects, we obtain the structure of space-time as shown in Fig 106(a). The core dimension of the real cone takes the coil structure to reach to the dark liquid ocean ending with the point of singularity.

The Universe we live is at the surface, where it is a spacious vacuum, in which we have six directions such as Up-Down, Right-Left and Forward-Reverse governed by the conventional graph, Fig 106(b & c) this is helpful in understanding the variation in local reality, however human perspective has developed the decimal number system that is separated by reference zero causing the duality of positive and negative phases.

Fig 107(a) shows this graph to be on the surface (i.e.) base of the shadow cone in wide dimension. Means it almost loses the contact with the core dimension. Also, the base dimension with a duality of cause and consequence in reality is changed into four quadrants with the combination of (x, y), (-x, y), (-x, -y), (x, -y) in the six directional graphs. The shadow cones are multi-directional whose positions are more than the minimum of six directions shown in the Fig. However, it is casting its shadow over the details about the depth of space-time and holding human understanding to remain only at the surface level.

[115]

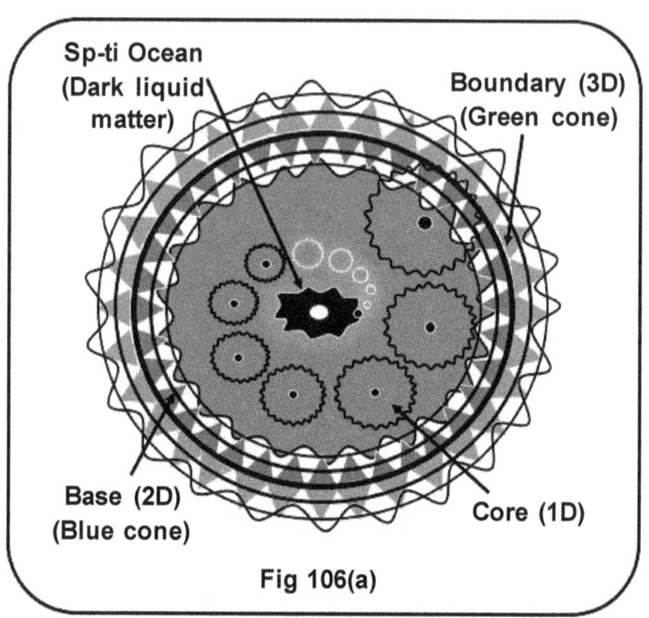

Fig 106(a)

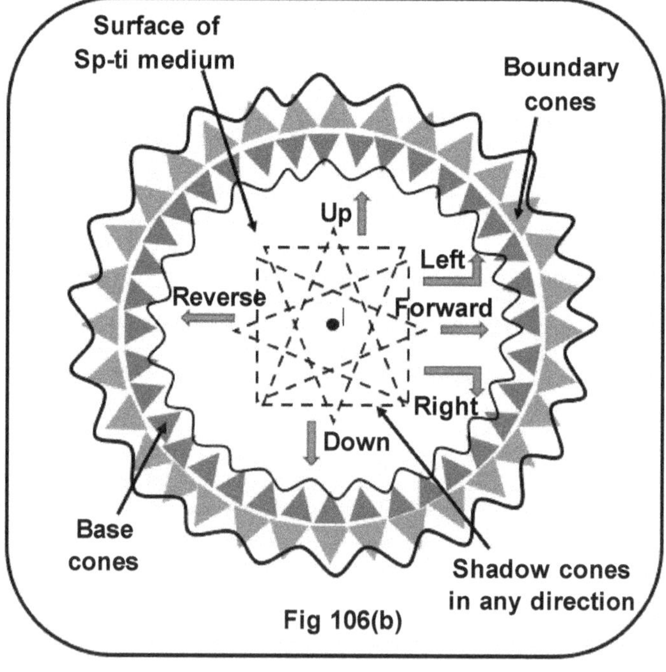

Fig 106(b)

[116]

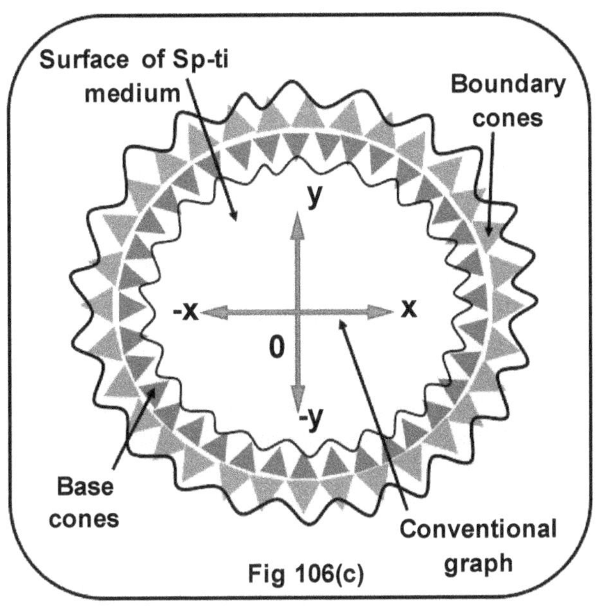

Fig 106(c)

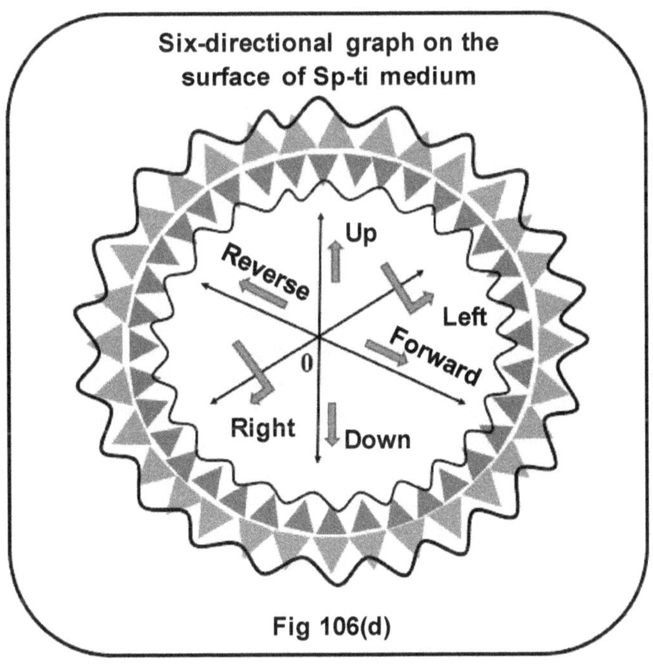

Fig 106(d)

Shadow cone of real dimensions

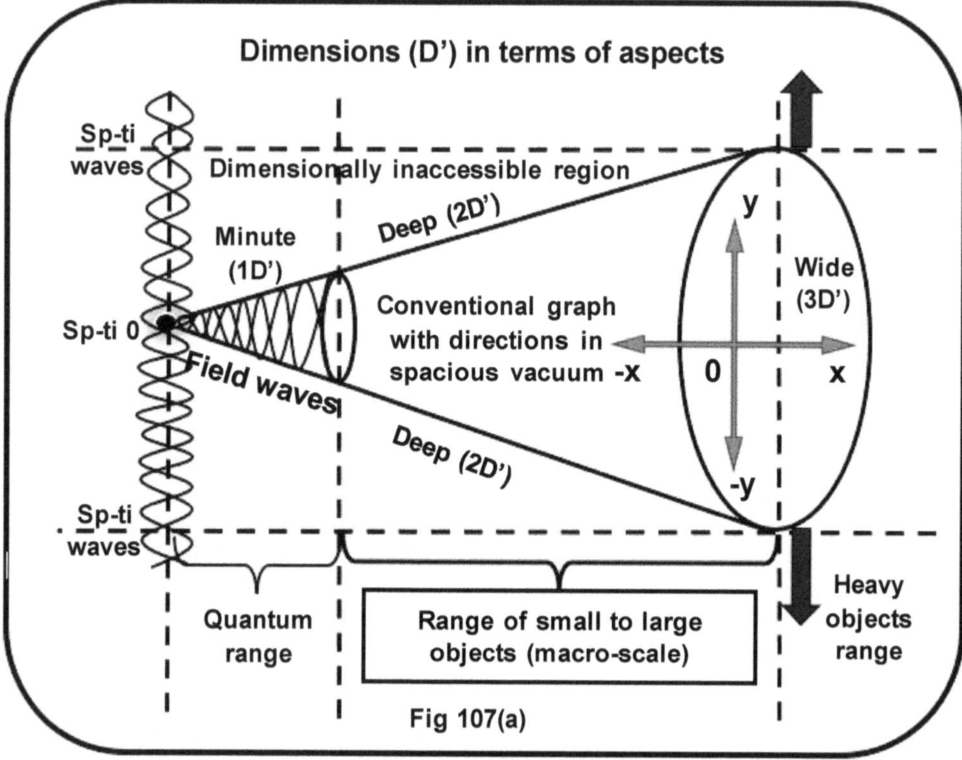

From Fig 107(a), we see sp-ti 0 and sp-ti waves of the medium from which the fundamental field waves are emerging out. The real dimensions in terms of aspects are marked along with the conventional graph. The quantum range holds the fundamental fields from which the particles evolve. Next to this is a range of small to large objects. This begins with minimum of smallest possible object below which the objects are minute and incapable of bending sp-ti grid lines with its volume. On the other extreme it ends with a maximum of largest possible object, which does not bend the sp-ti grid lines with its mass. Beyond this mass density, the object is said to be heavy as it bends the sp-ti grid lines. Even then there is again a limit for heavy objects also, to be within sp-ti tolerance max. The heavy objects range holds the fourth dimensional aspect of Gravitation-Orbitation duality. Further beyond this range comes the black holes that has no connection with gravitation, as it is believed so in existing research works.

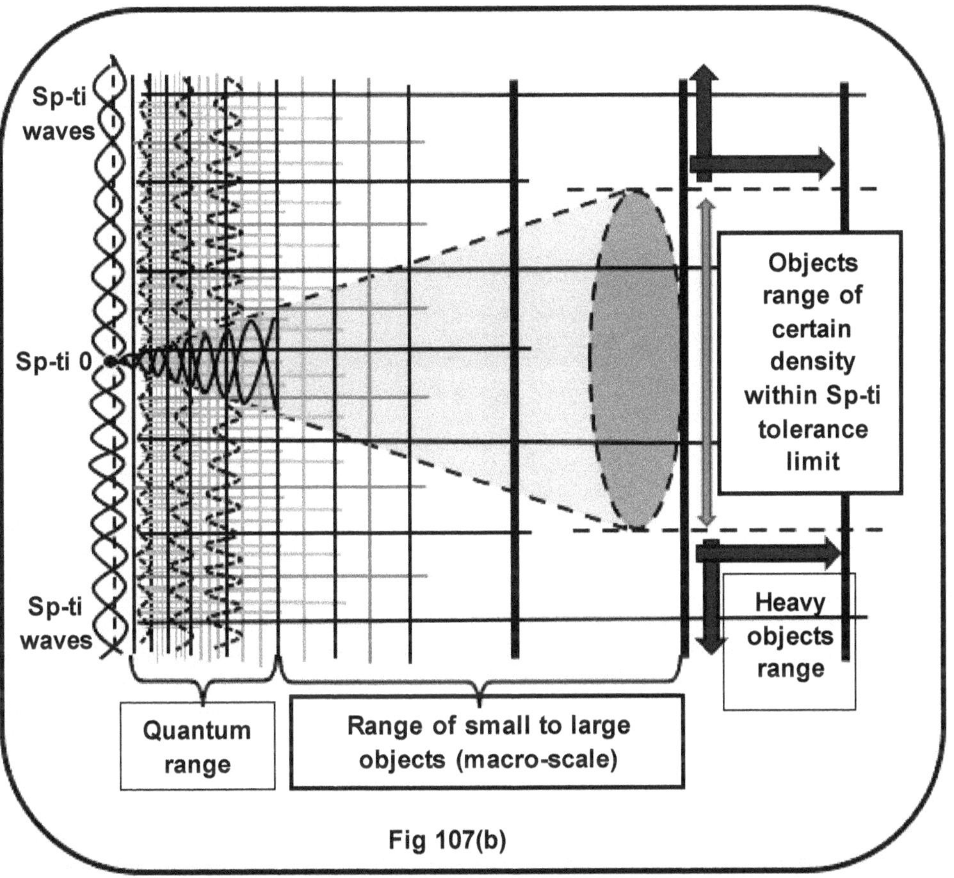

Fig 107(b)

The Fig 107(a) also shows a dimensionally inaccessible region to fall in the representation. However, this is actually same as the real dimensional cone, which is a cut piece of a sphere, to be understood.

Even in the real cone we are accessing the surface or base of the cone which is the wide dimension where, moving in six directions is possible. The deep dimension of the cone is theoretical and imagined only using shadow cone illustrations. This is the reason why light photons are wrongly thought to be on the same surface level we live, without considering the real dimensions at its background.

[119]

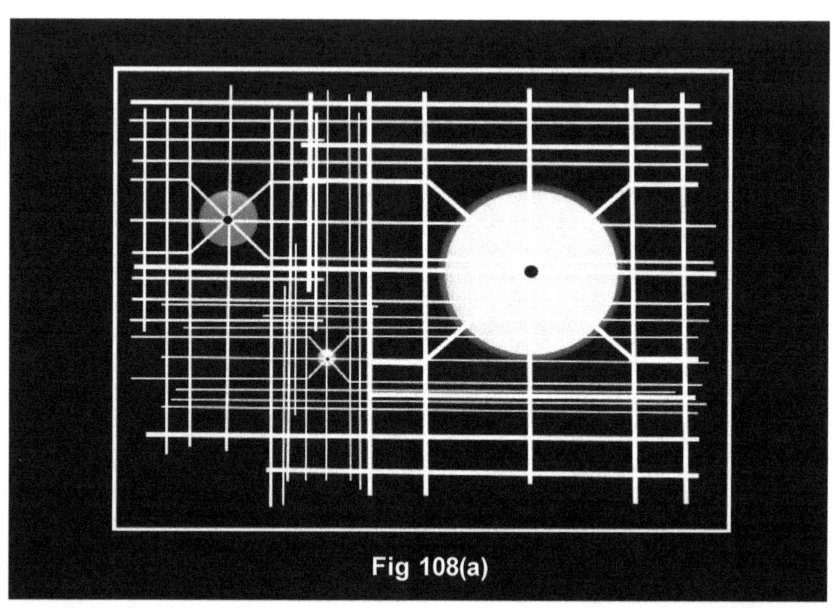

Fig 108(a)

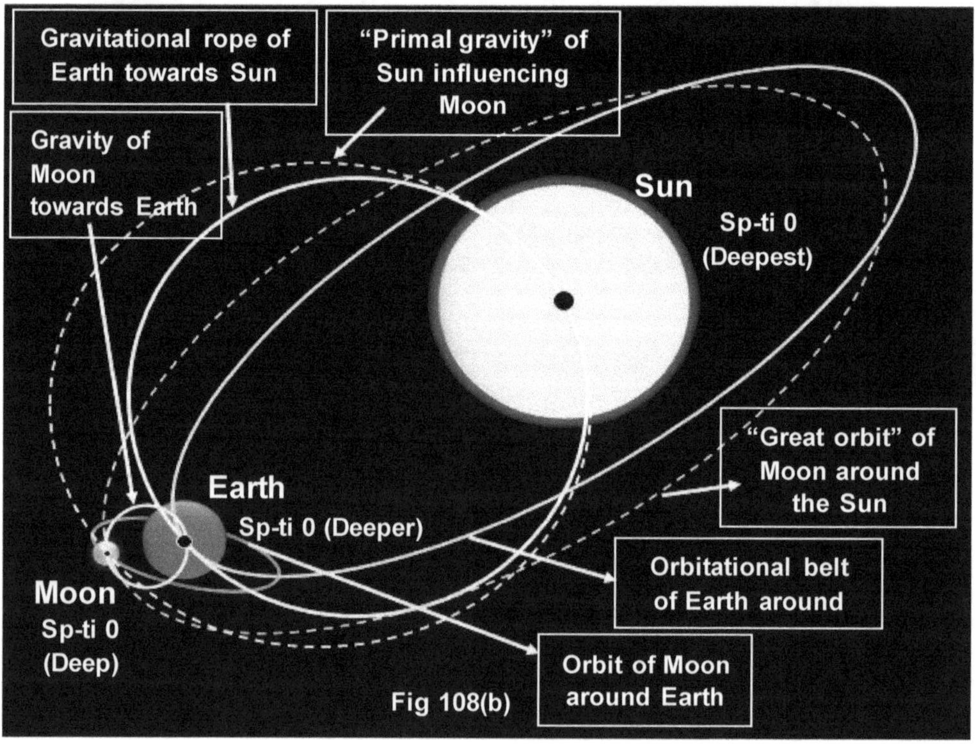

Gravitational rope of Earth towards Sun
"Primal gravity" of Sun influencing Moon
Gravity of Moon towards Earth
Sun
Sp-ti 0 (Deepest)
"Great orbit" of Moon around the Sun
Earth
Sp-ti 0 (Deeper)
Orbitational belt of Earth around
Moon
Sp-ti 0 (Deep)
Orbit of Moon around Earth
Fig 108(b)

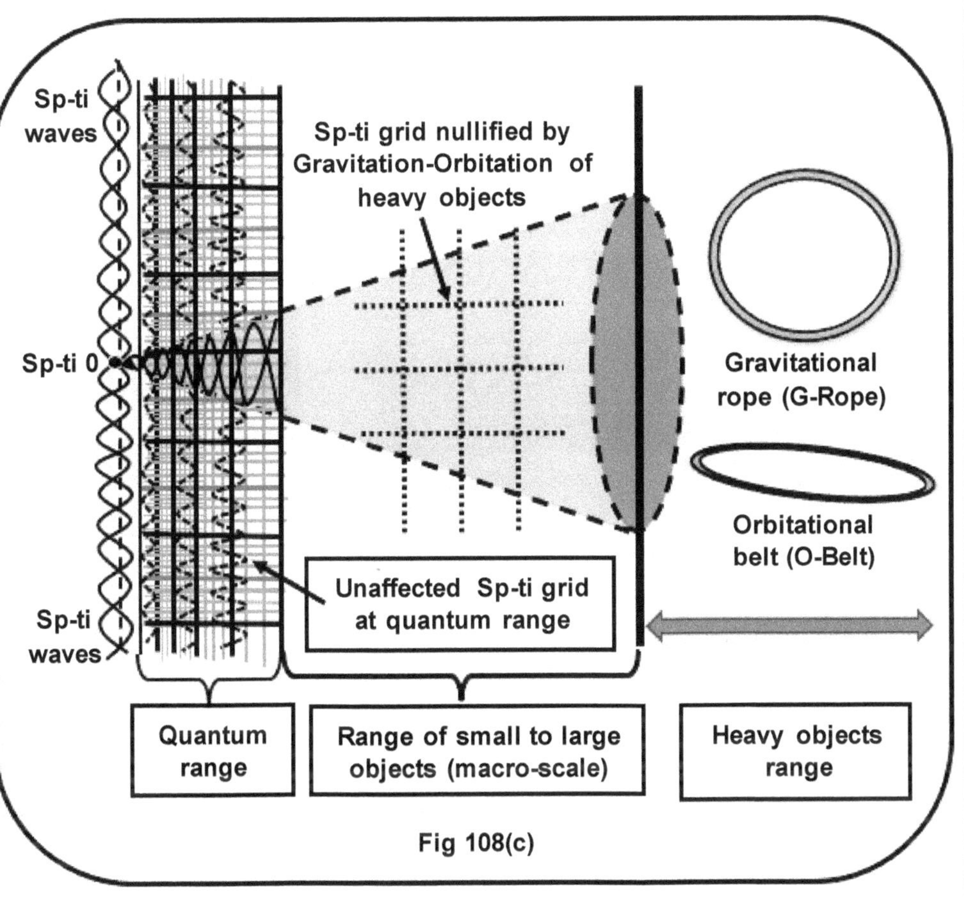

Fig 108(c)

Gravitation is an arrow head pointed towards Sp-ti 0 of every single object at its core and its flow is a downstream from surface to depth of space-time medium through Sp-ti 0 (deep) – Sp-ti 0 (deeper) – Sp-ti 0 (deepest). At the overall surface we live, this flow is made as solid circular loop between two objects (minimum) like a rope which would catch hold of each other, so that the evolved objects do not collapse back into nothing. In addition to this comes the orbitation, that the tied objects based on its depth level of Sp-ti 0 core, one object revolves around the other object (later deeper than the former).

This **Gravitational rope** and **Orbitational belt** are invisible, as these aspects are falling in fourth dimension yet their functioning is observed in terms of **force of attraction** and **path of revolution** respectively.

[121]

Thus, the G-Rope and O-belt could not be cut or interfered by the 3D objects but only to abide by the way it is by nature. Means, space-time medium serves the background and thus have absolute control over the life of evolving, sustaining & fading away of objects in it.

Fig 108(c) shows the nullified sp-ti grid in macro-scale range due to G-rope and O-belt whereas sp-ti grid at quantum range remains unaffected and said to be present everywhere in the existence.

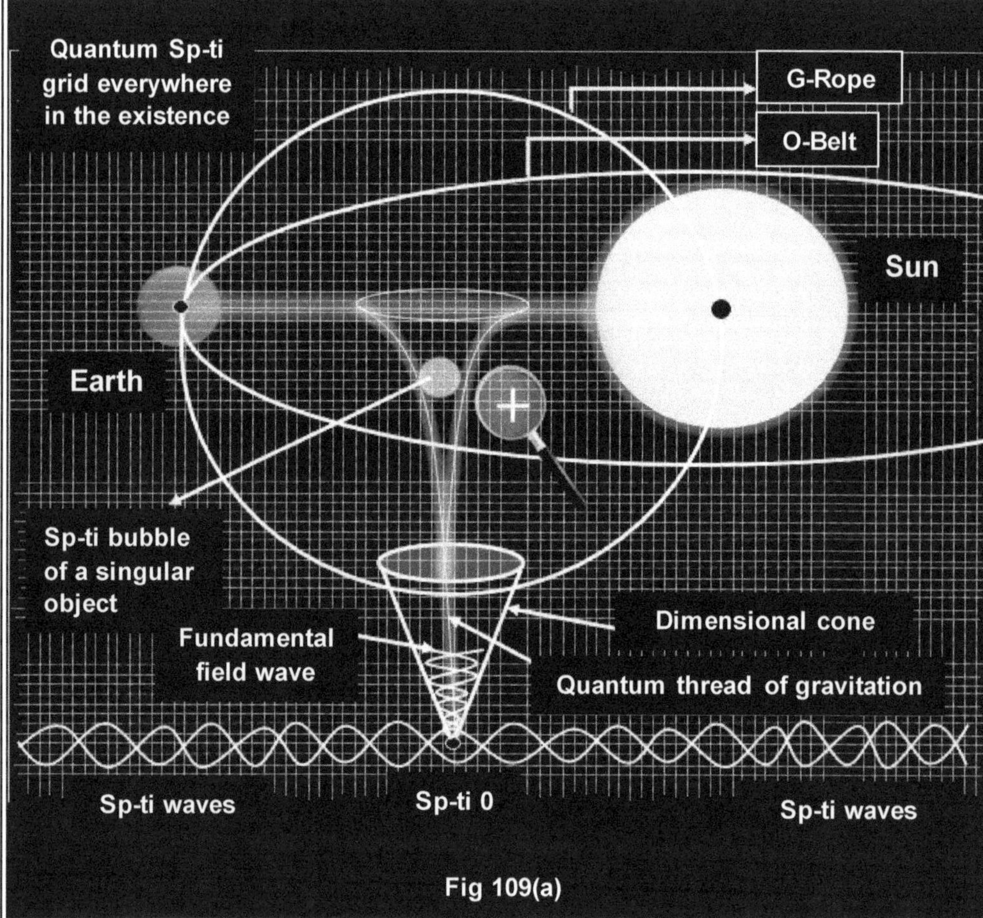

Fig 109(a)

The quantum thread of gravitation or quantum gravity is a connection among all the objects in the existence. Fig 109(b) shows the connection among Earth, Moon and the Sun with quantum thread. There is a dancing

[122]

note on the bed of space-time at every sp-ti 0 called as **quanta**, the pulse of the existence (everywhere). The quantum gravitational channel being the center one, is associated with hot and cold streams on its either side responsible for creation of any object in the Universe and blowing the bubble of space-time medium itself, to be noted.

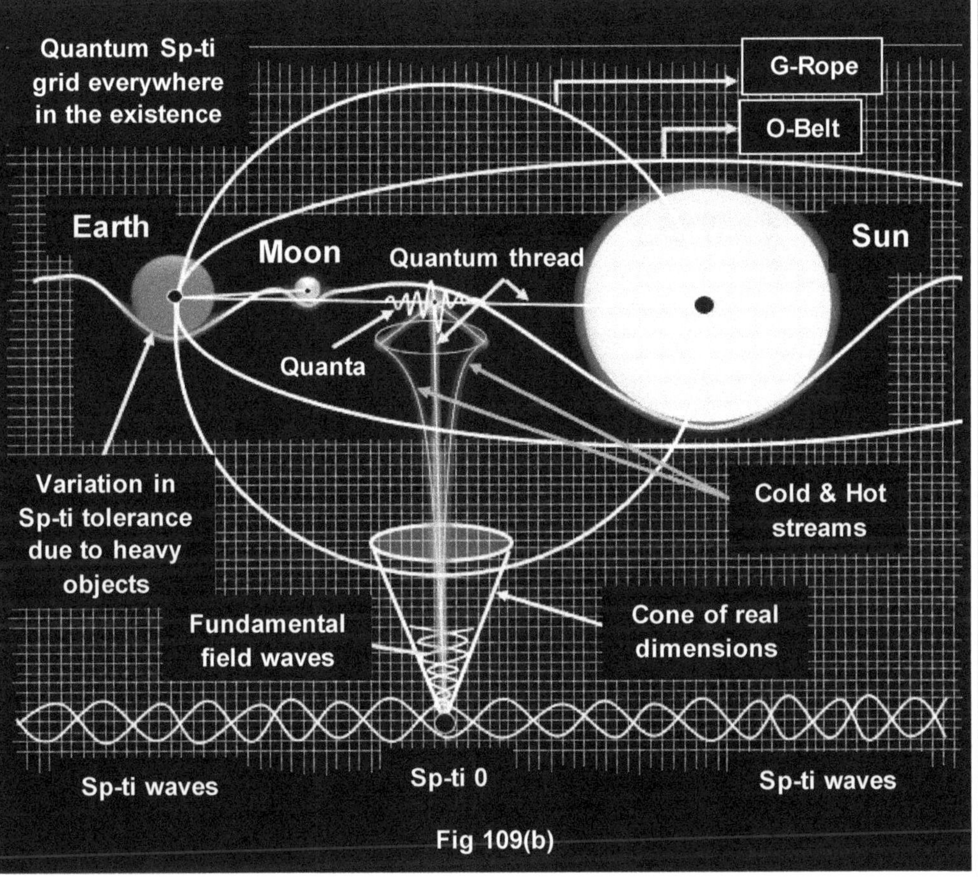

Fig 109(b)

The singularity study also includes string theory which says the fundamental particles are actually strings and has unique characteristics from one another. However, the theory failed to bring the connectivity to the science at the surface of the medium we live, simply due to lack of real dimensions. Fig 110 utilizes core dimension to explain the concept. Shape of the particle is a wave which is same as the field path in which it moves in a closed circular loop.

[123]

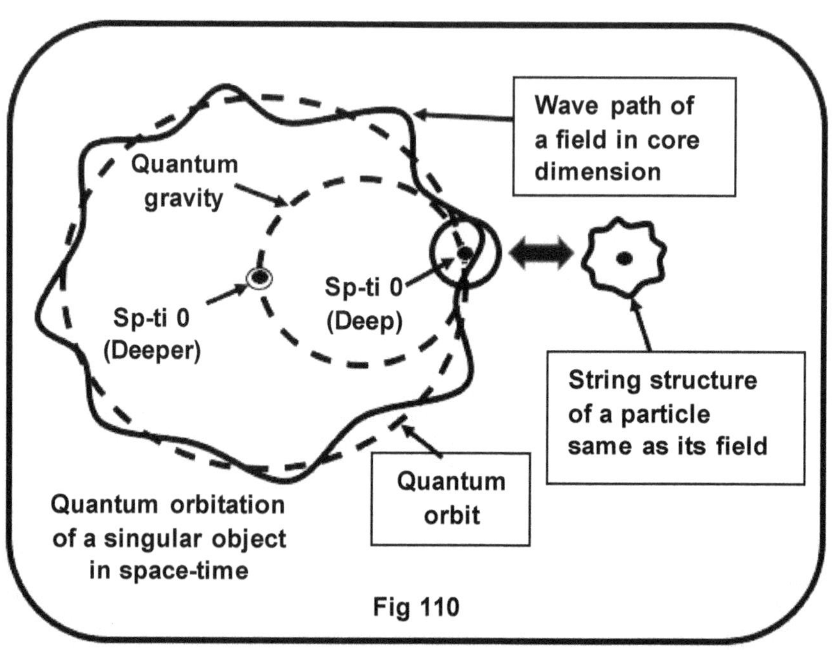

Fig 110

16.0 CONVENTIONAL VS DIMENSIONAL GRAPH

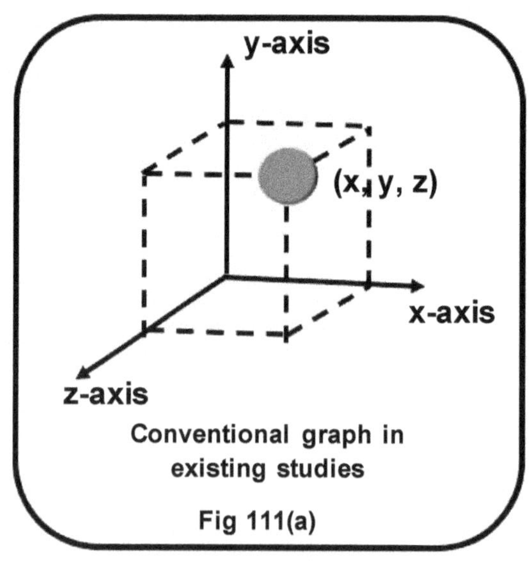

Conventional graph in
existing studies

Fig 111(a)

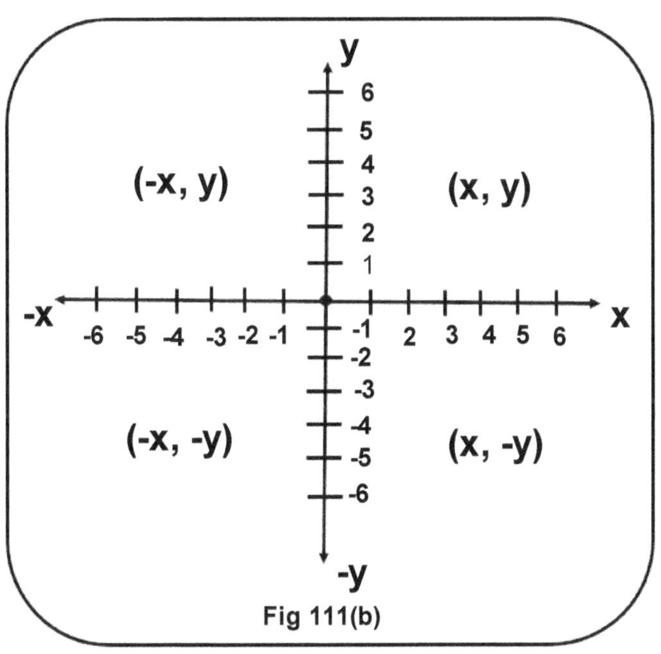

Fig 111(b)

Sp-ti dimensional graph at the background of conventional graph,

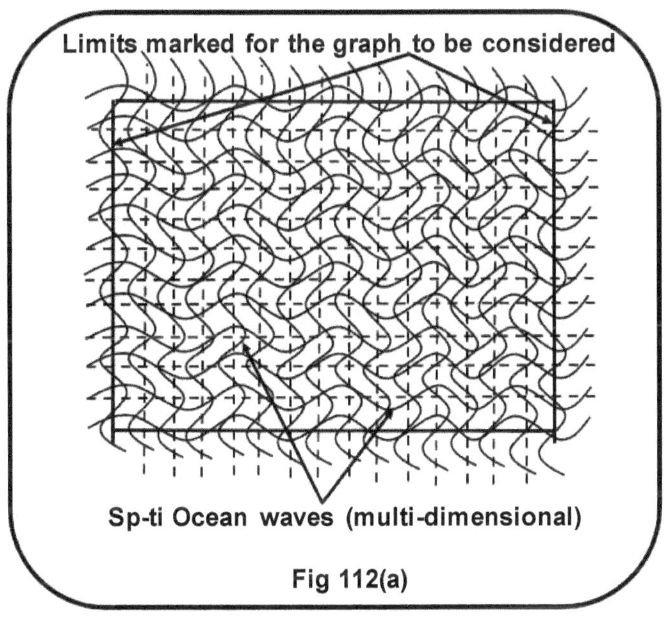

Fig 112(a)

[125]

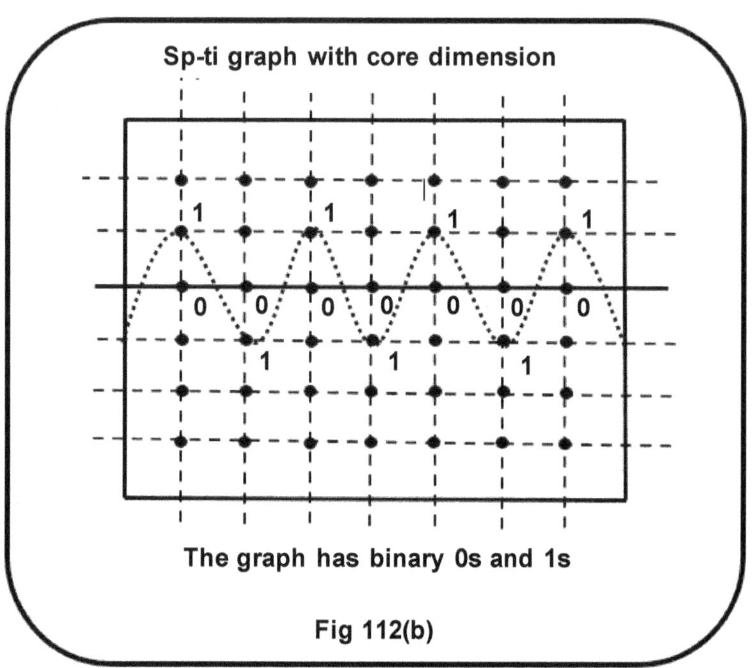

Fig 112(b)

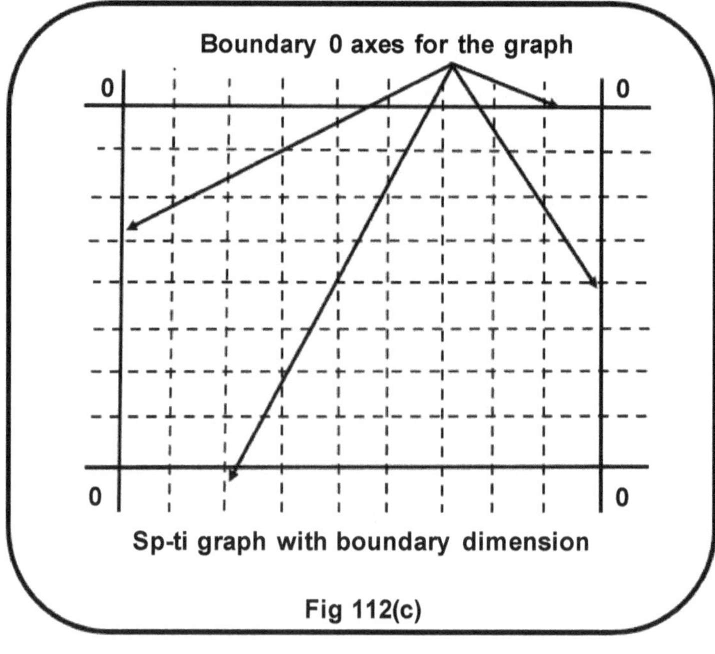

Fig 112(c)

[126]

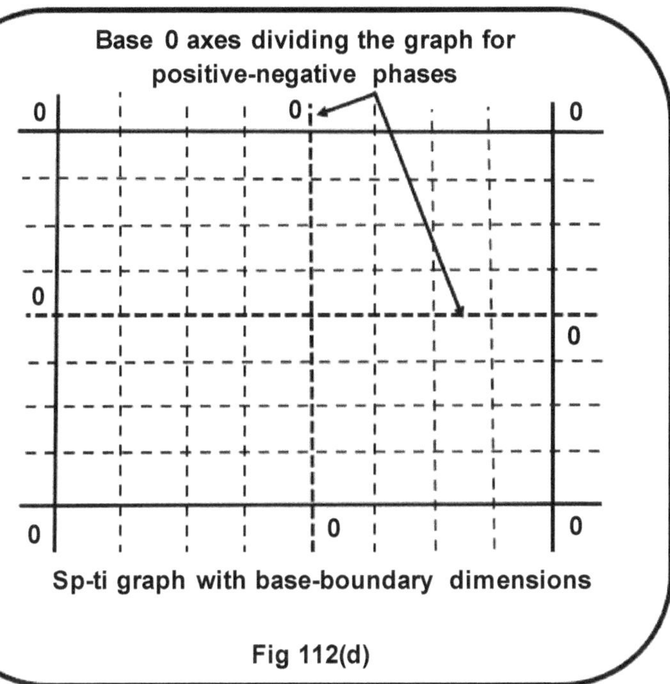

Sp-ti graph with base-boundary dimensions

Fig 112(d)

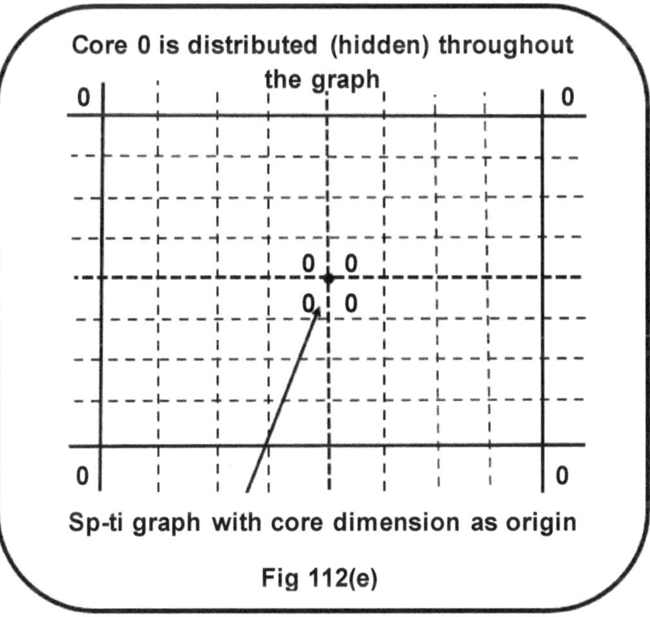

Sp-ti graph with core dimension as origin

Fig 112(e)

[127]

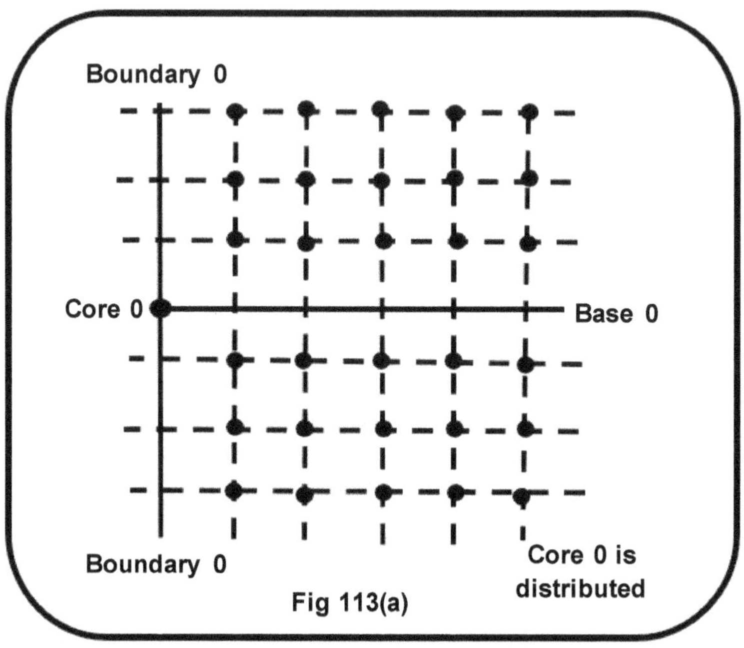

Fig 113(a)

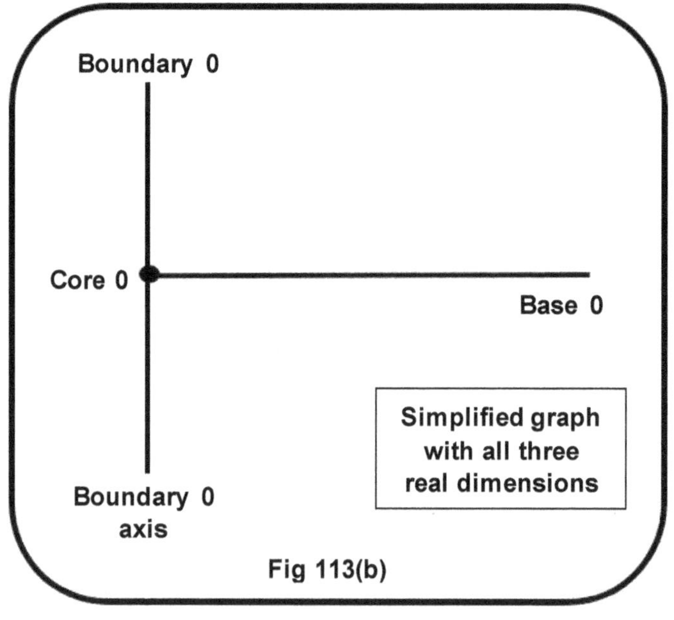

Fig 113(b)

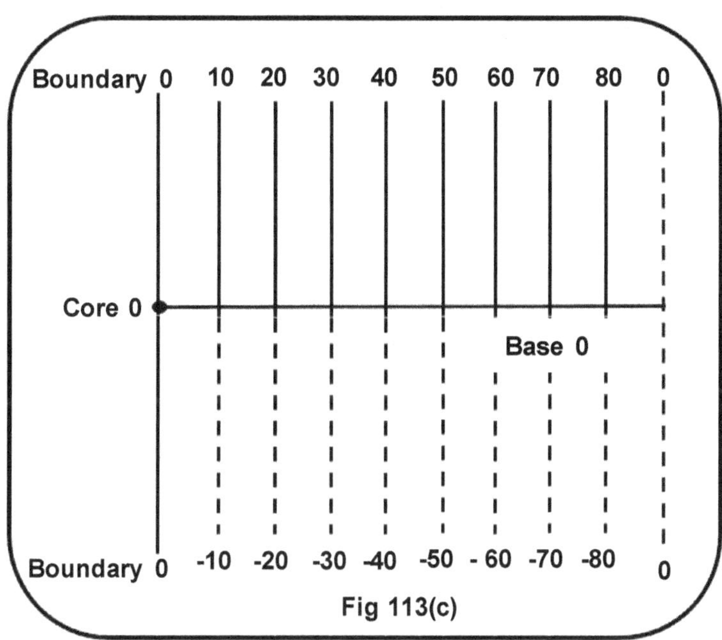

Fig 113(c)

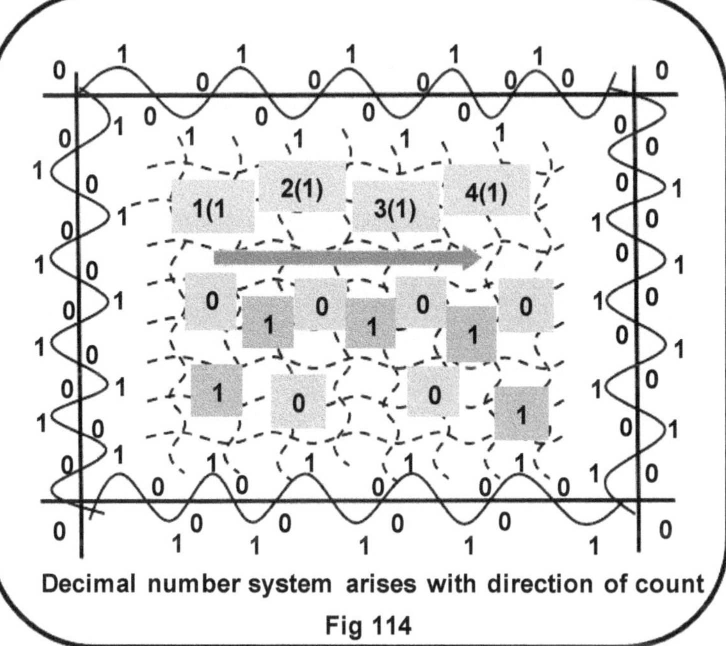

Decimal number system arises with direction of count

Fig 114

[129]

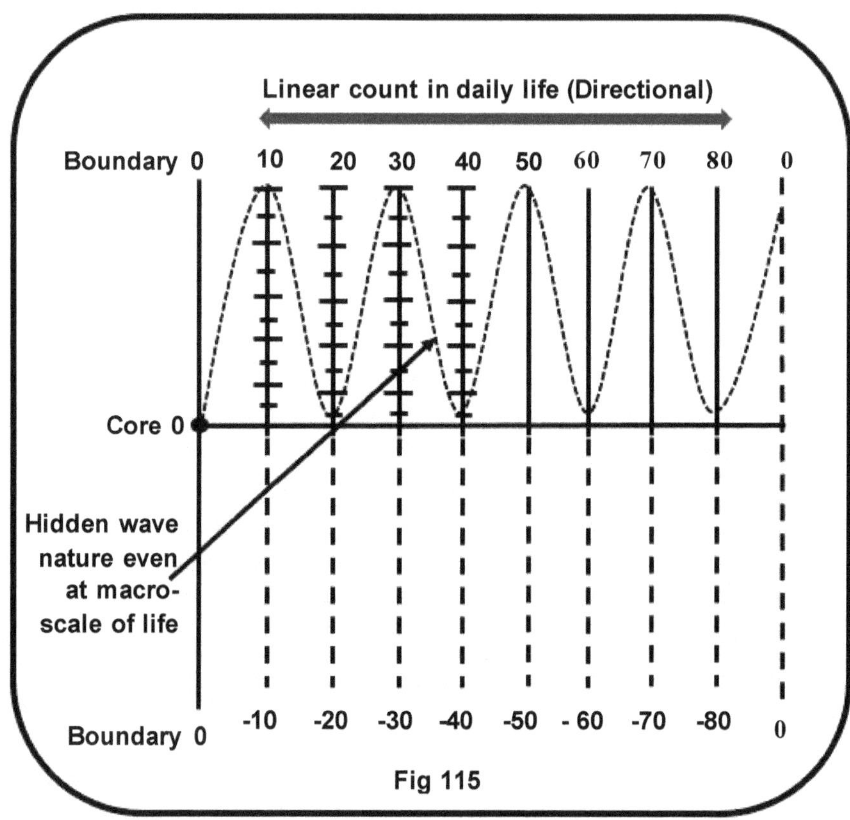

17.0 THEORY OF RELATIVITY - SOLVED FOR ITS DUALITY

The application of Sp-ti graph could be seen with the following examples.

Now, we will see some known thought experiments based on relativity and how their drawbacks are unnoticed in existing studies. And then plot them in singular perspective with the dimensional graph.

1) Observation on relative speed between train and a ball.
2) Twin theory paradox (aging difference with speed of light).

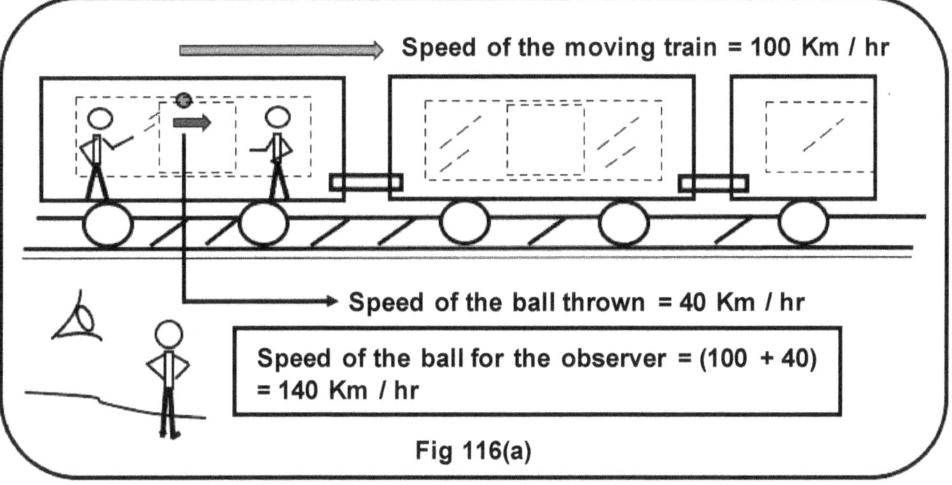

According to relativity, there are two convenient values for one situation in terms of observation,

1) Children playing within the train compartment as shown in Fig 116(a) experiences the ball with the speed of 40 Km / hr.
2) The observer away from the train, sees the speed of the ball is already 100 Km / hr with the moving train and so the total speed is 140 Km / hr.

Now, we will see what the misconceptions with this are thought experiment in duality (relativity) and its solution in singular perspective.

We use the **Sp-ti dimensional graph** to plot the speed of the ball and the hidden factors associated with it.

Important Note: The speed of the train and the ball shall not be compared to be a mutual aspect, as the train has a constant acceleration from its driving energy source whereas the ball is thrown with the force of the person whose speed persist only for a while. And also, the ball is a dependent object as long as it is travelling in the train.

[131]

NEW INTERPRETATIONS IN SINGULAR PERSPECTIVE

- Speed of the moving train = 100 Km/hr.
- The children playing with the ball thrown between them has a speed of 40 Km/hr within the compartment. The ball is a part of train, as long as one driving energy source of the train is considered.
- As soon as the ball is released (thrown) from the hand in the direction of motion of the train, it loses the previous source of acceleration and thus its initial acceleration point is not zero but lags by -100 Km/hr.
- This speed held by the object (ball) is called as **credit speed**. This credit speed is actually provided by the moving train to the ball (at rest position in it). Now, if the ball is thrown at a speed less than the speed of moving train (Within the credit range of 0 to 100 Km/hr), it results in two case studies,

- **Case1:** When the ball is considered for a forward throw, the train speed is available as credit speed of the ball. So, as soon as the ball takes its new speed, it has to account for the previous speed accordingly, which could be termed as **speed compensation**.

- **Case2:** If the ball is thrown opposite to the direction of motion of train, the credit speed still has opposite face however this time, reverse throw assists for quick speed compensation than the previous case.

- The path of the ball entering into new speed value is shown to jump from +100 to -100 initially and then has to go through speed compensation to reach 0 first.
- From zero, the ball has to again approach the speed of train through which, at any point in its approaching path, it is caught by the chasing speed of the train which is trying to cancel it, for the ball to attain the initial credit speed (come back to its rest position).
- However, this cancellation is not happening due to catch-throw-catch played between the two children alternatively, changing the direction (forward and reverse) of the ball.

➢ Only after all the compensation of speed with the previous source active with +100 Km/hr, the ball could be assumed for its actual speed calculation.

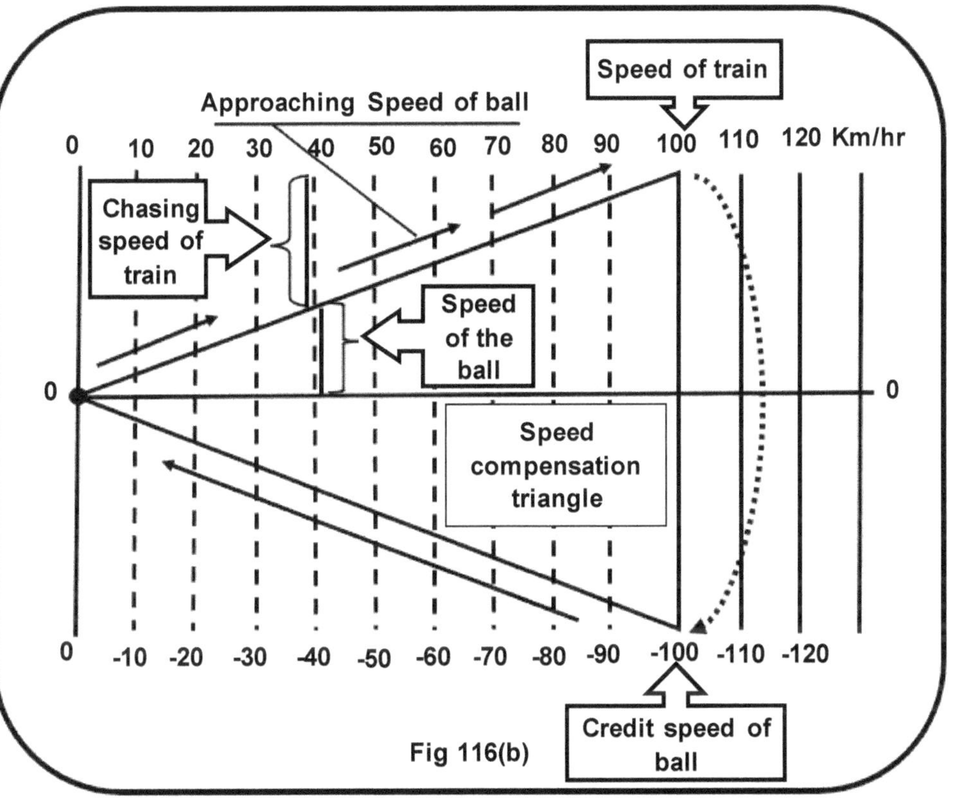

Fig 116(b)

➢ So, the dimensional graph of space-time clearly plots and traces the path of the ball entering and leaving the other unobserved dual symmetry of life.

➢ Thus, the speed of the ball is not relative at any point of space-time. And it could not be taken for two granted values such as 40 Km/hr for the children playing and 140 Km/hr for a person not involved in the activity and observing the train from a distance.

➢ **Case 3:** If the ball is thrown more than the speed of moving train (say) 120 Km/hr now, its actual speed is 20 Km/hr in singular perspective (observed by nobody).

[133]

> Now, to what extent this value is real or is it possible to realize this speed in daily life? As this value is not seemed to be applicable for the children experiencing their play speed inside the compartment (40 Km/hr) or the person observing the ball speed from outside the train (140 Km/hr) either.

> Of course, this value could be realized in the same situation. The children playing within the compartment will never know the chasing speed of the train. The ball could be hit by the train for the following two reasons,
> a) The speed of the ball does not have a constant acceleration and just thrown with a force that keeps dropping down its speed.
> b) Even if some constant accelerating source maintains the ball speed but it is less than the train speed, then also the train hits the ball.

This could be realized if one of the children possibly stand in the first compartment and throw the ball right in front of the moving train, where it is not caught by his partner but it is only the train that catches the ball at every point in its travelling path.

> It literally means that the real values obtained at some other point of space-time as in this illustration, does not apply for human **observation point of view from different reference frames.**

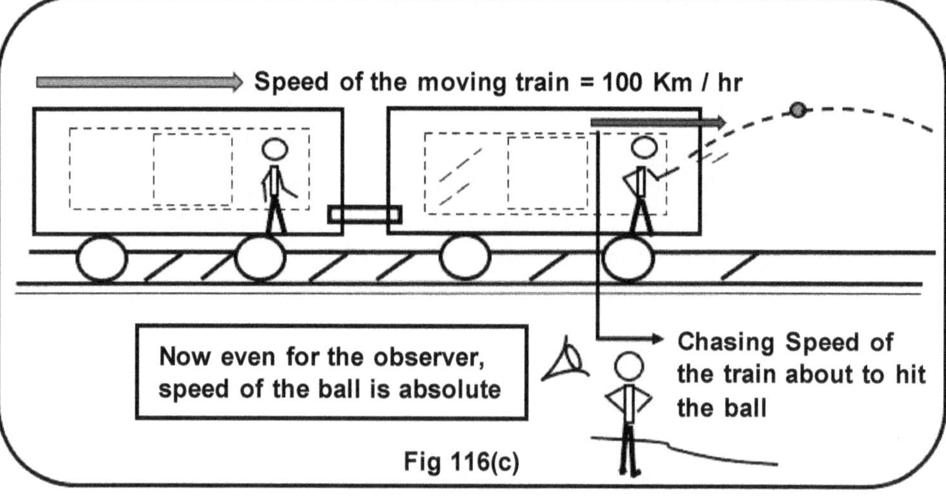

Fig 116(c)

Thus, the reality is filtered for every individual consciousness varying from one another to serve each one's life purpose separately, which is possible only in terms of **Sp-ti frames**, to be discussed in the following topics.

18.0 PARTICLE PHYSICS; PART-2 (Continued...)

e) Double slit experiment

The double slit experiment by scientist Thomas Young is famous for showing the dual nature of a particle to behave as a particle as well as wave. However, the mysteries of how and when the transition of wave into particle or particle being in probabilistic wave is unknown in physics. Let us reveal the truth behind this with technical explanations.

First, we see the way experiment is conducted and the results obtained. The experimental setup is as follows,

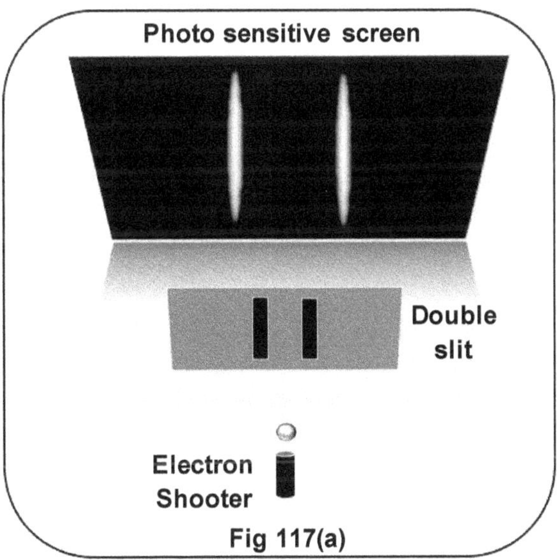

Fig 41(a) shows a pattern on the screen which is obviously expected one, as the electron shooter continue to shoot the electrons through the double slit, only two-line pattern should be sensed on the screen, Fig 117(a). But the actual pattern observed was different and unexpected as shown in Fig 117(b).

[135]

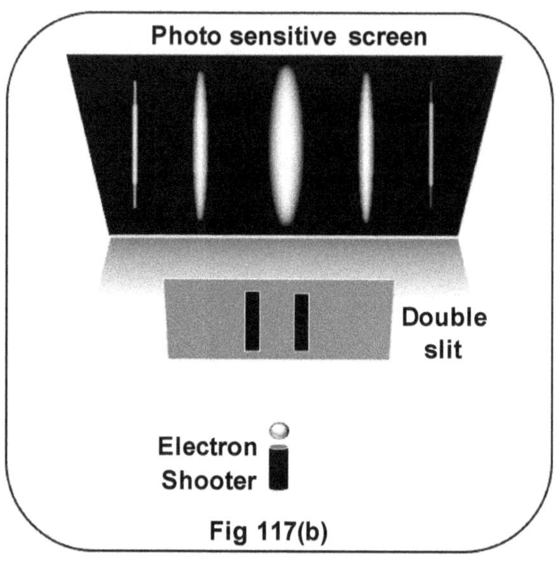

Fig 117(b)

The experimentation results are as follows,

1) The unexpected pattern, which is a mismatching of lines in the screen not pertaining to the count of two slits through which the electrons must have passed.

2) The expected pattern of two lines is obtained in the screen when an observation is made. Again, pattern of many lines resulted on the screen when unobserved.

Here, the first point is understood for particle to have behaved like a wave. However, the second point is clear that, when an observation is made, the two-line pattern is obtained which means, the particle behaved like a particle as well, entering properly through two slits at two different times resulting in expected pattern on screen.

When there is no observation made, the electron while passing through the double slits entered like water waves, Fig 117(c). The mystery about the experimentation is the wave pattern (multiple line) changes to particle pattern (double lines) immediately with the observation made on it.

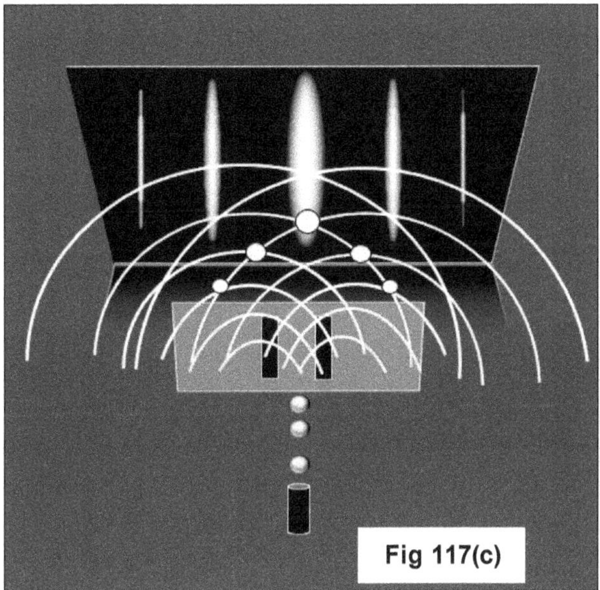

Fig 117(c)

So, for this mystery there was an idea of checking which way the electron entered one of the two slits at a time or else when the electron changes from particle to wave nature resulting in wave pattern on the screen.

An observation is made on the electron released from the shooter before obtaining the pattern results, Fig 117(d). Now, the electron behaved like a particle with two-line pattern on screen confirming particle nature.

Again, when the observation is not made then multiple lines appeared. This made the scientist wonder how the results varied based on observation made.

This time, a detector is placed to check if experimentation is about human conscious of observing the particle. When the detector is ON, the particle shooting resulted in two-line pattern and when detector is switched OFF wave pattern appeared, Fig 117(d & e).

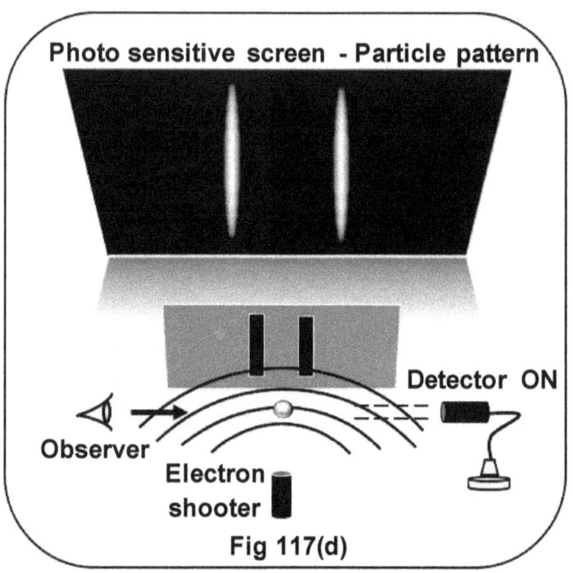

From this, it is concluded that human consciousness is not the factor however, the observation made either by human or detector it is still a confusing part that affected the results.

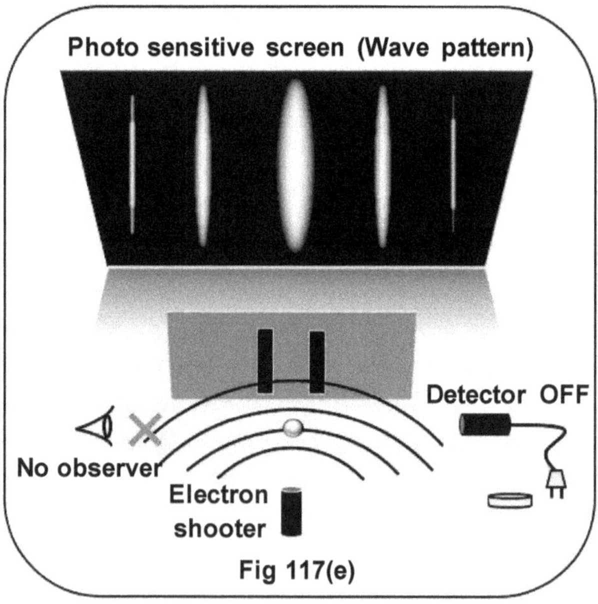

So, it is further thought for placing the detector after the double slit so as to see if the electron changes its result pattern depending upon the hidden observation made on it, Fig 41(f).

Again, the same is repeated that, when observation is made particle pattern appeared and when unobserved (i.e.) detector is switched off, wave pattern appeared on the screen.

Hence, it is concluded for particle to behave like particle as well as wave however, the point where it switches depending upon the observation made on it, is unknown in existing studies. The moment particle is tried to locate, the probability wave collapses into a particle.

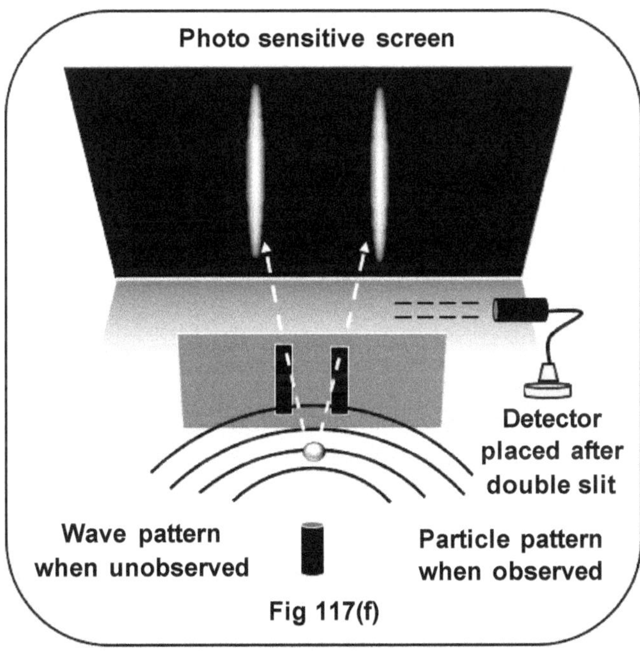

Fig 117(f)

We will see the solution for the above experimentation results in detail by applying real dimensions. First of all, let us analyze the problem logically. Here, there are only two results such as particle and wave pattern when observed and unobserved respectively. It is also cross checked if it is about human observation affecting the results, but it worked for the detector kept in ON/OFF positions too. However, the pattern is matching with detector ON same as observation made and OFF position as unobserved.

[139]

It is clearly the situation where the first object such as a fundamental particle and a final object such a human is meeting up. The one thing that is singular or common between both is their purpose of existence. It is only the human who have the consciousness to experiment all things of the Universe and it is obvious that there must be a point where the observer is equal to or same as every other observing object.

The working of the detector, that records the patterns is also meant for human knowledge. Now, to think how the pattern changes pertaining to whether an observation made or not is wrong. The solution for the problem is about the perspective itself, the observer has to include himself in the experimentation as the life-happenings are beyond human mind. The happenings are pre-recorded in space-time and the human is just undergoing the motion picture frames without realizing that he is subjected to it.

Whether he decides to observe at one time and other time not, those moving frames are already containing the information that the observer will undergo the way it is. The observer could never doubt on this and feels to work with free-will but the results clearly says that the observer, observing object and the whole experimentation setup altogether moving in terms of sp-ti frames.

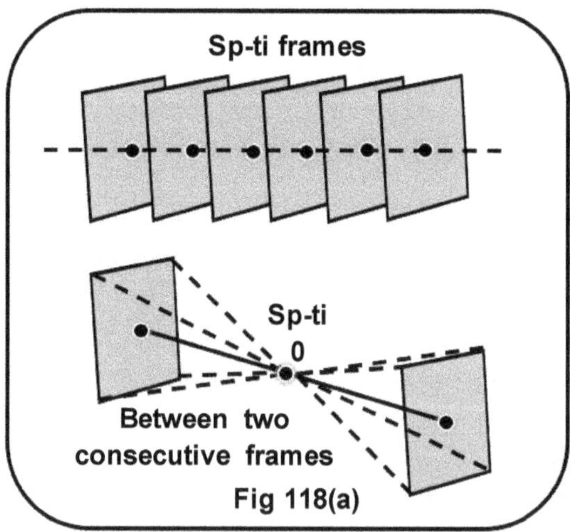

It is hard for the scientists to accept the fact, as it literally means life is inevitable rather than free-will. However, at this point there is no way as it demands to give up oneself and step forward blindly for further analysis. So, the observer deciding to make observation or not and even changing his mind every time without any order, are still said to be subjected to pre-determined sp-ti frames as shown in Fig 118(b).

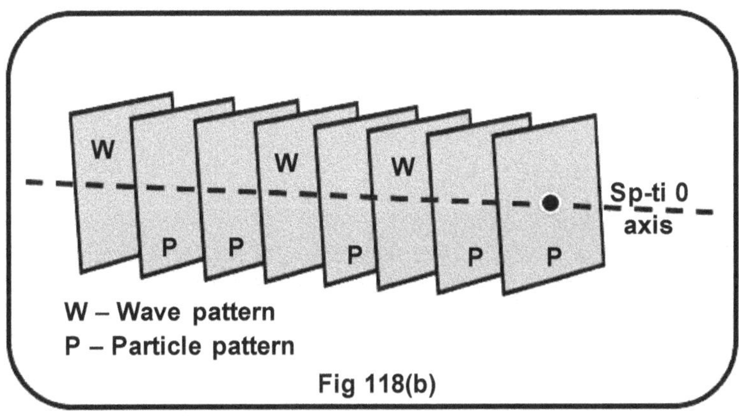

Fig 118(b)

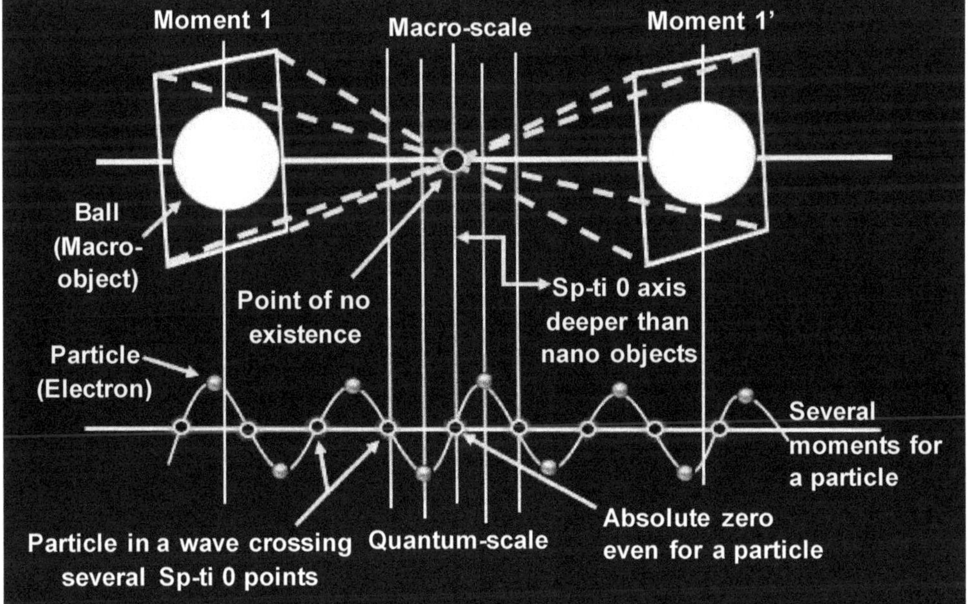

Fig 119

Now, let us compare two consecutive moments of human with the moments of a quantum-scale object such as an electron, Fig 119. There is a point of non-existence of space-time itself whose Sp-ti 0 is not only common between quantum and macro-scale objects but also deeper than the two.

There is one more case study that even by placing (hiding) the detector after the double-slit, the results remained the same which made the scientists think, how come the electron could foresee whether an observation is made or not and change its pattern on the screen accordingly or is it travelling back and forth in time and knowing whether a detector is placed for recording or not, in the experimentation. In this way, the electron or the particle physics itself is believed to be the future deciding factor of life. What is wrong in this assumption could be clearly understood with the live experimentation.

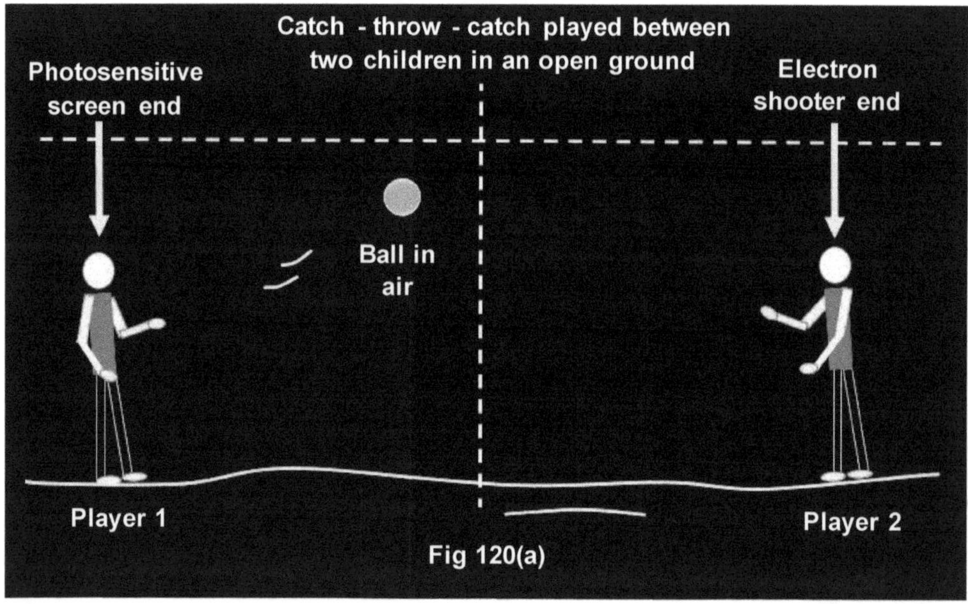

We will see a real-time illustration to reveal the above mystery in singular perspective.

The children are playing catch-throw-catch in an open ground whose situation could be assumed for the setup of double slit experimentation. The scientist keeps the detector before and after the double slit which is not required, as player 1 represent the photo-sensitive screen while player 2 on the electron shooter end and the observation is live and experienced directly. The ball represents the electron in macro-world.

In case of open ground as shown in the fig 120(a), the whole setup is a present frame. Both the players see each other, the time when the ball is released from the hand and the path of the ball in air is known by both of them.

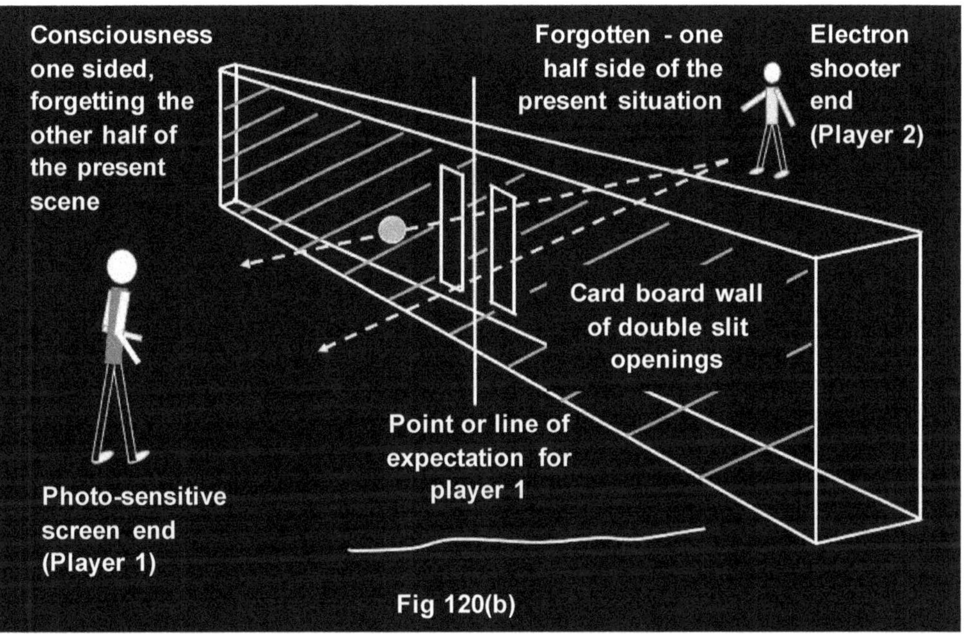

Fig 120(b)

Now, assume that some third person interferes in the game by keeping a double slit cardboard wall in between the two players such that one person cannot see the other. The ball thrown by one player has to pass through one of the double slits. The player on the other side keeps an eye only on the slits and forgets the other player. The expectation of which way the ball would come out between one of the two slits makes the consciousness one sided.

This means that, at no point the single (whole) present frame could be sub-divided into past, present and future sections as required by observer. We know the players always existed and were moving in sp-ti frames altogether along with the ball, Fig 122. This way of understanding is singular and there is no difference between observer

[143]

Photo-sensitive screen end
Line of double slit
Electron shooter end
Player 1
Player 2
Sp-ti frame 1
Past
Sp-ti frame 2
Present
Sp-ti frame 3
Future
Sp-ti frame 4

Fig 121

[144]

and an observing object in the picture, the whole setup is moving in sp-ti frames.

Conclusion: At certain point human have to realize that he is undergoing the pre-determined sp-ti frames of life. Thinking to live or free-will is just an ignorance where mind is the confusing part to identify oneself different from reality. Whatever way the person thinks to make an observation or not and changes the sequence of doing it to test the electron, has no use. It is still between two patterns on the screen which means he is involved in two kinds of situations and have to include himself in the experimentation same as the electron.

The conversation between the scientist and the electron would be as follows,

Scientist: I kept the detector before the double slit to check the point where your particle nature is converting into wave nature. As long as the detector is ON you are showing a particle nature of two lines pattern and when detector is OFF, showing wave nature of multiple lines pattern.

Electron: Yes, I serve the purpose of life in terms of information (basic unit of an atom). As a single electron I am a part of sp-ti frame which is holding the picture of life. Even if I am left unattended or unobserved, I would be readily available in the non-directional region of quantum range. To exist as an electron, I need a direction to choose the solid particle nature otherwise just remain as a wave in fluid nature of Sp-ti medium.

Scientist: Alright, now tell me, when I keep the detector after the double slit, how do you know that it is switched ON/ OFF for recording (i.e.) an observation is made or not?

Electron: I am not bothered about your observation or experimentation; I just reach my destination as determined for every single frame. I don't have a consciousness as human does. I don't see whether the detector is before or after the double-slit. I am not from any future and determine the present. I just move from source point to destination in every single present sp-ti frame.

In double slit experimentation, as the wave pattern occurs when unobserved, it makes the scientists to think, how come the photons travelling all the way from a new Universe from far away distances in light years, knows that there is someone to receive it and must carry the information for them without fail. These photons must be waves, carrying no information if it is not received or left unobserved by anyone.

In that case, now it is hard to accept that photon particle is emerging in every single sp-ti frame from a point. As even if we track the photons, frame by frame in the reverse direction, it will reach to the point of newly formed Universe in the past, from where it had started.

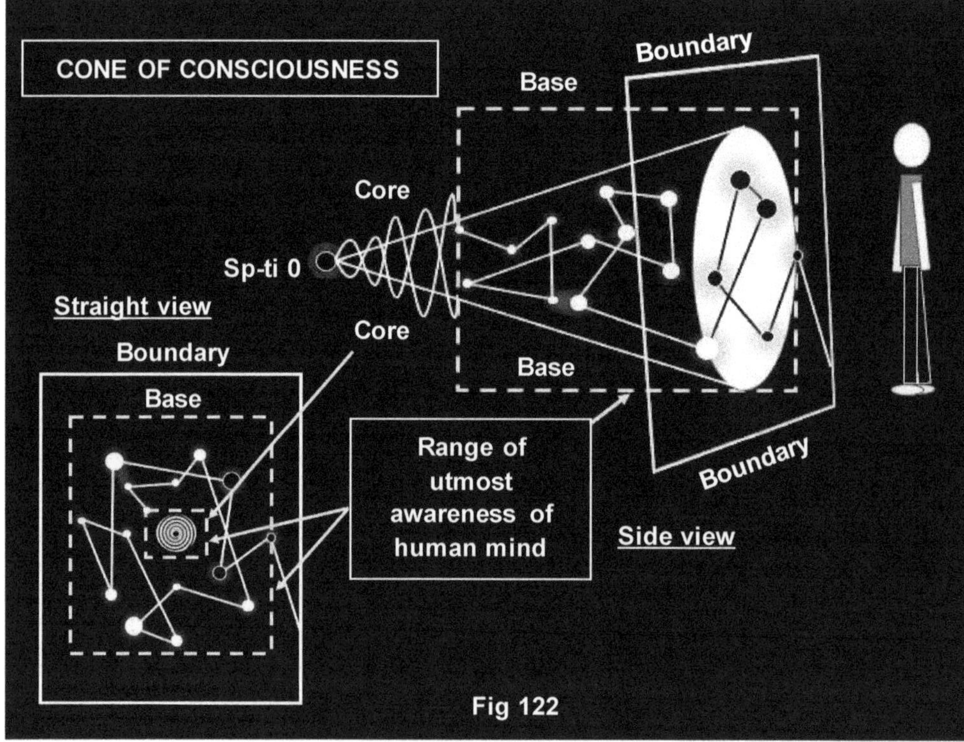

Fig 122

There is an evident misconception with existing studies that, assuming the detector placed after the double slit and near to the photo-sensitive screen, it observes the electron coming through the slit which is actually

[146]

said to come from future into the present. Thus, it is believed that particle physics from the future is deciding the present life while the same idea is interpreted in the opposite way that the photons carrying the information of new Universe from far away distances, having reached the telescopes, is said to come from past into present.

To clarify the above said problems, comes the **cone of consciousness**. The cone of depth we discussed so far is external and understood with base-boundary dimensions however, the core dimension is beyond the human mind. In Fig 121, the cone appears to be outside the observer but it is inward and goes deeper than mind.

Thus, the cone of consciousness solves the mystery in such a way that, every single frame is said to be the present however with certain time period. In this frame the photons are not carrying any information over distances from the past or know the present from future either, even if it is logically right in physics.

Means, this is the point where the logical subjects such as physics and mathematics are limited. Beyond this point, it is a different study that breakup with logical calculations and completely associated with consciousness. So, the photons are already containing the information and emerge at a point in the cone of consciousness whose base is said to be the pre-recorded sp-ti frame to pass from time to time and simultaneously human mind is going through the same.

In fact, the sp-ti frame holding the picture of life, itself is an information rather than understanding photons to carry or contain any information.

So, the range of utmost awareness of mind is shown in Fig 121. The core dimension is always behind human awareness that one cannot find the point of initiation of a single sp-ti frame or where the time starts in present sp-ti frame. It is all about the limitations of human mind failing to have a complete awareness of life of every present moment.

19.0 QUANTUM ENTANGLEMENT PATH

The particle physics in existing studies is only three dimensional and hence the communication between two particles in terms of quantum entanglement is unknown. It is scientifically proven to exist through some connection called quantum tunnel which could not be seen physically.

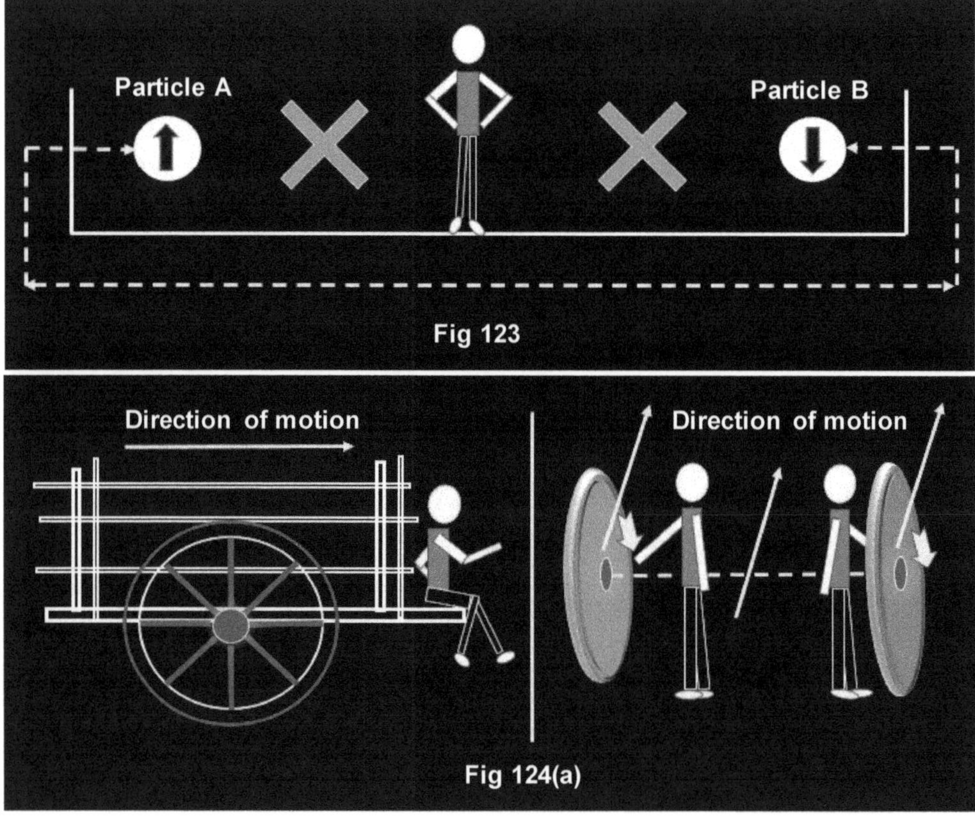

In case of an observer travelling in a bullock cart, he is positioned in between the two cart wheels. Now, even though the cart is moving in one particular direction, if he turn towards the left-side wheel, it rotates in the clockwise direction and facing the right-side wheel, it rotates in the anticlockwise direction. However, the observer could get down from the cart to position himself to see both the wheels to rotate in either clockwise or anticlockwise direction as shown in Fig 124(b). In case of

[148]

two entangled particles, it is not possible so. Means particle physics is dimensionally greater than human perspective that its path of communication or connection is made through fourth dimension which could not be interfered. Thus, as far as quantum entanglement is concerned, one of the particles is said to be always at the background of human mind and could not be thought based on the visibility of two considered entangled particles A & B, observed at a time.

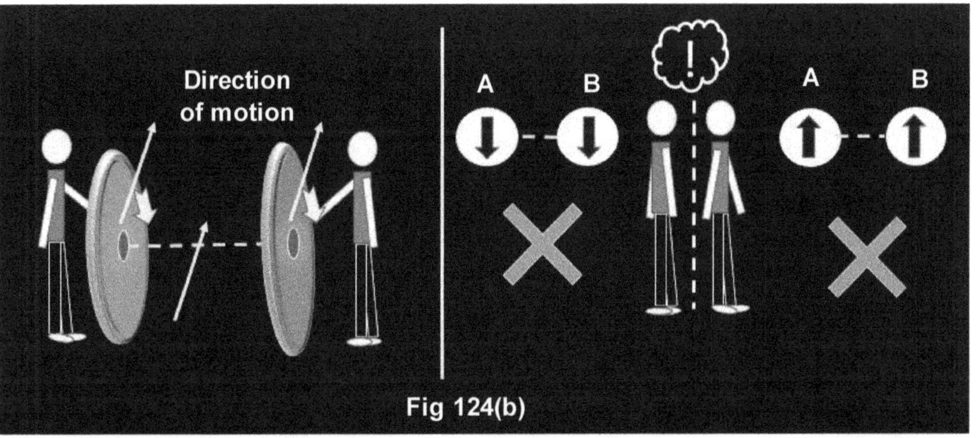

Fig 124(b)

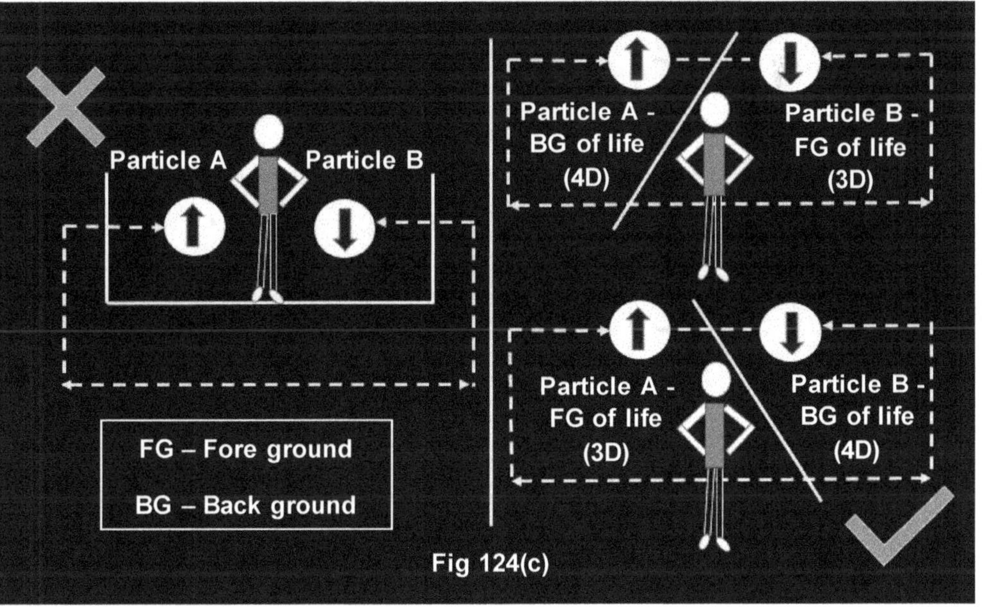

Fig 124(c)

Applying the real dimensions between two entangled particles A & B, the path of entanglement is traced dimensionally as shown in Fig 125.

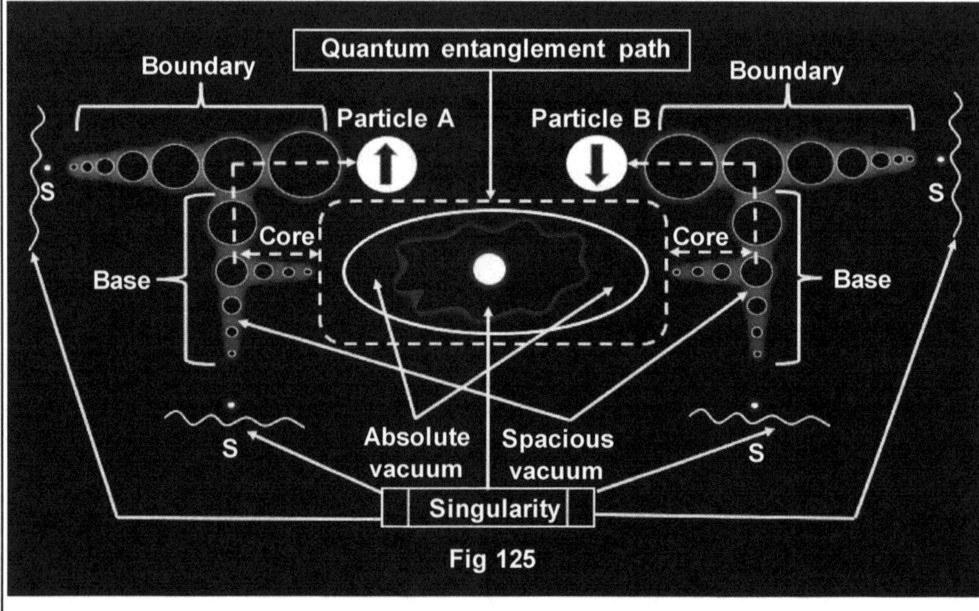

Fig 125

20.0 FUNDAMENTAL NUMBERS OF SPACE-TIME – (ZERO, ONE & INFINITY)

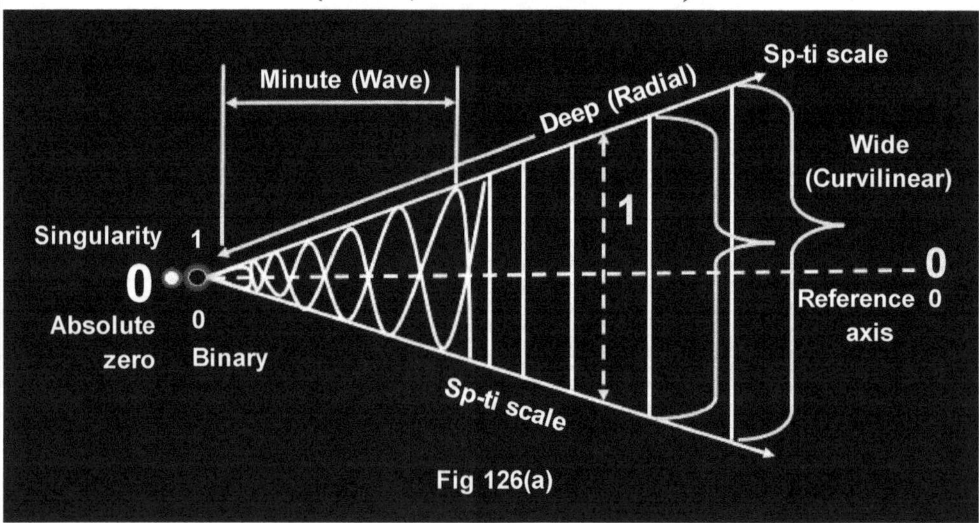

Fig 126(a)

- Absolute 0 is singular and an ever-existing nature.
- Binary 0 represents absence of life or consciousness.
- Value 1 is always vertical and projected as existence of life in space-time scale from depth to the surface.
- Reference 0 is the axis for time intervals of existence to be crossed between +1 and -1 through 0s.

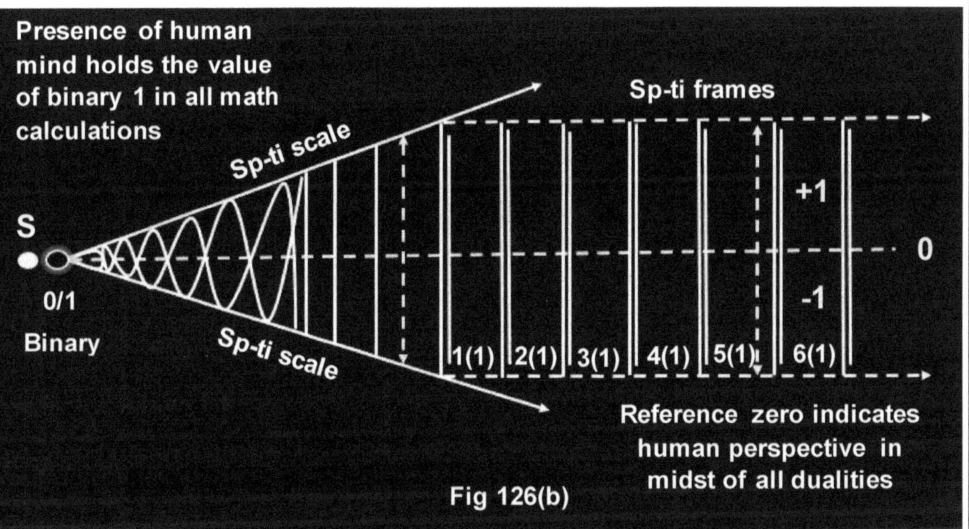

Let us consider shades between white and black, which could be easily understood in a linear as well as reversible way, Fig 127. This is more like a continuous cycle of full moon to new moon and vice versa.

For simple understanding,
- The existence of moon is represented by one.
- Any point along its cycle is infinity. Infinity exists as long as the moon exists with its cycle.
- The time when the moon itself does not exist is absolute zero.
- New moon is a binary zero,
- Axis separating the two half cycles of moon is the reference zero.

In mathematics,

$$1/0 = \infty \implies 1 = 0 \times \infty \implies 1 = 0?$$

Here, when it comes to 1 divided by 0, this zero takes the value of binary 1 which represents the presence of human mind in the existence to do

[151]

this calculation. Binary 0 represents absence of mind or unobserving state of mind not involving in calculation. And infinity acquires the value of 1 representing the presence of object or existence itself under observation or consideration. Also, the infinity always has the minimum value of 1 indicating the cycle and could only exists as long as the value 1 exists.

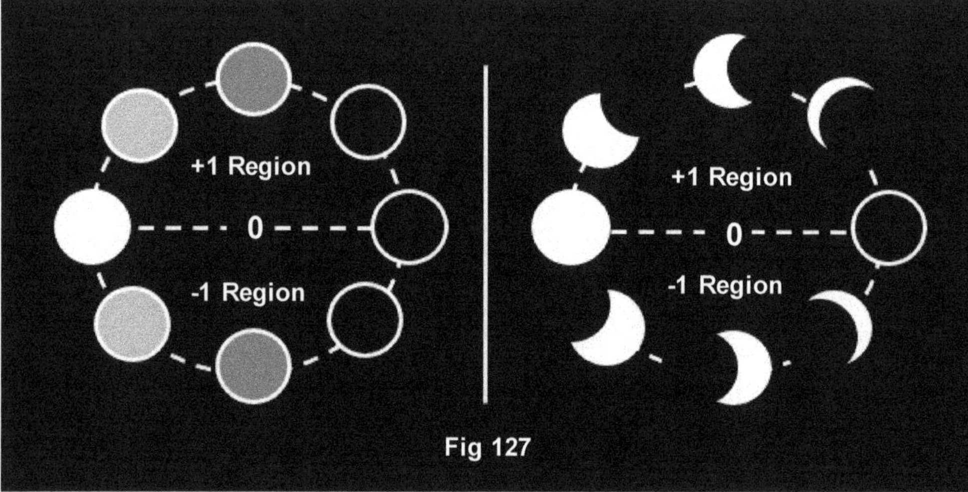

Fig 127

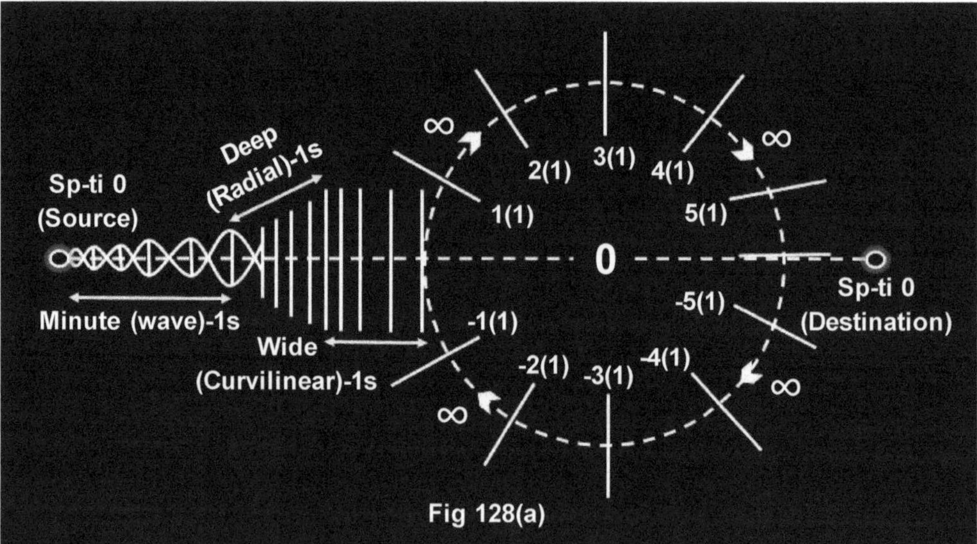

Fig 128(a)

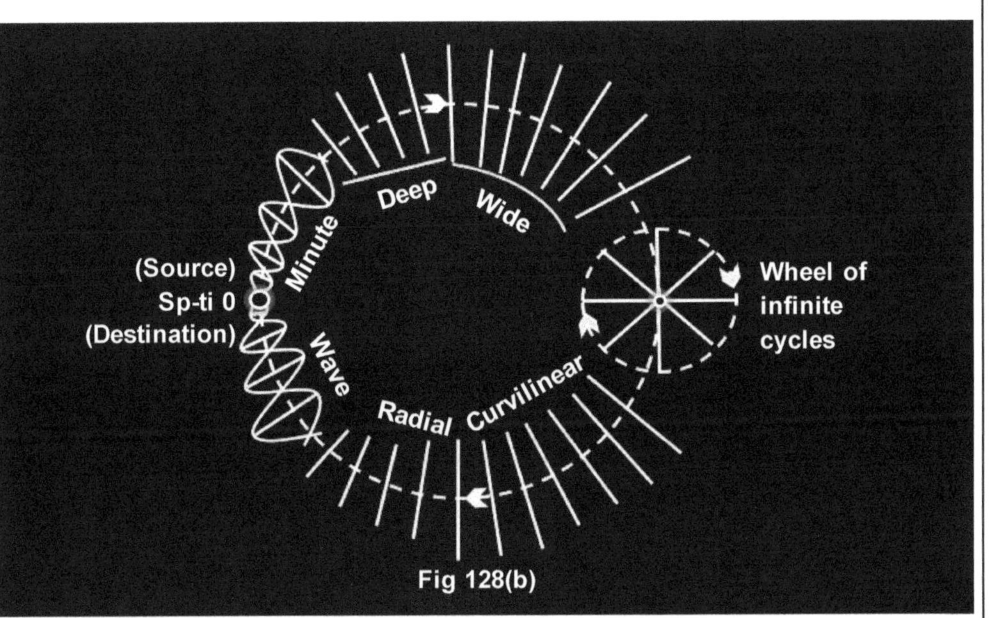

Fig 128(b)

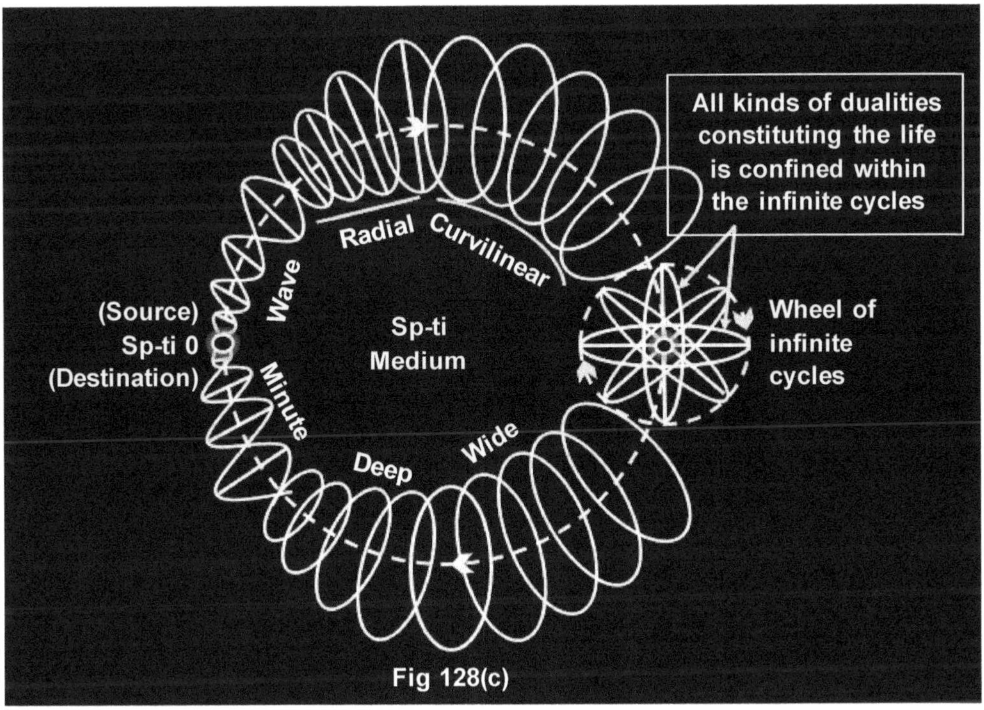

Fig 128(c)

21.0 BLACK HOLES

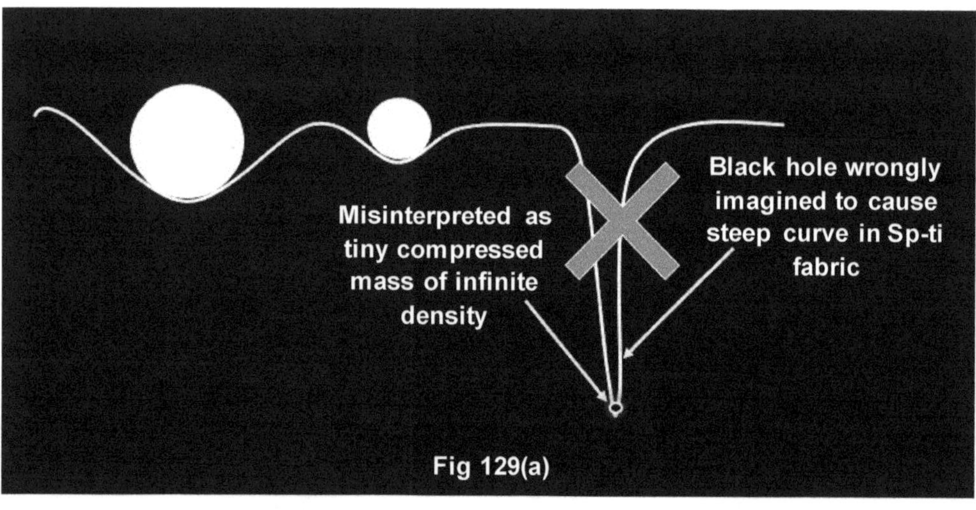

Fig 129(a)

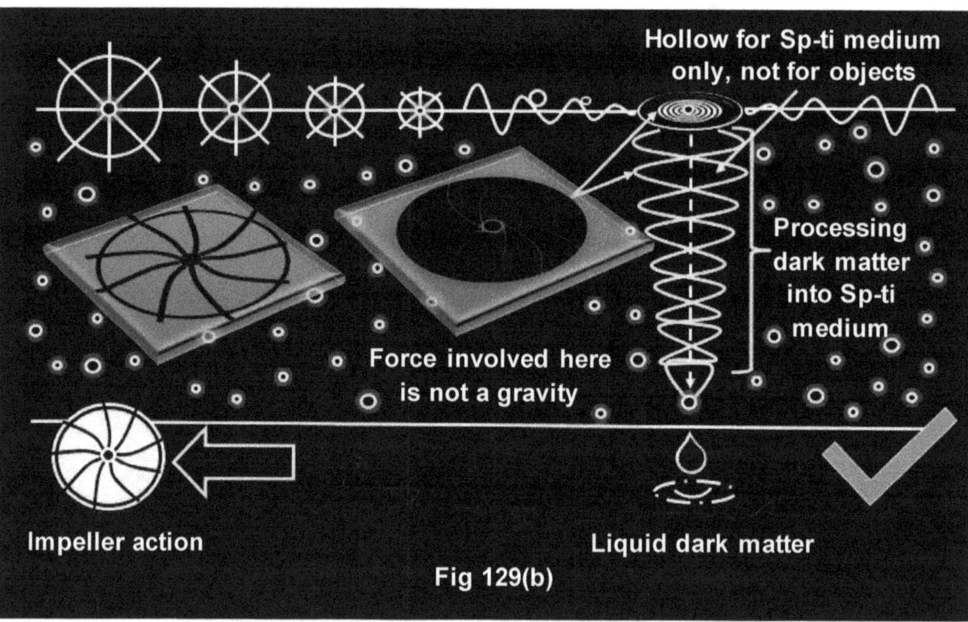

Fig 129(b)

[154]

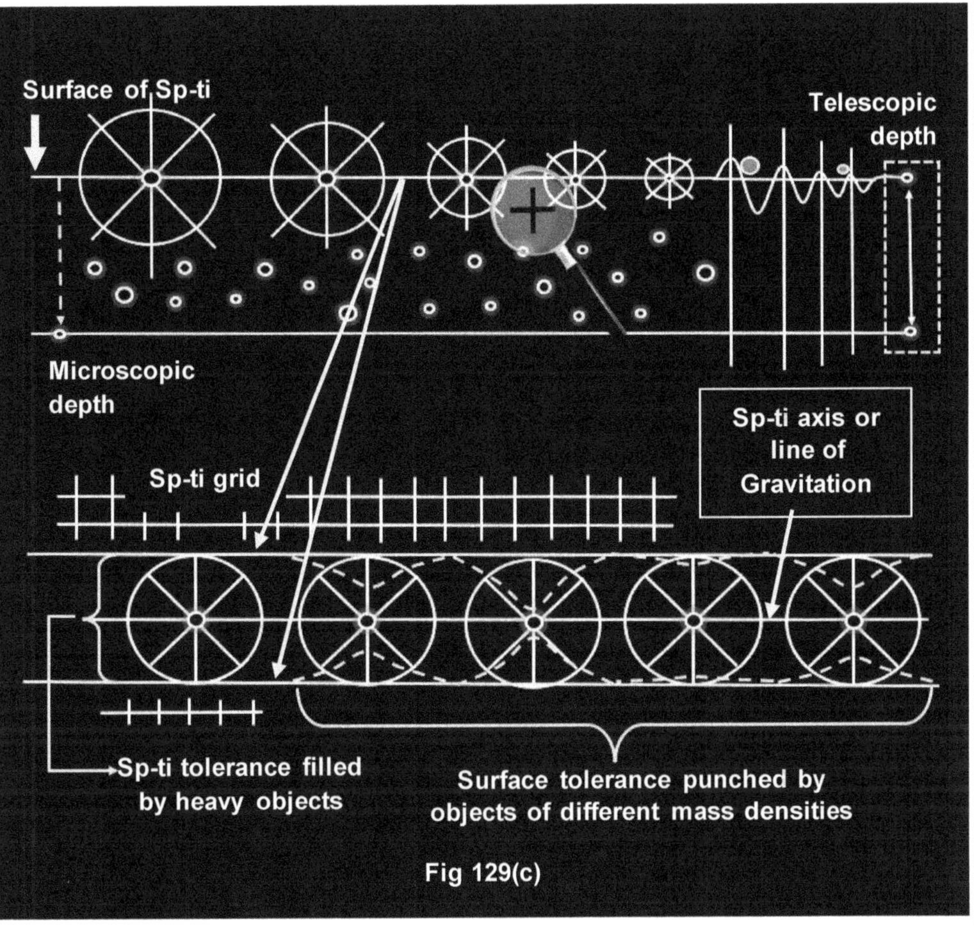

Fig 129(c)

The surface of space-time medium is a double line between which the sp-ti tolerance exists, Fig 129(c). This tolerance holds the heavy objects till certain limit, up to which there is an availability of mobile space-time. Beyond this limit, the object starts biting the tolerance as shown in Fig 129(c). When the bending tolerance lines touches the sp-ti 0 at the center of the object, the object becomes independent. This is in case of neutron star at various stages, Fig 130. The object is said to be sinking in Sp-ti medium. It is clearly the line of gravitation is no more at the center but terminates at the edge of the object. The process inside the star continues until it settles down with the medium. During this process,

[155]

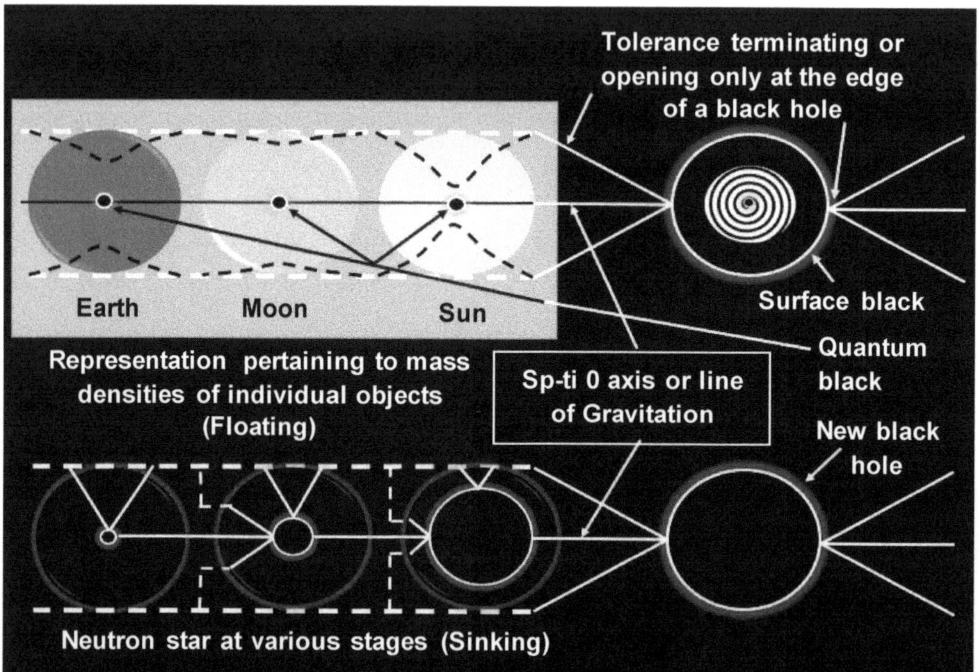

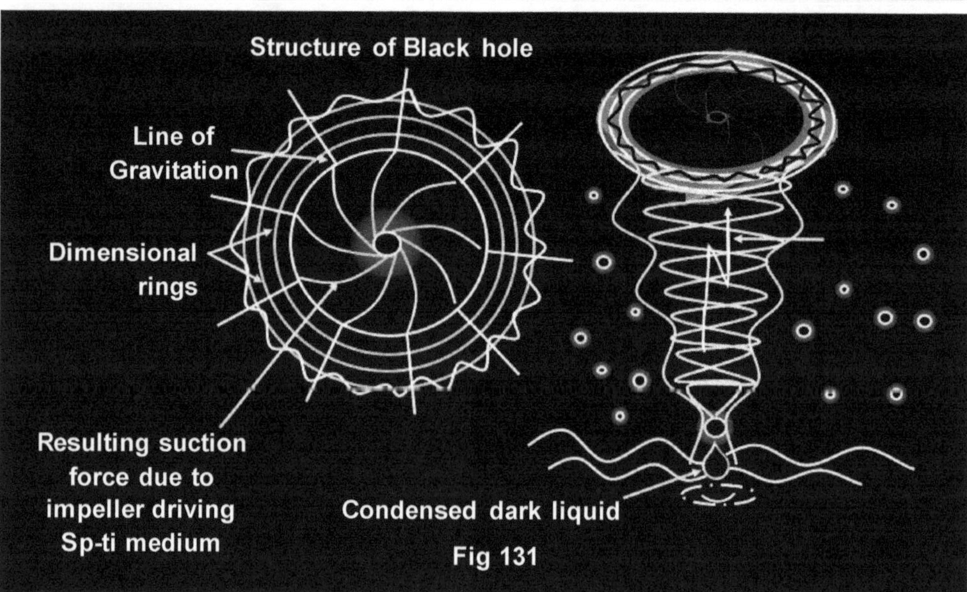

Fig 130

Fig 131

the hollow dark appearance covers the same without a clue of any visibility, which is termed as **Black hole**.

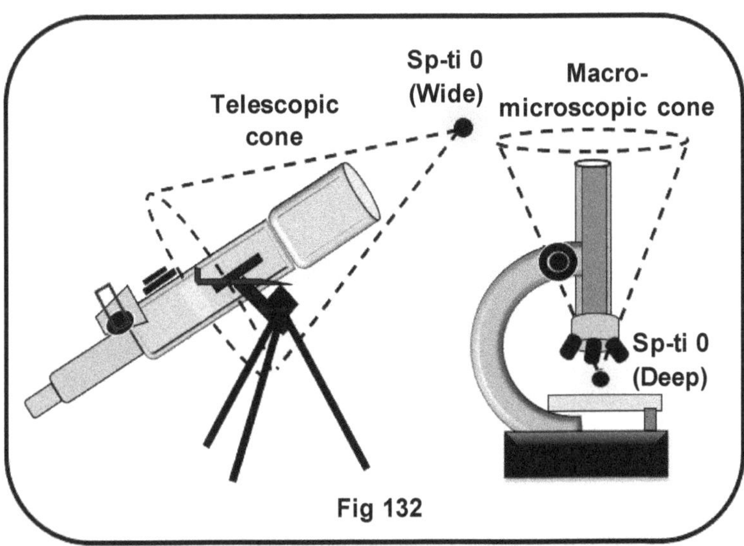

Fig 132

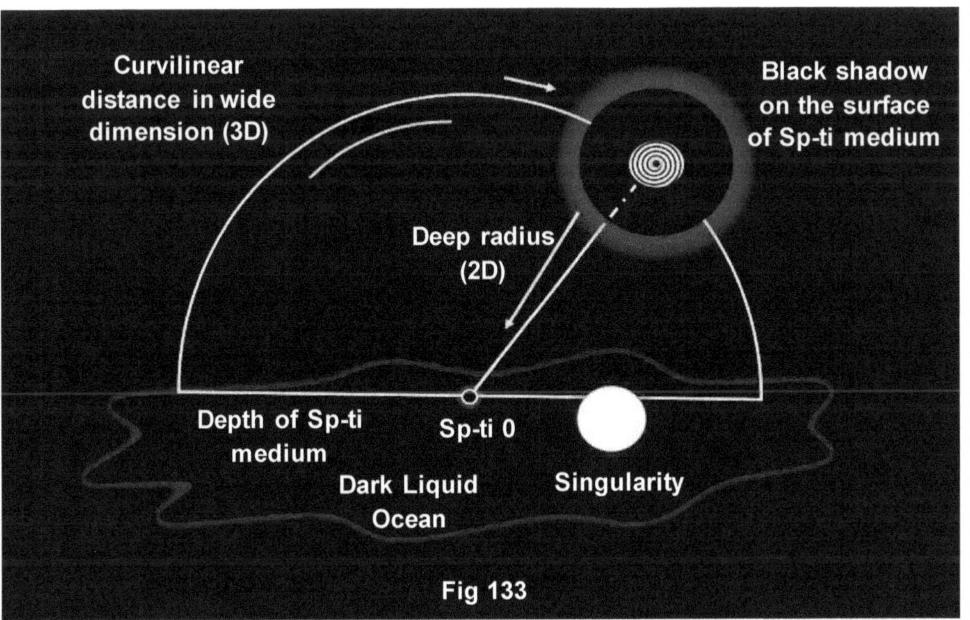

Fig 133

[157]

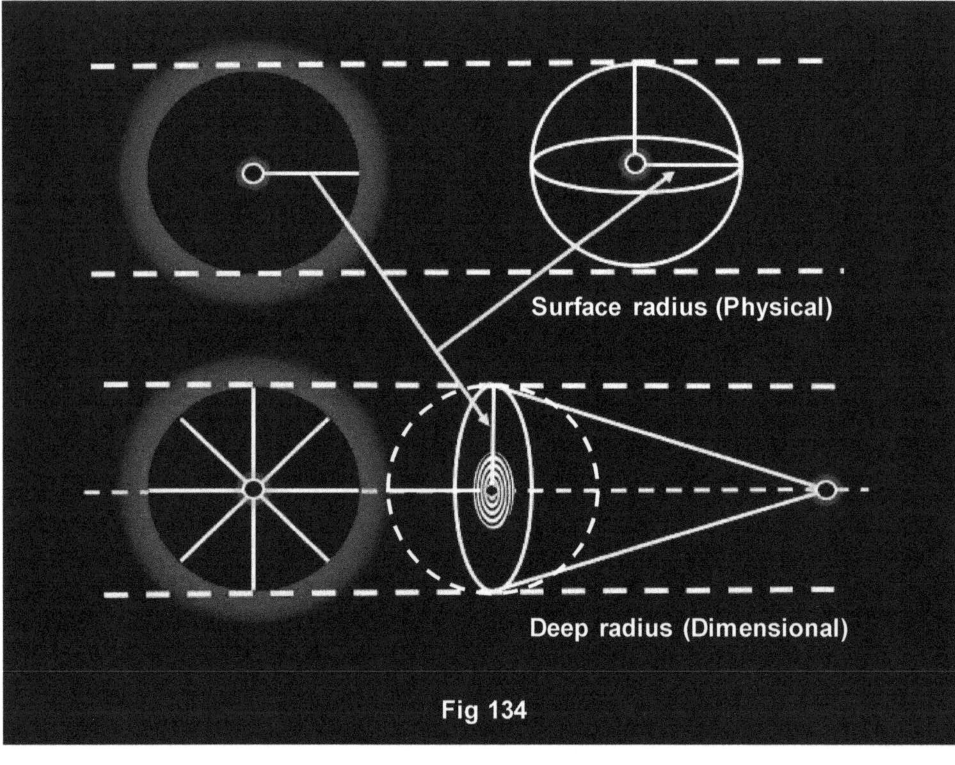

Interpretation of Black holes in terms of dimensions

1) An idle black hole with no effects is simply said to be a shadow on the surface of the medium, whose depth is leading to the dark liquid ocean. This shadow has no connection with the process happening at that point.

2) What if an observer decides to reach an inactive black hole and enter into it? He never reaches the black hole. If a location near to black hole is viewed through a telescope, marked and tried to reach, the black shadow would recenter itself.

3) The observer reaching the marked location, will not see a black hole and it will be same as normal space-time medium out there. Means it is a well-like depth however, one can never fall into it.

4) When the black hole is active (i.e.) there is a process of destruction, it is happening due to the impeller force at the depth of space-time medium, whose effect is seen as swirl pulling the objects on the surface of space-time.

5) During this destruction process, there is an opening from surface to depth of the medium with the impeller force and the shadow of the existence accumulates and hides what is happening out there.

6) It is possible for the observer to fall along with the big destruction where there is a connection between surface and depth. It is like a person wants to burn himself by entering a house on fire.

7) For an idle black hole, observer will keep on trying to reach near to it, but faces one of the following two cases,
    i)   The shadow relocates either by shifting forward.
    ii)   Disappears in half-way and gets re-centered even to the point where the observer started his journey itself.

8) Let us consider two observers Ram and Laxman watching an inactive black hole through a telescope. Ram decides to reach the black hole and on reaching there he would wave his hand to his brother Laxman.

9) Laxman finds no changes with Ram as he moves towards the black hole. However, Ram would see the appearance of black hole growing in size bigger and bigger and after certain point he would not see the black hole at all.

10) But Laxman still sees Ram as well as the destination of black hole to be reached to be the same.

11) Now, Ram reaches the destination and stops but sees no black hole there, looks back and get surprised by seeing the black hole near to Laxman.

12) Laxman unaware of this, happily shows his hand to Ram for having successfully reached the destination and saying that he could see him standing next to the black hole, which is another surprise for Ram.

13) Laxman now asks his brother Ram to further move into the event horizon of the black hole. Ram steps forwards and Laxman could no longer see him.

14) Ram could not see Laxman either and finds him to have entered into event horizon too. This is the duality concept of black hole for its appearance in 3D.

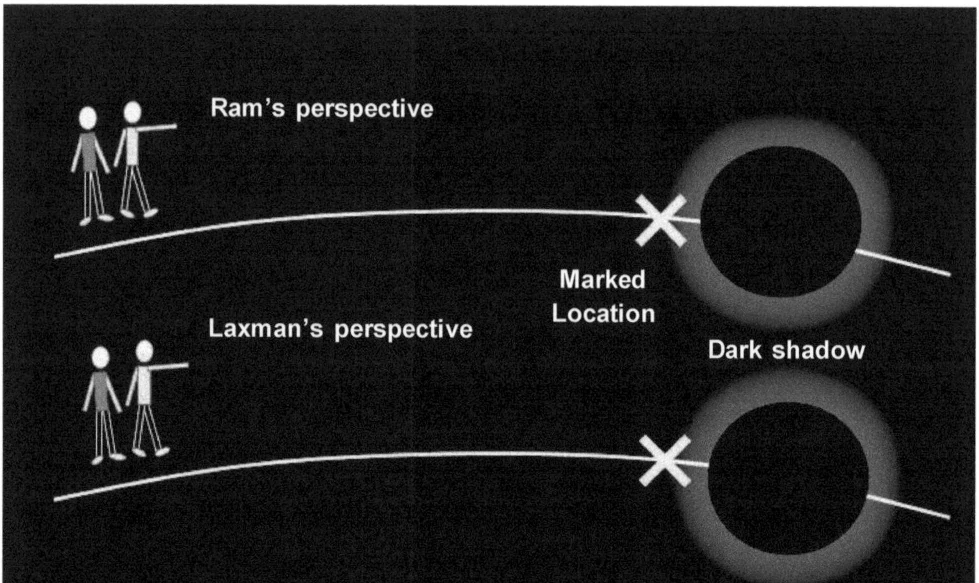

Ram's perspective
Laxman's perspective
Marked Location
Dark shadow
Fig 135(a)

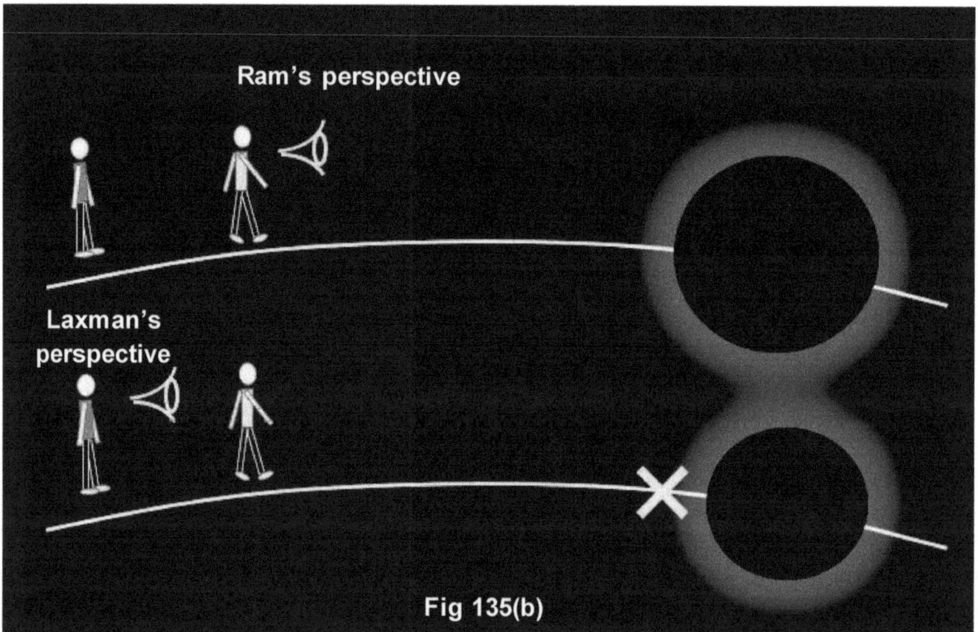

Ram's perspective
Laxman's perspective
Fig 135(b)

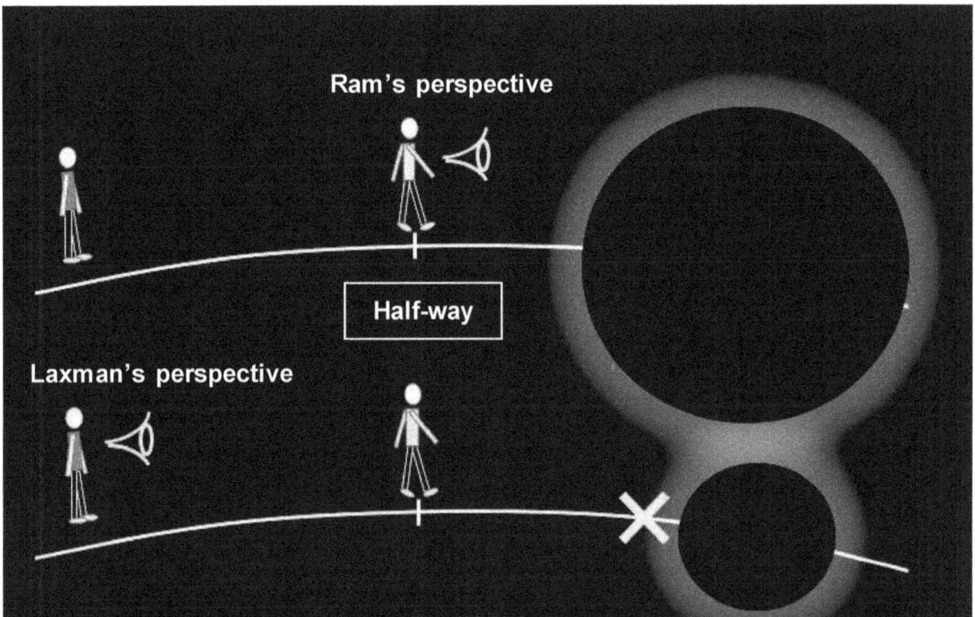

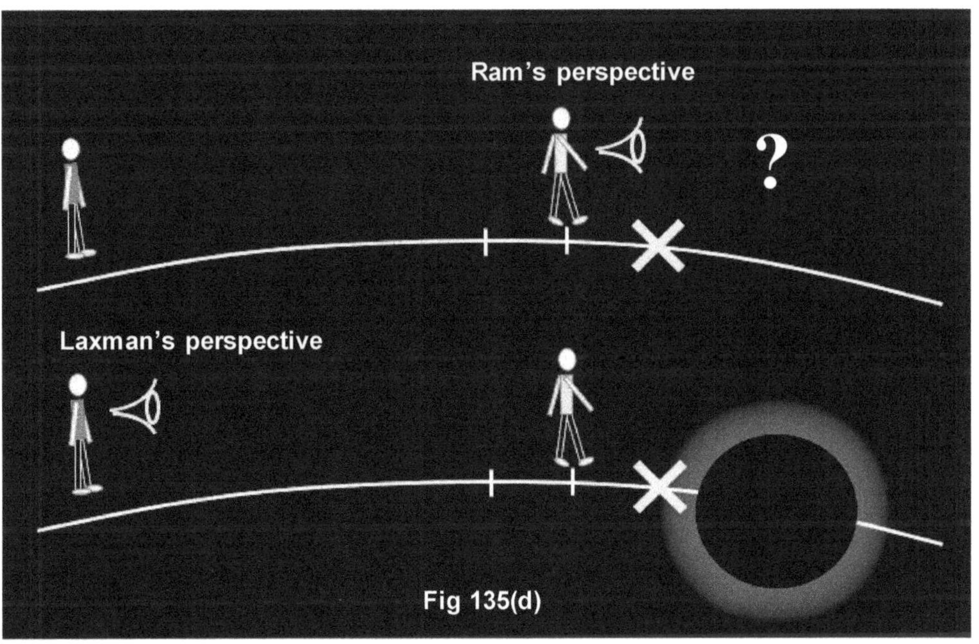

[161]

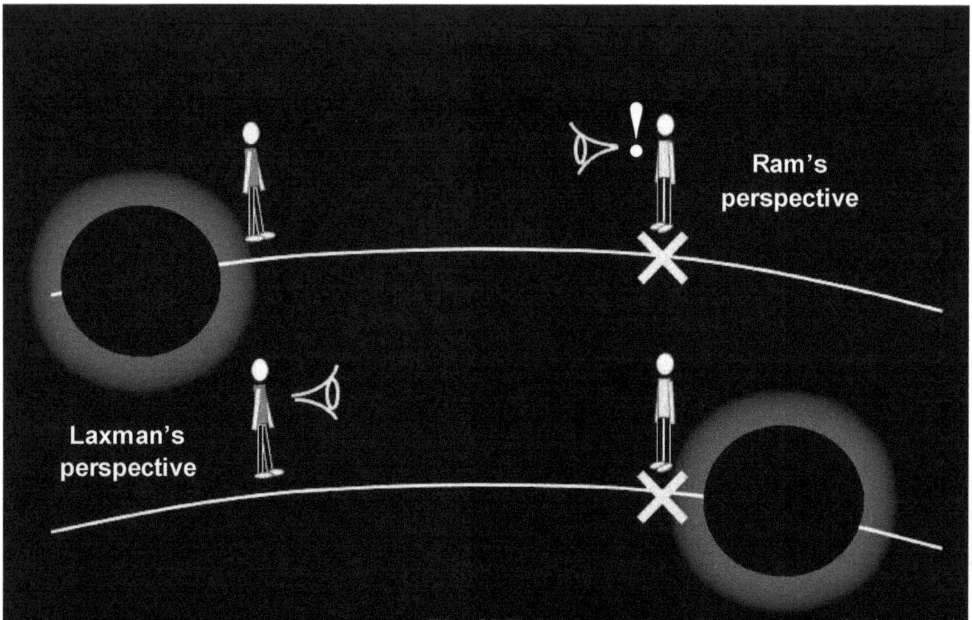

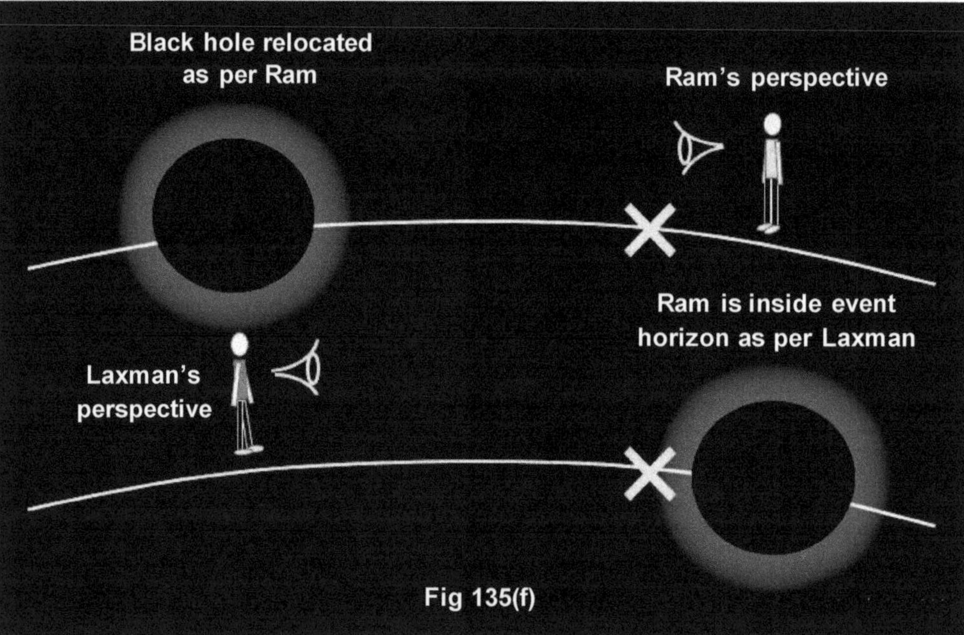
Ram's
perspective
Laxman's
perspective
Fig 135(e)

Black hole relocated
as per Ram
Ram's perspective
Ram is inside event
horizon as per Laxman
Laxman's
perspective
Fig 135(f)

The meaning for above illustration of black holes conveys an unbelievable truth that when people of the world believed Earth to be flat, later sky objects were observed through telescope and found planets including Earth are spherical. Now, the real dimensions of space-time say galaxy is a sphere which could not be realized with a telescope which captures its appearance as a disc to human perspective. The massive blackholes at the center of the galaxy is actually deep, which could not be reached. Hence, it is the core of the galaxy indicating surface and depth of space-time medium, to be understood.

22.0 BENDING PATH OF LIGHT

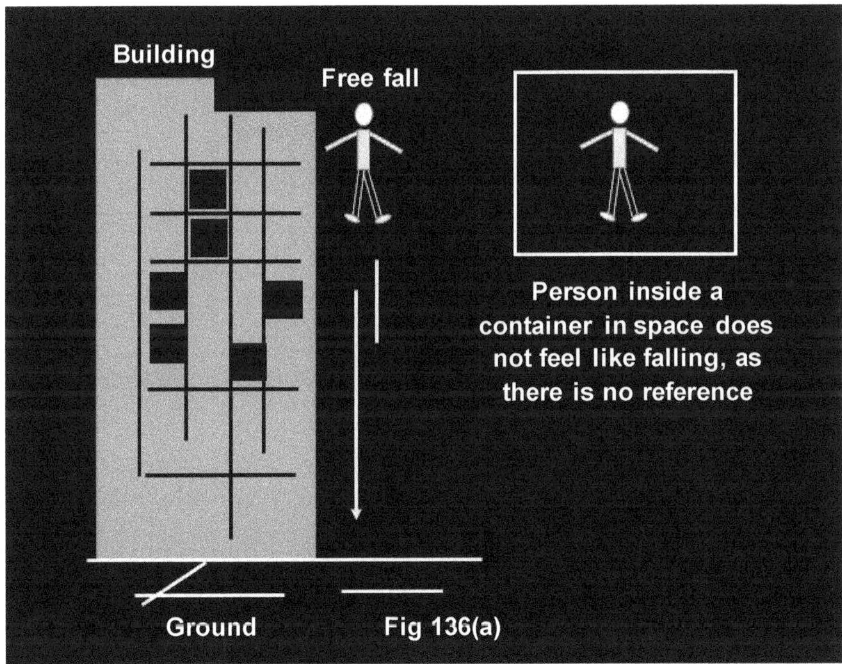

There is an idea of bending of light path along with the gravitational field. Gravitation is said to bend for speed, which could be understood with the real-time illustration (as in the existing studies). Fig 136(a) shows the person jump off a building feels his falling downward towards the ground. Whereas, in space the person inside a container moving down at a speed does not feel like falling, as there is no reference. However, in case of elevator, Fig 136(b) when its moves downwards

[163]

with the minimum acceleration of 9.8 m/s^2 onwards the observer and a ball placed on the floor surface does not feel its weight. Now, when the elevator moves in upward direction accelerated for the same, both observer and the object each experiences their own weight.

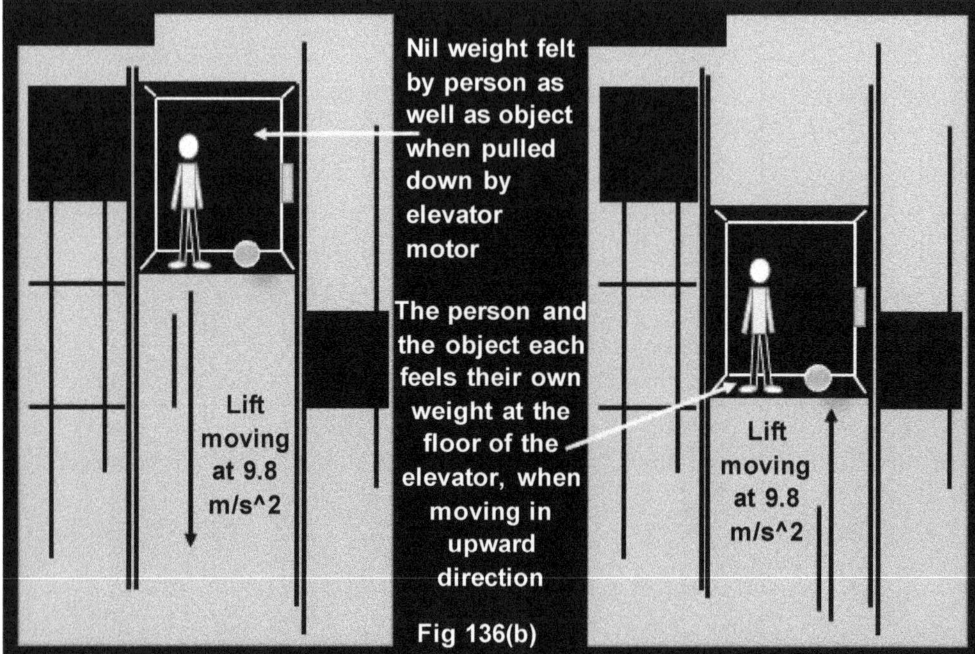

Consider, the ball is thrown by the observer to the wall, the path of the ball is straight when the lift is not moving however, when the lift is moving in upward direction the path of the ball bends as shown in Fig 137(a) and try to be with the ground for its stability based on local gravity. Same way, the light beam is imagined such that the straight-line path of the light bends with the gravity.

This phenomenon is verified by the scientists, based on the fact that gravitational field of Sun is greater than Earth, during a solar eclipse the Moon hides the Sun exactly to show only the shadow to be seen from the Earth. So, at this time, the picture of objects such as stars located far away from the sun on its other side, must be carried by the photons which bends along the curved space around the sun to reach the observer's telescope. The image of stars is captured at certain point proving

[164]

Einstein's prediction of Space-time to behave like a fabric is true and so the gravitational field associated with the heavy objects.

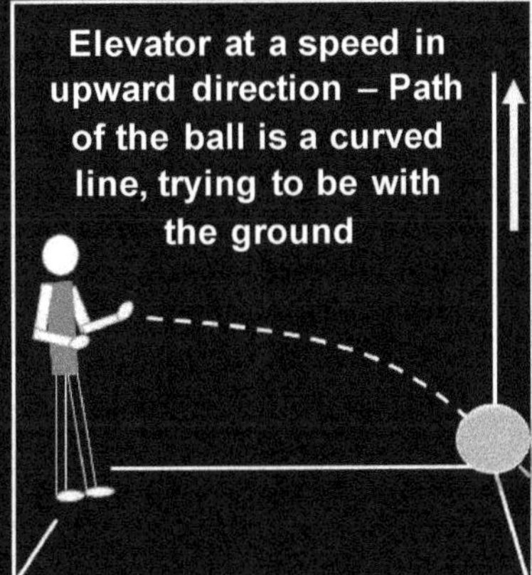

Ball thrown by the person to the wall of the elevator

Fig 137(a)

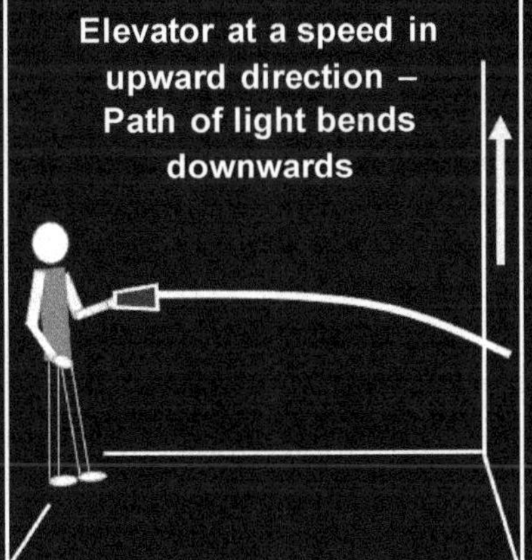

Light beam pointed by the person to the wall of the elevator

Fig 137(b)

[165]

Now, the path of bending light beam in case of elevator is not the same with bend in gravitational field which is assumed to be a curvature caused by heavy objects, not clearly differentiated in existing studies, to be noted. For more understanding let us assume the speed of the elevator moving in upward direction is not accelerating at 9.8 m/s^2 but at the speed of the light itself. As we said the path of the light beam bends, then to what extent the path bends and the limit which the light curve does not exceed could be understood with the following diagram.

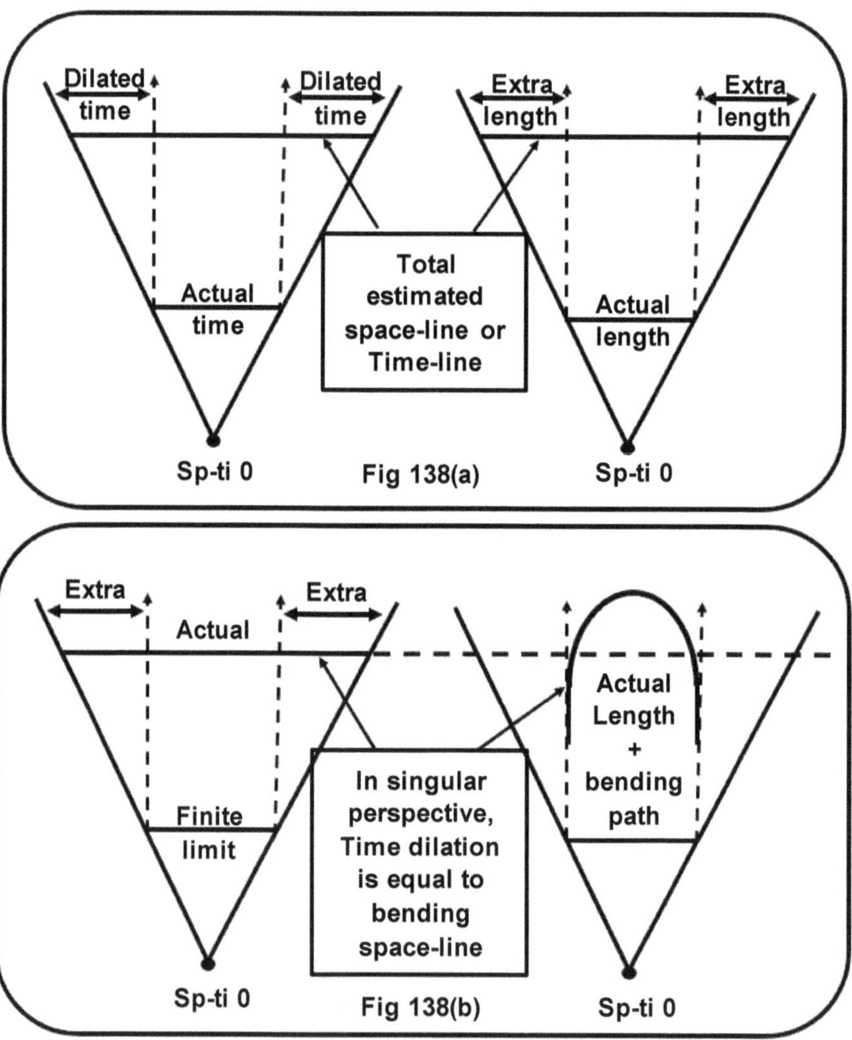

Since we have introduced sp-ti frames, the bending must be traced with surface and depth of sp-ti medium for space as well as with the moving frames for time, hence called as **Sp-ti frames**. The path of light beam observed within the elevator does not serve a complete thought experiment. It must be bent on either side and curve to be within limits as shown in Fig 138(c). This could be further clarified with moving light clock illustration in modern days in understanding time dilation. However, it is also a misconception but the idea is good and shall be utilized to understand length extension and actual time delay (topic follows)

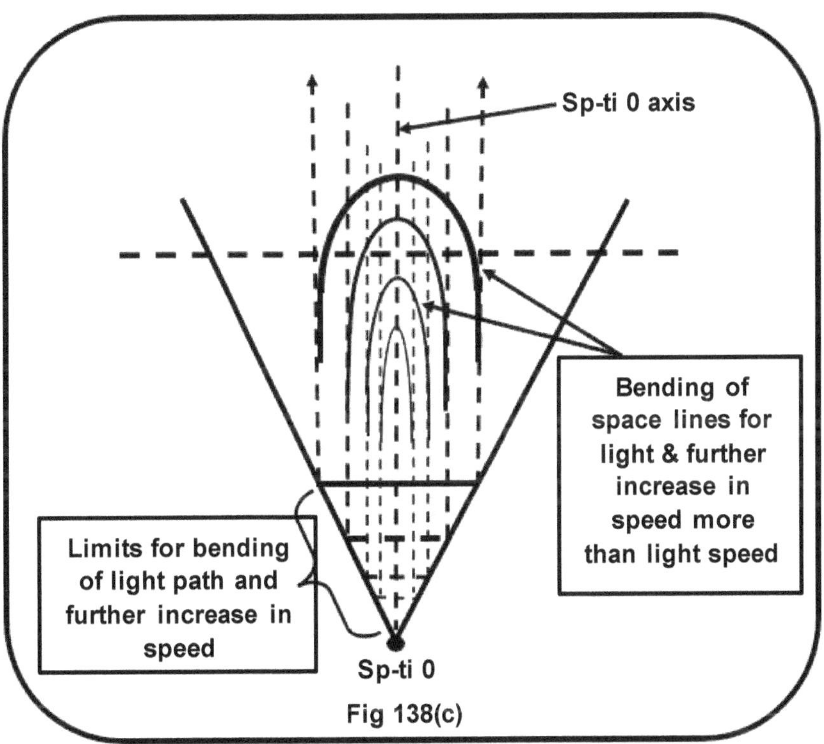

Fig 138(c)

The bending of space lines for light speed and further increase in speed more than light speed are shown in Fig 138(c).

Time dilation = [Actual curved length of light + Bending path of light]

[167]

The actual curved length of light means the length of the light beam in one sp-ti frame for a moment whereas the bending curved path of light means how deep this actual length from surface to depth of sp-ti medium. This could be clearly understood in the following topic.

23.0 LENGTH EXTENSION AND ACTUAL TIME DELAY (Light clock illustration)

The path of light is said to be at the depth and the observer lives on the surface of Sp-ti medium, what is the impact when the light is experimented by the observer is the most important technique of analyzing space-time. We shall understand the same with the light clock, a method of understanding length contraction and time dilation. However, it is applied in the opposite way in favor of relativity. Let us see the illustration clearly.

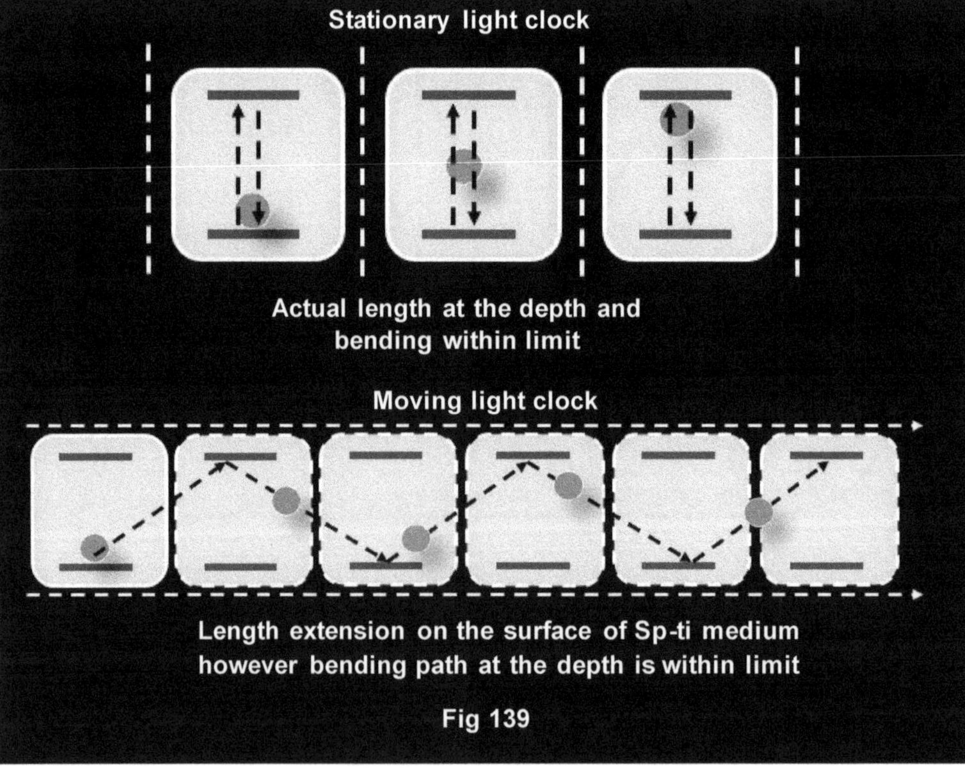

Fig 139

The above illustration with light clock is wrongly convincing for length extension instead of contraction and making actual time delay instead of time dilation. This could be cleared with v-diagram representation, Fig 140(a).

Here, besides the curved length of light at the depth, the bending of its path along the scale also to be noted. The speed more than the light speed causes more bending as well as thinning of lines towards the vertical Sp-ti 0 axis is shown. The limits for further increase in speed more that light is also shown to reduce to reach Sp-ti 0 point or axis, Fig 138(c).

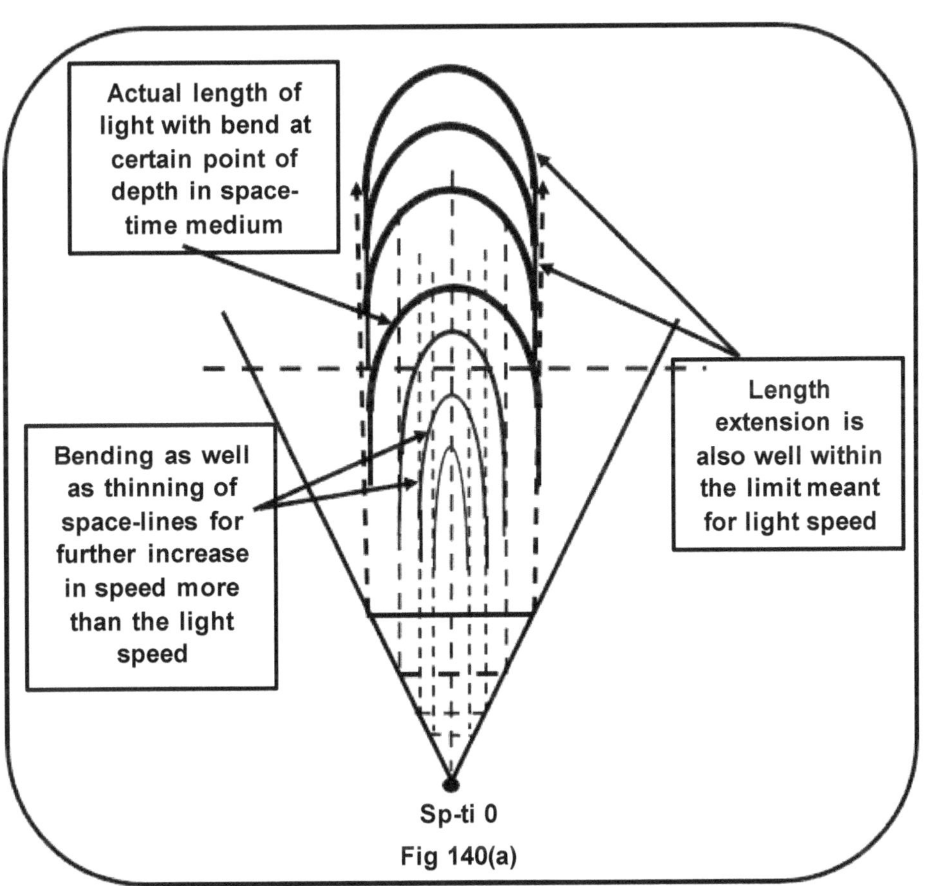

Fig 140(a)

[169]

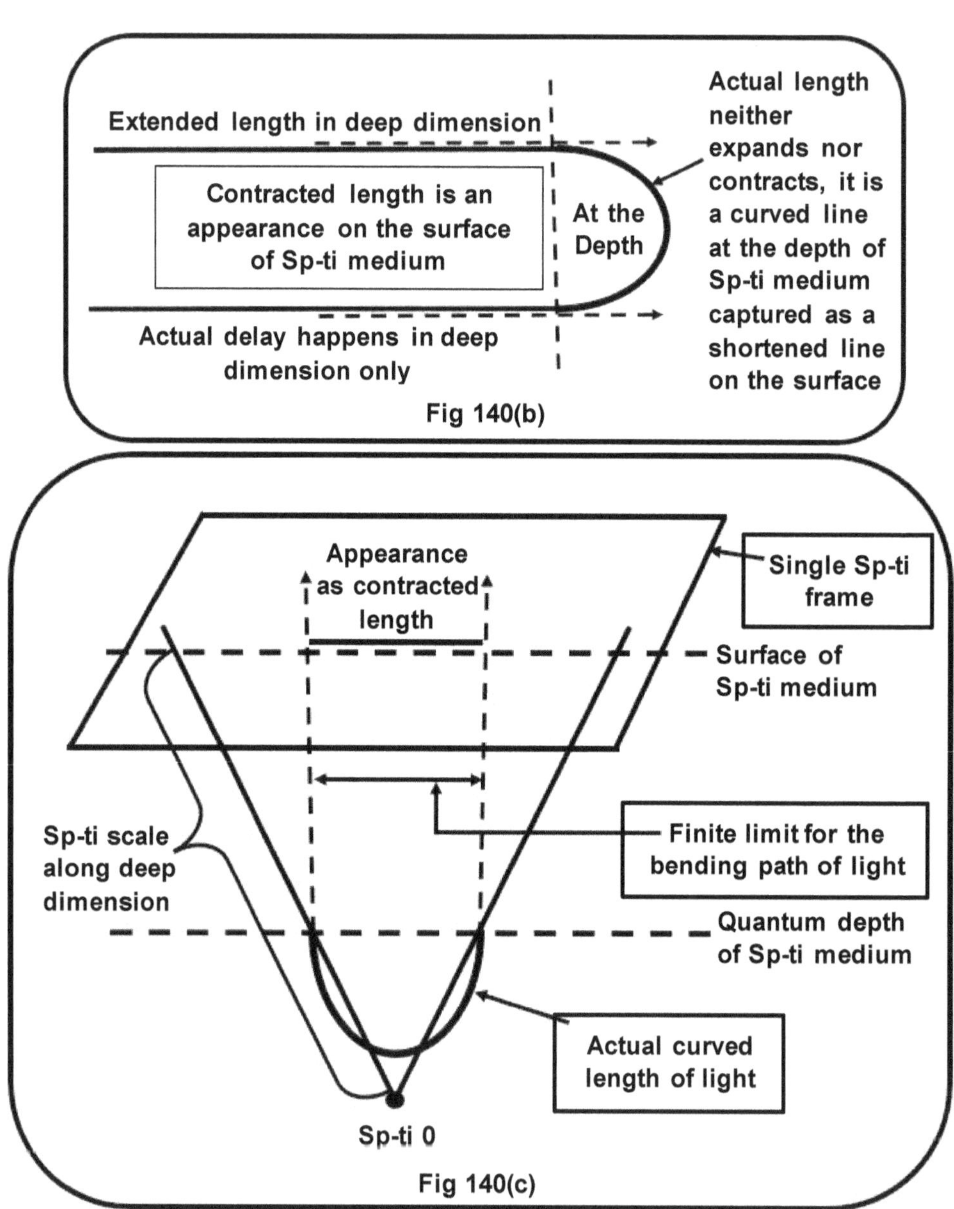

Important note: Fig 140(c) shows, even for length extension more than the actual curved length of light happening in light-clock illustration, it is not visible in wide dimension, it happens radially along deep

[170]

dimension. Only the shortened length appearance could be seen on the surface of sp-ti medium we live. The curved length of light is shown at the bottom in the representation so as to distinguish its quantum depth from the surface of the medium. However, we have already discussed that the real cone of depth is not physical but dimensional and only its shadow could be realized on the surface. Hence, for theoretical understanding the real depth is projected through V-diagram.

24.0 GENERAL DISCUSSION & CONCLUSION

a) V- Diagram Representation: Relativity and singularity have only one thing in common, it is the point that could be simply denoted by the English alphabet 'V'. In which way it is further derived leads to the two straight opposite understandings. However, relativity just remains a concept even though many of the ideas of Sir Einstein proved in recent studies. It is a very deep insight, missing of which relativity sounds absolutely right. Evidently, relativity does not lead to quantum mechanics and controversial too. General theory of relativity (GR) is applicable only for macro-scale objects and quantum mechanics (QM) is another branch of physics to explain the nature of quantum-scale objects. Relativity did not serve the fundamental theory of everything. The term relativity itself means a duality whose path fails to lead to singularity and projected in opposite direction indeed.

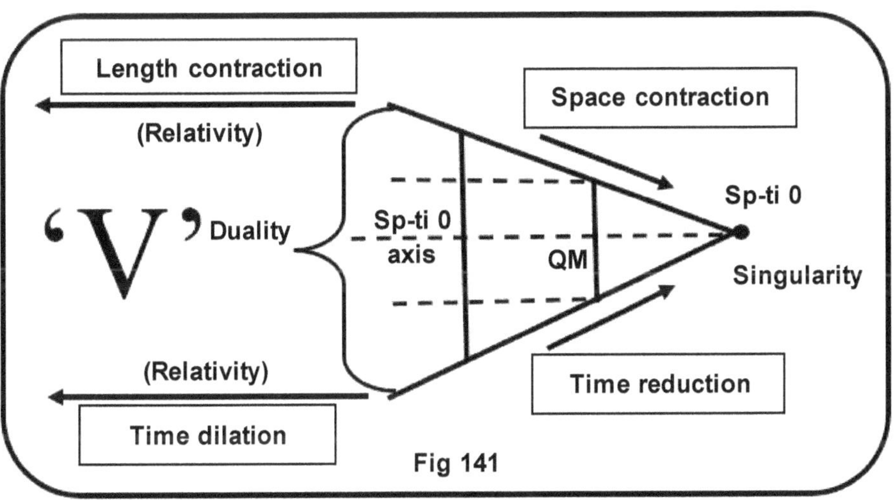

Fig 141

The concept of relativity is same like the threads that are twisted out would not be let into the loop hole of the needle to serve the purpose of stitching. The true findings such as length contraction and time dilation are dual observations in nature. One does not exist without the other and hence each one does not mean anything like instantaneous travelling with zero distance, moving back and forth in time etc. In short, theory of relativity is derived or understood in the way opposite to quantum mechanics and that is the reason for its contradiction. In reality, both the observations together reduce in a scale, pass through the quantum range and then to reach the point of **nothing** or the ultimate single deepest point of all Sp-ti 0s called as **Singularity.**

b) Symmetry-Asymmetry duality

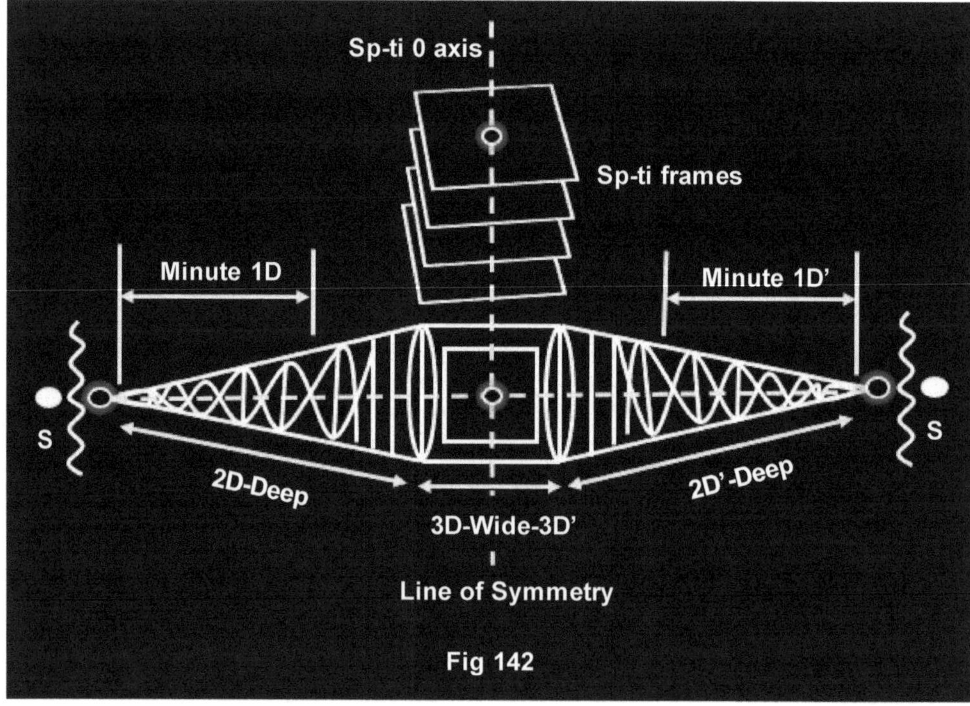

The Sp-ti scale begins at Sp-ti 0 but where it ends? We know the Sp-ti tolerance along the surface of Sp-ti medium. There is a maximum point beyond which the object breaks the tolerance string and becomes a black hole. Beyond this point, the object itself does not exist, it is ending up to the start point by becoming the space-time medium itself.

[172]

In fact, the Sp-ti scale could be said to end with Sp-ti tolerance minimum itself as after this point only the mass density of the object increases and not the volume. As the dimensions and perspectives cannot be projecting infinitely, the point after the wide dimension is closed with symmetry, which is a mirror of the real dimensional cone.

c) Tree of Gravitation

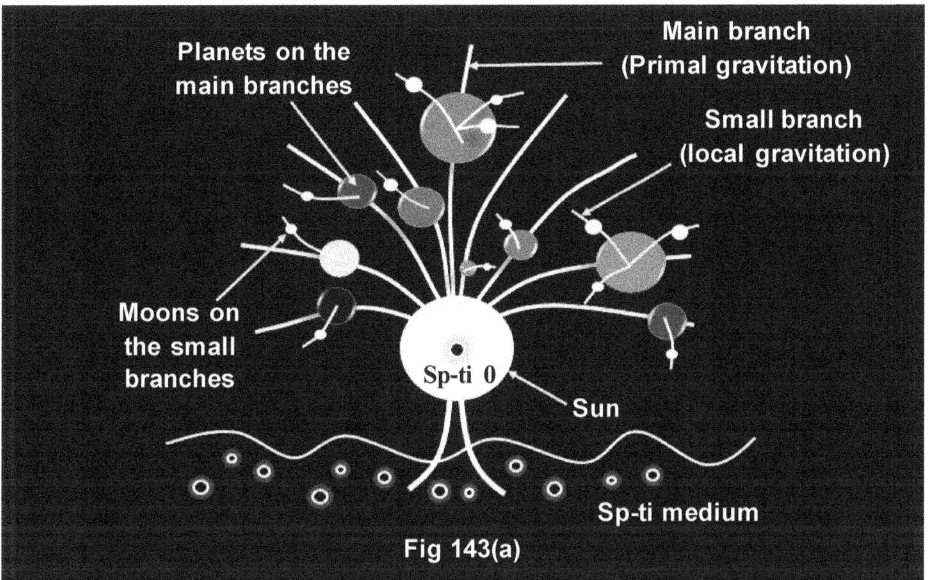

We have seen the gravitation at point level and clearly distinguished primal gravity different from local gravitation. Also, the model of quantum gravity-orbit is the basic for planetary gravitation-orbitation happening at macro-scale. So, it is possible for two galaxies to merge to form a new galaxy such a way that two systematic things combine to form a new system without collapsing too.

Gravitation could be simply represented as a tree diagram for a set of heavy objects like solar system. But entire gravitation network from its point of emergence and its branching could not be tracked. However, Fig 143(b & c) reduces the complication through the representations in 0D and 4D for simple way of understanding it's working. To conclude, Gravitation is neither a force nor a field and it is also not the curvature caused in sp-ti fabric, it is a channel that conducts the energy flow and even responsible for the creation of the very existence called spacetime.

[173]

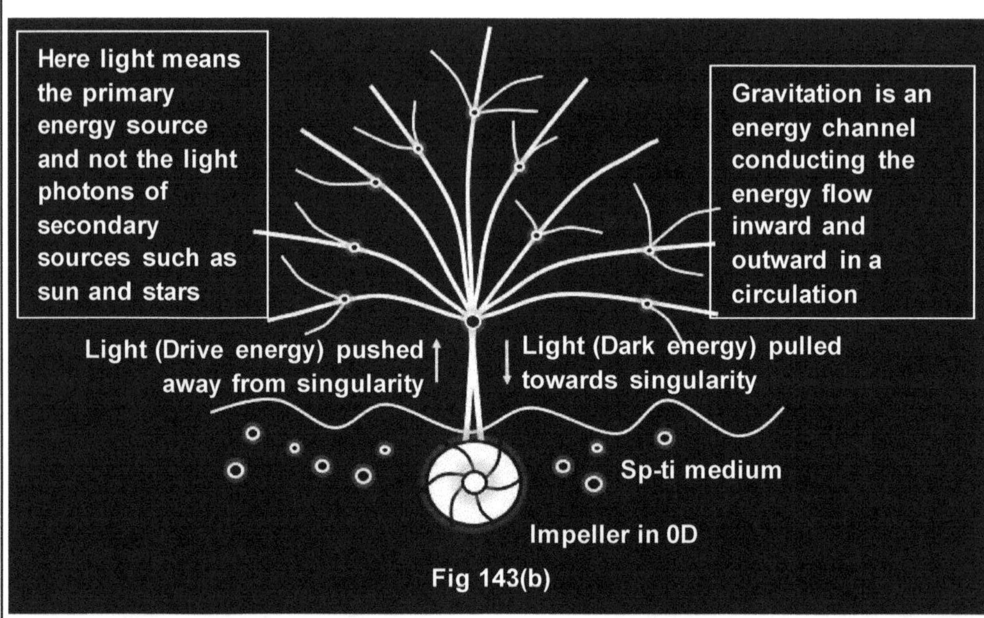

Fig 143(b)

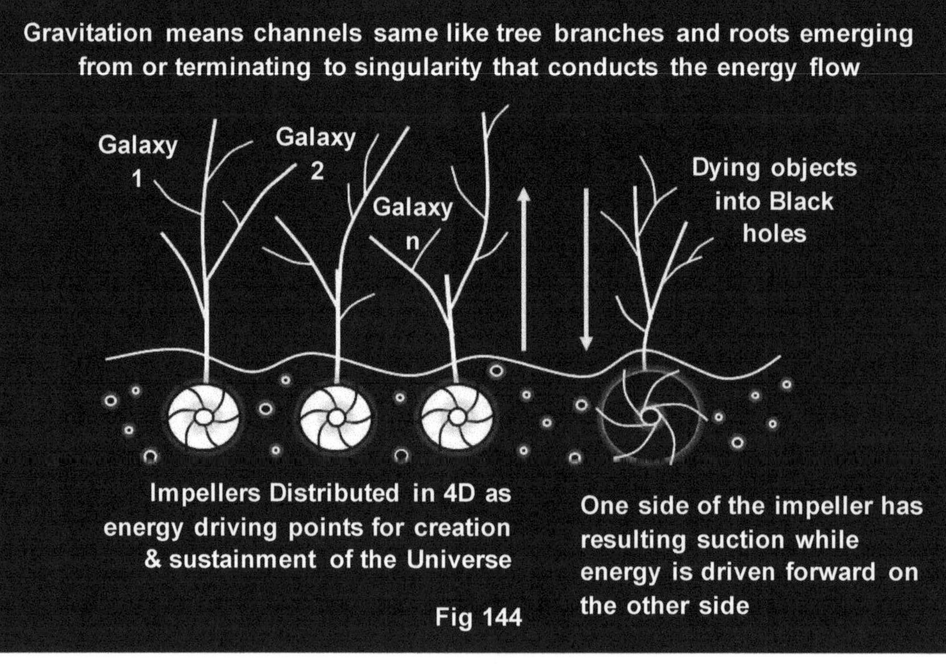

Fig 144

[174]

d) <u>Table of real dimensions of space-time</u>

S. No.	Geometrical Aspects (Shadow cone)	Non-Geometrical Aspects (Real cone)
1(a)	Wide (3D) - Length	Boundary (3D)
1(b)	Wide (3D) - Width	
1(c)	Wide (3D) - Height	
1(d)	Wide (3D) - Radius	
2	Deep (2D) - Deep radius	Base (2D)
3	Minute (1D) - Waveform	Core (1D)
4	Singularity (0D)	Singularity (4D)

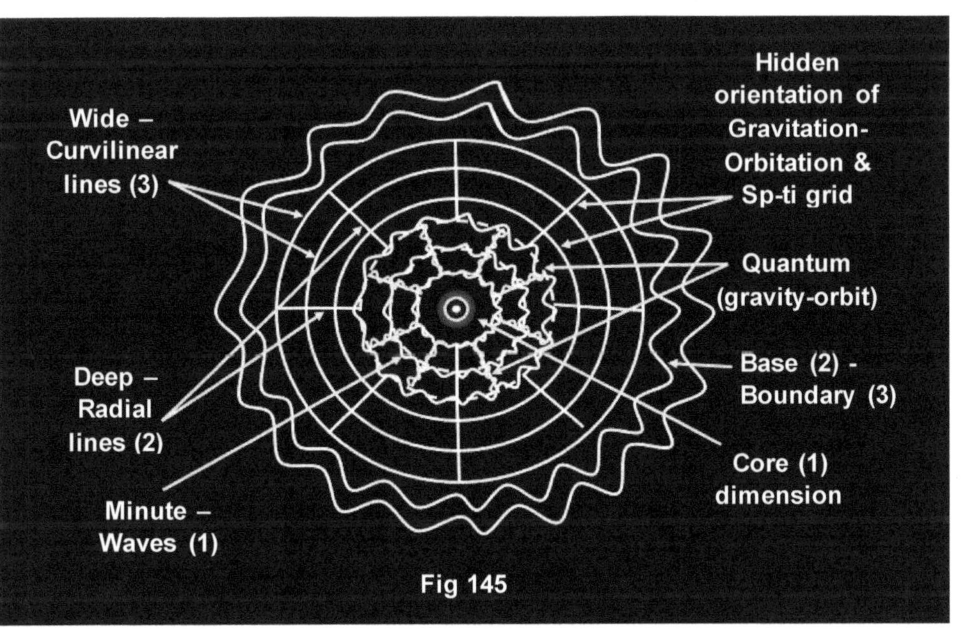

e) FTS – Real-time understanding

Consider a person standing near a building (green) sees another building of same size at some far away distance. It appears small. Now moving towards that distant building (white) and on reaching the same, now if the person turns back and see the green building where he started, it appears small same as the white building appeared before.

Here, it is the shadow cone that shifts its apex or point of depth sp-ti 0 in two opposite directions by switching the source and destination on reaching one of the two opposite sides.

Dark liquid ocean is distributed as inaccessible droplets at the surface of sp-ti medium and considering each point, it is a point of ocean. On the other hand, going dimensionally deep into space-time medium there is a dark ocean in which the Universe we live is a dot or point. However, clearly the cone of depth is not physical but dimensional which means, it is possible only through real dimensions, Fig 147.

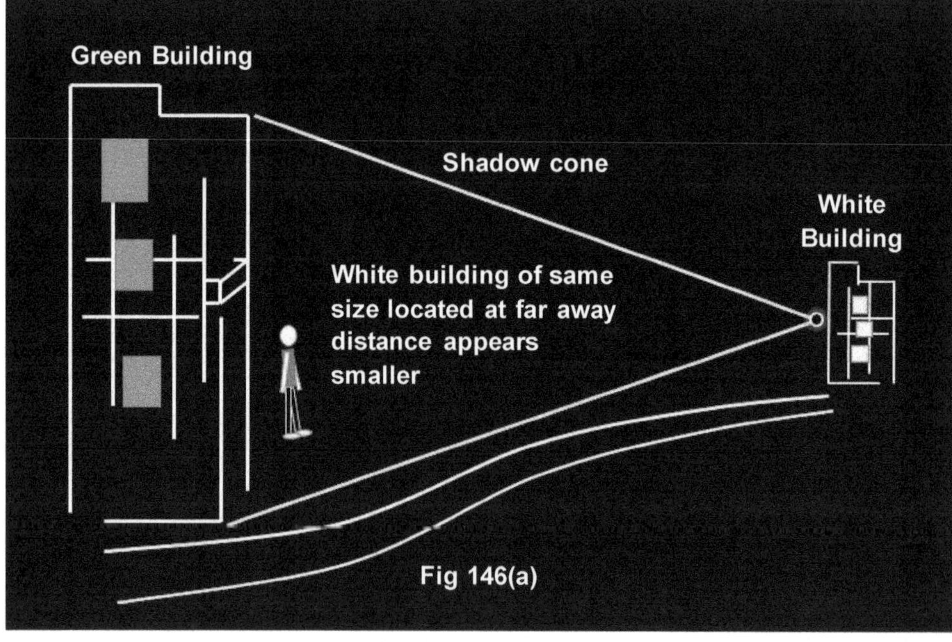

Fig 146(a)

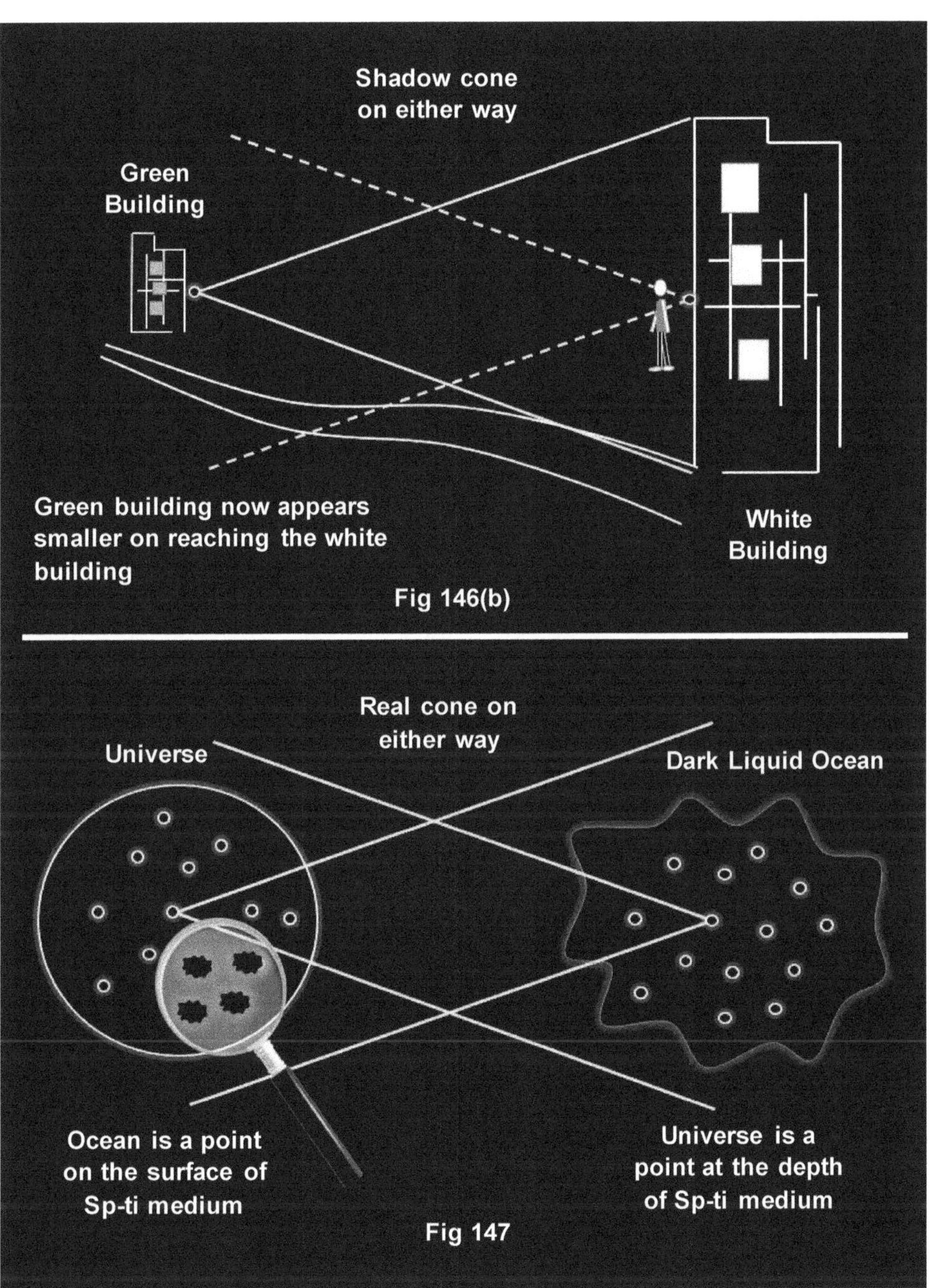

Shadow cone
on either way
Green
Building
Green building now appears
smaller on reaching the white
building
White
Building
Fig 146(b)
Real cone on
either way
Universe
Dark Liquid Ocean
Ocean is a point
on the surface of
Sp-ti medium
Universe is a
point at the depth
of Sp-ti medium
Fig 147

f) Finite structure of space-time

Fig 148 shows the finite structure of space-time. It includes all six real dimensions in terms of geometrical and non-geometrical aspects such as wide, deep & minute and boundary, base & core dimensions respectively. The singularity is at the core point of the structure as well as beyond the boundary dimension. At 4D, with or without human intervention, all the points of sp-ti 0s are light spots of same size distributed without any dimensions and at 0D this light is a single spot whose size is big or small is unobserved by nobody and thus nothing or non-existence means this **primary & ever-existing light source** of God nature.

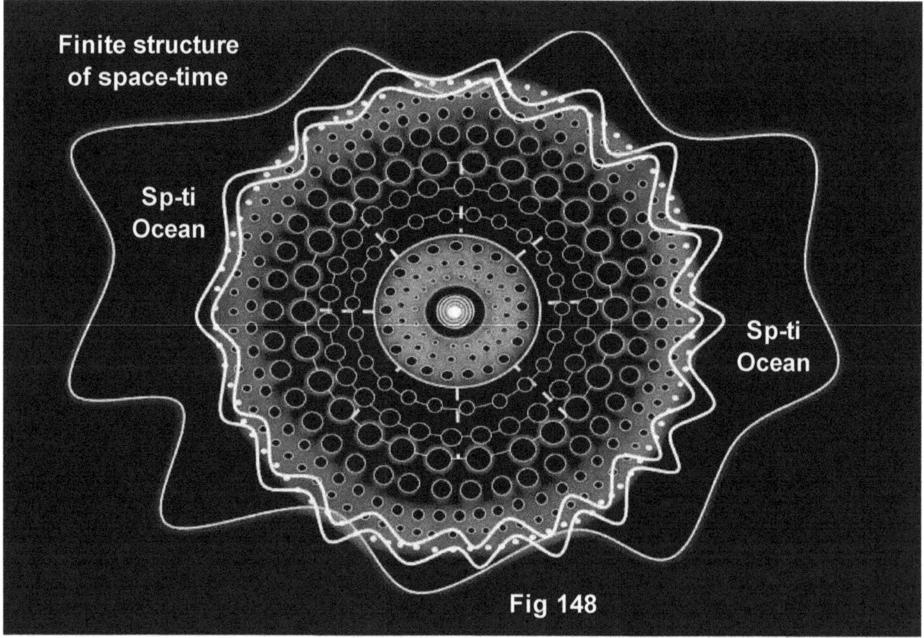

Philosophy: Whether the existence, is considered with trillions of galaxies or hand-held amount of it, the structure of space-time is finite. One may always wonder that how everything came out of nothing. Who created nothing? The answer is as simple as that when you think of nothing one should include his consciousness also to collapse into nothing. If there is nobody to think about nothing, then there is no point of asking who created nothing.

[178]

Nothing has the self-conscious of everything. Human is the ultimate creation who could access only a part of this knowledge through his consciousness using the tool called mind. To be with everything or nothing one should give up his mind and there by flow with the life, the way it goes to reach the destination. Life is distributed in terms of sp-ti frames. Human have to go through all the situations and gain the absolute knowledge through one-eye perspective free from all dualities.

All the problems along with their solutions are always available in the existence same like a library. Even this piece of work is a book from the library of space-time. However, the period of time when the theory of relativity to be revealed and later, when the theory of singularity to be revealed to people of the world, everything is pre-determined. Human is a puppet in the hands of time, still he can serve great purpose if he realizes the same. Whether, the mankind wants to be natural or artificial, everything is contained in sp-ti frames. Means, whichever way one chooses, it leads ahead and has its own results or consequences. Aliens too are not exceptional in life.

g) Misconception about mass (Existing studies)

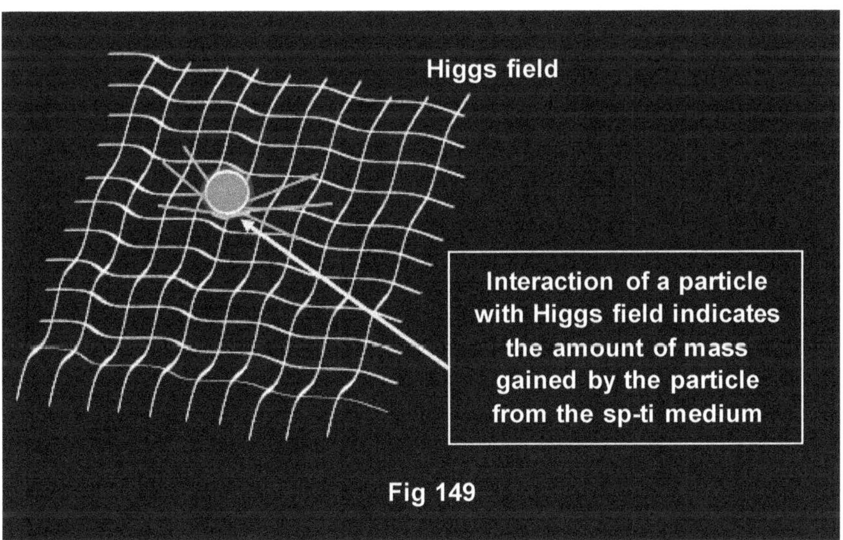

Human perspective about mass of a particle says, to what extent the particle interacts with Higgs field that much amount of mass is gained

[179]

by it. And Higgs field is responsible for all masses of the objects in the existence. In singular perspective, mass is not due to the interaction between particle and Higgs filed. However, the interaction is just an indication of amount of mass already provided to the evolving particle. Means, Higgs field is some constructive way through which a particle carry mass from space-time medium itself and hence not responsible for the source of mass, to be noted.

The amount of mass is equal to amount of liquid dark matter evolving into a particle pushed by drive energy. Mass is one of the characteristics in space-time, however it is not about a solid nature. There is no solidity in space-time, it is only due to the perception of objects on the same surface level. Space-time is a fluid medium (mechanism). Objects are said to be moving for understanding, but in reality, everything is floating & swimming in space and flowing in time.

We have seen the Sp-ti 0 points deeper than Higg's field and also the deepest point or region called singularity. However, Higg's field unlike other fundamental fields, indicates the amount of mass gained by the particles through interaction which in turn differs upon its intensity.

To understand this idea in real-time, consider an open tank with full of water at ground level. Pick a tumbler and fetch water from it, now slide the bottom of the tumbler on the surface of the tank water, this action is same as the interaction of a particle with Higgs field. Now take a bucket full of water and slide it on the surface of tank water, the impact would be more. This difference in interaction actually indicates the difference in amount of water already fetched in the containers of different sizes.

Literally, the space-time medium arises or blown out from the liquid matter of darkness. So, the Higgs field spread on top of it shows the amount of interaction made by particle with its field while the particle has already gained mass from the medium itself. Thus, Higgs boson termed to be God's particle in existing studies shall be modified as **God's mediating particle** meant to connect two opposite realities.

In the existing studies, there is nothing wrong to have assumed particles are gaining mass due to the interaction with Higg's field because without the real dimensions it is unknown to see things deeper than fundamental fields such as dark matter. And that is the reason, particle is thought to have dual nature of particle as well as wave. In our new study of singularity, we have visualized how the wave nature is pertaining to sp-ti fluid medium only.

h) Male-Female Energy duality

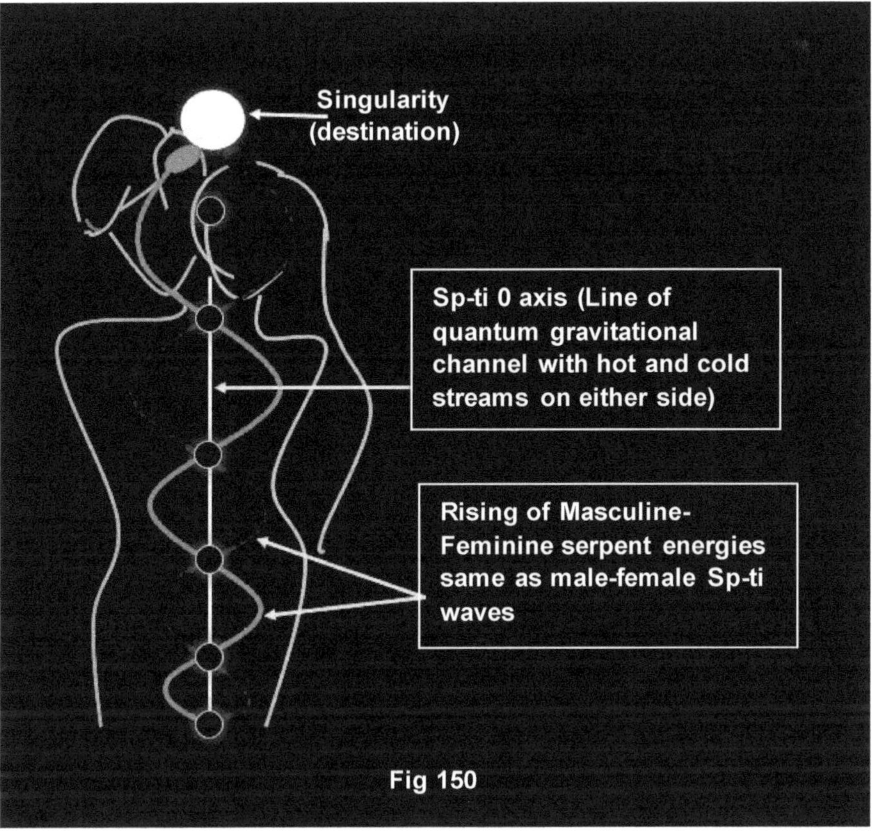

> The evidence for male-female sp-ti waves of the liquid dark ocean is nothing but the objects evolved from fundamental fields has reached a full-fledged ultimate creation called human (man and woman).

> The creation and existence of all living and non-living objects basically have the male-female energy combination.

> This dual energy of the existence is the first and foremost duality of all the other dualities of nature.

---------------------- End of chapters ----------------------

<table>
<tr><td colspan="4"><h2 align="center">Acknowledgement of Book issuance</h2></td></tr>
<tr><th>S. No.</th><th>Name of the educational institution / School (Address seal)</th><th>No. of copies issued</th><th>Authorized signatory with date</th></tr>
<tr><td></td><td></td><td></td><td></td></tr>
<tr><td></td><td></td><td></td><td></td></tr>
<tr><td></td><td></td><td></td><td></td></tr>
<tr><td colspan="4">Comment / Feedback:

</td></tr>
</table>

PUBLISHED ARTICLES FOR REFERENCE

[1] Self-reference_12: Fundamental Theory of Singularity; Formulated study – 3. [Volume 11, Issue 01, 2024]. (IJARPS – www.arcjournals.org).

[2] Self-reference_11: Fundamental Theory of Singularity; Formulated study – 2. [Volume 10, Issue 10, 2023]. (IJARPS – www.arcjournals.org).

[3] Self-reference_10: Fundamental Theory of Singularity; Formulated study – 1. [Volume 10, Issue 08, 2023]. (IJARPS – www.arcjournals.org).

[4] Self-reference_9: New Study of Gravitation in Singularity. [Volume 10, Issue 04, 2023]. (IJARPS –www.arcjournals.org).

[5] Self-reference_8: Fundamental Theory of Singularity. [Volume 10, Issue 03, 2023]. (IJARPS –www.arcjournals.org).

[6] Self-reference_7: Fourth dimension of space-time – Study of gravitation; part-2. [Volume 10, Issue 02, 2023]. (IJARPS – www.arcjournals.org).

[7] Self-reference_6: Fourth dimension of space-time – Study of gravitation; part-1. [Volume 10, Issue 01, 2023]. (IJARPS – www.arcjournals.org).

[8] Self-reference_5: Fundamental study of space-time – (Zero, One and Infinity). [Volume 10, Issue 01, 2023]. (IJARPS – www.arcjournals.org).

[9] Self-reference_4: Particle physics based on real dimensions of space-time. [Volume 9, Issue 10, 2022]. (IJARPS – www.arcjournals.org).

[10] Self-reference_3: General relativity Vs Quantum mechanics; Incompatibility solved with real dimensions of space-time. [Volume 9, Issue-9, 2022]. (IJARPS – www.arcjournals.org).

[11] Self-reference_2: Length contraction and time dilation are experimental but non-physical variations in space-time. [Volume-9, Issue-8, 2022]. (IJARPS – www.arcjournals.org).

S. No.	Name of the College / University (Address seal)	No. of copies issued	Authorized signatory with date

Acknowledgement of Book issuance

Comment / Feedback:

[12] Self-reference_1: Length contraction and time dilation with real dimensions of space-time. [Volume-9, Issue-8, 2022]. (International Journal of Advanced Research in Physical Science (IJARPS) – www.arcjournals.org).

ISSN No. (Online) 2349-7882 [For above published articles].

> ❖ Self-Published e-book in Amazon Kindle Direct Publishing (KDP).

Titled: **"INVITATION FOR NEW DISCOVERY IN SPACE SCIENCE – Real dimensions of space-time"**. – Dec 2021.

Objective of the work: This book is a sample work to segregate all the ideas, drawings and explanations to bring it in a format. Every single topic could be elaborated and only the basics are discussed here. The work required to be reviewed by the educationists and finalized once. Awaiting response call for the same.

Further, the fair document of this book for the purpose of education shall be standardized with proper choice of words, minute modifications, and more details for connectivity and so on. It is quite difficult to explain fourth dimension in a lecture without having proper sequence of explanations & technical drawings, as hand notes. The four-dimensional representations throughout this book are explored in all possible ways and hope the theory of singularity serves the fundamental for existing science without doubt.

Self-Declaration: The content of this book is true to my knowledge and I take the sole responsibility to declare that, it is still under creation, imagination, perspective and literary work of my own until it is recognized as the subject of space-time study.

<table>
<tr><td colspan="4" align="center">Acknowledgement of Book issuance</td></tr>
<tr>
<td align="center">S. No.</td>
<td align="center">Name of the Distributor / Wholesaler / Retailer (Address seal)</td>
<td align="center">No. of copies issued</td>
<td align="center">Authorized signatory with date</td>
</tr>
<tr><td></td><td></td><td></td><td></td></tr>
<tr><td></td><td></td><td></td><td></td></tr>
<tr><td></td><td></td><td></td><td></td></tr>
<tr><td colspan="4">Comment / Feedback:</td></tr>
</table>

AUTHOR'S BIOGRAPHY

Prabhakaran Natesan,

Bachelor's degree in Electrical and Electronics Engineering (2011) – Affiliated to Anna University, Chennai, Tamil Nadu, India.

Email: [prabhakar3112@gmail.com]

Contact: [+91 9600167756; 8056031636]

The science world is seeking for the unified theory that accommodates the two major branches of physics such as *General theory of relativity (Classical physics) and Quantum mechanics (Modern physics)* that contradicts each other. Hope our new work titled **Fundamental Theory of Singularity (FTS)** serves the basic for study of space-time for oncoming generations. It demanded a great effort and hark work to formulate it in an understandable way even to publish as articles.

The scientific drawings in this book could convey the details of space-time more than the words do. The knowledge of space-time is so concentrated that it cannot be diluted through open discussions with the words of our routine life. The ultimate truth is always an unspoken reality whose major part is as big as an ocean while the level of truth one can seek is self-realization which means, there is nothing to identify oneself different from the existence.

To work on space-time, had some space and time during covid-19 pandemic. Initially, I just wanted to solve the mystery of incompatibility between general relativity and quantum mechanics. The invitation booklet published for new discovery in space science in the year 2021, itself has this problem solved dimensionally that the sp-ti lines are left unbent at the depth of space-time and thus, restored in its original form of wave nature. This key point solves the contradiction between macro and quantum scale objects. Later on, the work progressed towards formulating the theory and published the papers in the following years. Space-time could be studied or analyzed only through diagrammatic representations containing the real dimensions (discussed in this book).

Acknowledgement of Book issuance			
S. No.	Name of the Individual (Student / Teacher / Lecturer / Professor)	No. of copies issued	Signature with date

Comment / Feedback:

APPENDIX

[New scientific terms & key words introduced in this book]

Sp-ti 0; Sp-ti 0 axis, Surface radius, Deep radius, Real dimensions, Fourth dimensional aspects, Gravitation-Orbitation duality, Gravitational stopper, Gravitational filters, Line of gravitation, Circle of orbitation, Primal gravity, Local gravity, Great orbit, Local orbit, Sp-ti grid, Sp-ti bubble, Liquid dark matter, Dimensional rings, Dimensional ribbons, Spacious Sp-ti 0s, Dimensional Sp-ti 0s, Structure of black holes, Open surface black hole, Closed quantum black hole, Surface and depth of space-time, Singularity, Finite structure of space-time, Wave-particle, Path of quantum entanglement, Fundamental numbers of sp-ti, Overflowing & Flickering nature of sp-ti, Fluid fountain mechanism of sp-ti, Sp-ti frames, Point of non-existence of sp-ti, Impeller action, Spacious vacuum, Absolute vacuum, Retained dark matter, Primary & secondary sources of light, Human consciousness in duality, Abode of god in singularity, Telescopic depth, Microscopic depth, Shadow cone, Real Dimensional cone, Sp-ti waves, Sp-ti pond, Sp-ti ocean, Male-Female dark energies, Sp-ti womb, Space contraction, Time reduction, credit speed, Length Extension, Dimensionally reduced sp-ti scale, Virtual resistance, Virtual delay, Absolute zero, Binary zero, Reference zero, 4D with Symmetry-Asymmetry, Cone of consciousness, V-Diagram representation, Primary Light as Drive energy & Dark energy, Dark shadow, Gravitational filters & stoppers, Hot & Cold streams, Gravitation - Energy channels, Tree of gravitation and God's mediating particle.

THANK YOU

Acknowledgement of Book issuance			
S. No.	Name of the Individual (Scholars / Professionals / Govt. officials)	No. of copies issued	Signature with date

Comment / Feedback:

Acknowledgement of Book issuance

S. No.	Name of the Organization / Committee / Council / Sector (Address seal)	No. of copies issued	Authorized signatory with date

Comment / Feedback:

Acknowledgement of Book issuance

S. No.	Name of the Academy / Association / School / College (Address seal)	No. of copies issued	Authorized signatory with date

Comment / Feedback: